Creative Art & Activities

Fun with Art!

Mary Mayesky

THOMSON
DELMAR LEARNING

Australia   Canada   Mexico   Singapore   Spain   United Kingdom   United States

Creative Art and Activities: Fun with Art!
Mary Mayesky

Vice President, Career Education SBU:
Dawn Gerrain

Director of Editorial:
Sherry Gomoll

Senior Acquisitions Editor:
Erin O'Connor

Director of Production:
Wendy A. Troeger

Production Coordinator:
Nina Tucciarelli

Director of Marketing:
Wendy E. Mapstone

Library of Congress Cataloging-in-Publication Card Number: 1401880967

NOTICE TO THE READER

Publisher does not warrant or guarantee any of the products described herein or perform any independent analysis in connection with any of the product information contained herein. Publisher does not assume, and expressly disclaims, any obligation to obtain and include information other than that provided to it by the manufacturer.

The reader is expressly warned to consider and adopt all safety precautions that might be indicated by the activities herein and to avoid all potential hazards. By following the instructions contained herein, the reader willingly assumes all risks in connection with such instructions.

The Publisher makes no representation or warranties of any kind, including but not limited to, the warranties of fitness for particular purpose or merchantability, nor are any such representations implied with respect to the material set forth herein, and the publisher takes no responsibility with respect to such material. The publisher shall not be liable for any special, consequential, or exemplary damages resulting, in whole or part, from the readers' use of, or reliance upon, this material.

With thanks

To teachers around the world who everyday give the best of themselves

to the youngest of our citizens.

—MM

Contents

PART II   Crayons, Chalk, and Markers 67

ACTIVITIES *continued*

ACTIVITIES

CONTENTS **ix**

ACTIVITIES *continued*

ACTIVITIES

Preface

The book you are holding in your hands is designed with **you** in mind. It is right for you **if** you are interested in fun, creative and easy-to-do art activities with young children. It is also right for you **if** you want creative activities that involve everyday, recycled, and easy-to-find materials. And it is perfect for you **if** you need activities that are easy to do even if you feel you are not the "artsy" type!

This book covers basic art materials and forms that are found in early-childhood programs everywhere. The six parts of the book are:

1. Clay, Play Dough, and Modeling Materials
2. Crayons, Chalk, and Markers
3. Painting
4. Puppets
5. Print Making
6. Paper Art

In each of these parts, the focus is on the process of creating, not the product. The main reason for each activity is to allow children the joy of creating, exploring materials, and discovering how things look and work. In other words, forget how the finished product looks and concentrate on the fun of **doing.**

All activities are designed to be user-friendly. You will find all you need on one page—including required materials, helpful hints, preparation tips, step-by-step instructions, ideas for variations, and even a place for notes for next time. Illustrations give more details to help you in using the activity.

The activities in each part are designed for children aged 2 through 8. An icon representing a suggested age for the activity is listed at the top of each activity. However, use your knowledge of the child to guide you in choosing and using the activities in this book. Wherever possible, information is provided on how to adapt the activity for children over age 8.

USING SAFE ART MATERIALS

In each part, you will find information on using, storing, and preparing to use materials specific to that part. In all of these activities, be sure to use safe art supplies. Read labels on all art materials. Check materials for age appropriateness. The Art and Creative Materials Institute (ACMI) labels art materials "AP" (approved product) and "CL" (certified label). Products with these labels are certified safe for use by young children.

Some basic safety hints for art activities are:

- Always use products that are appropriate for the child.
- Never use products for skin painting or food preparation unless the products are intended for those uses.

- Keep art materials in their original containers. Do not transfer them to other containers. You will lose the valuable safety information on the product packages.
- Do not eat or drink while using art and craft materials. Wash after use. Clean yourself and your supplies.
- Be sure that your work area is well lighted and ventilated.

Some materials to avoid using are:

- Epoxy, instant glues, or other solvent-based glues. Use only water-based white glue.
- Paints that require solvents like turpentine to clean. Use only water-based paints.
- Cold water or commercial dyes that contain chemical additives. Use only natural vegetable dyes made from beets, onion skins, and so on.
- Permanent markers. Permanent markers may contain toxic solvents. Use only water-based markers.

Be aware of all children's allergies. Children with allergies to wheat, for example, may be irritated by the wheat paste used in papier-mache. Children allergic to peanuts must taste nothing with peanut butter. Other art materials that may cause allergic reactions include chalk or other dusty substances, water-based clay, and any material that contains petroleum products.

Also be aware of children's habits. Some young children put everything in their mouths. (This can be the case at any age.) Others may be shy and slow to try new materials. Use what you know about the child to help you plan art activities that are safe for all children.

Take the time to talk with the child about which things they may taste and which they may not. For example, when making anything mixed with glue, remind the children that glue is not to be tasted. You may find it helpful to use a large cutout of a smiley face with a tongue at the end of the smile to indicate an "edible activity." Make a copy of the smiley face and place a large black X over it to show a "no-taste activity."

CREATING A CHILD-FRIENDLY ENVIRONMENT

It is hard to be creative when you have to worry about keeping yourself and your work area clean. Cover all artwork areas with newspaper. A good idea is to tape the paper to the surface to avoid having markers or other materials seep through the spaces. Also, picking up a messy newspaper and throwing it away is so much easier than cleaning up a tabletop! Other cover-ups that work well are shower curtains and plastic tablecloths.

Remember to cover the children, too! Some good child cover-ups are men's shirts (with the sleeves cut off), aprons, pillowcases with holes cut for the head and arms, and smocks. Some fun alternatives to these are sets of old clothes or shoes that can be worn as "art clothes." These old clothes could become "art journals" as they become covered with the traces of various art activities.

ATTITUDE IS EVERYTHING

Don't forget that your attitude toward all activities with children, whether art or any other activities, affects children's attitudes as well. Being relaxed and positive is the best start to all activities in this book. Remember, you don't have to be an artist to use this book and the activities in it. You just have to expect to have fun, to explore, and to learn something new about art materials. Now, enter the fun world of arts and activities. Enjoy your *Fun with Art* trip!

PART I

Clay,
Play Dough,
and
Modeling
Materials

Fun with Clay, Play Dough, and Modeling Materials

Welcome to the world of clay and play dough! At all ages, work with clay and play dough gives children many chances for creative experiences. Most children like the damp feel of clay. They like to pound it, roll it, poke holes in it, and pull it apart.

The activities in this book are designed for children aged 2 through 8. An icon representing a suggested age for the activity is listed at the top of each activity. However, use your knowledge of the child's abilities to guide you in choosing and using the activities in this book. Wherever appropriate, information is provided on how to adapt the activity for children over age 8.

Through working with clay and play dough, children can express their creativity and discover and build their own unique styles of expression. Each child's work with clay differs from another child's, just as children's appearances and personalities differ.

Children who see clay as "messy" or "slimy" may not want to work with it. Never force the issue. Be patient and give these children lots of time and plenty of opportunities to see the fun others have with clay. Some adults find that involving timid children first in a "cleaner" aspect of clay work, such as mixing play dough, helps involve those children gradually. Hesitant children might feel more comfortable sitting near you as you pat the dough and describe how it feels. Acknowledge these simple participations. Eventually, when hesitant children feel more comfortable, they may try patting gently with you or a friend.

GETTING STARTED

Process vs. Product

The focus of this book and all early childhood art activities is on process, not product. This means that the process of creating, not the product, is the main reason for the activity. The joys of creating, exploring materials, and discovering how things look and work are all part of the creative process. How the product looks, what it is "supposed to be," is unimportant to the child, and it should be unimportant to the adult.

Young children delight in the experience, the exploration, and the experimentation of art activities. The adult's role is to provide interesting materials and an environment that encourages children's creativity. Stand back when you are tempted to "help" children working with clay. Instead, encourage all children to discover their own unique abilities.

Clay and play dough are especially good for creative expression because they are plastic materials, which means they are flexible. They can be rolled into one form, smashed, and then become another. This soft, plastic quality of clay and dough appeals to children of all ages.

Young children generally use dough and clay again and again rather than make and take objects home.

For special occasions, however, it is nice to allow pieces to harden and to then paint or color them. Two recipes in this book serve this purpose particularly well: Ornamental Clay and Baker's Dough.

Considering the Child

Young children find it hard to wait patiently to use materials in an activity. Often, the excitement of creativity and patience do not mix. In addition, it is sometimes difficult for young children to share. With young children, plan to have enough materials for each child. For example, having enough play dough for each child makes activities more fun and relaxed for young children.

Gathering Materials

Each activity in this book includes a list of required materials. It is important to gather all materials before starting an activity with children. Children's creative experiences are easily discouraged when they must sit and wait while the adult looks for play dough materials. Be sure to gather materials in a place the children can easily access. See **Figure 1** for more ideas on storing art materials.

Using Food Products

Many of the play dough recipes in this book involve the use of food. There are long-standing arguments for and against food use in art activities. For example, many teachers have long used potato printing as a traditional printing activity for young children. These teachers feel potatoes are an economical way to prepare printing objects for children. Using potatoes beyond their shelf life is an alternative to throwing them away. On the other hand, many teachers feel that food is for eating and should be used for nothing else.

This book has many activities that do not use food so that there will be options for teachers who oppose the use of food in art activities. Also, where possible, alternatives to food items are suggested. Whatever your opinion, creative activities in clay and dough are provided for your and the children's exploration and enjoyment.

You will also find recipes in this book for edible and nonedible play doughs. Edible play dough activities are marked with a smiley face with a tongue. When experiencing both kinds of activities, young children may be unclear as to what they can and cannot eat. When conducting these activities, take the time to talk with the children about which things they may taste and which they may not. For example, when making anything mixed with glue, remind the children that glue is not to be tasted.

To help remind young children about what they can and cannot eat, you may find it helpful to display an icon like the one used in this book. To show a "no-taste" activity, use the same smiley face icon under a large, black X. Displaying and reminding the children about the meanings of these symbols can help children avoid confusion about what they can and cannot taste.

Employing Safe Materials

For all activities in this book and for any art activities for young children, be sure to use safe art supplies. Read labels on all art materials. Check materials for age appropriateness. The Art and Creative Materials Institute (ACMI) labels art materials AP (approved product) and CL (certified label). Products with these labels are certified safe for use by young children.

FIGURE 1 · TIPS FOR STORING ART MATERIALS

CLAY

The ways materials, supplies, and space are arranged can make or break children's and teachers' art experiences. Following are suggestions for arranging supplies for art experiences:

1. *Scissor holders*. Holders can be made from gallon milk or bleach containers. Simply punch holes in the containers and place scissors in the holes with the scissor points to the inside. Egg cartons turned upside down with slits in each mound also make excellent holders.

2. *Paint containers*. Containers can range from muffin tins and plastic egg cartons to plastic soft-drink cartons with baby food jars in them. These work especially well outdoors as well as indoors, because they are large and not easily tipped. Place one brush in each container. This prevents colors from mixing and makes cleanup easier.

3. *Crayon containers*. Juice and vegetable cans painted or covered with contact paper work very well.

4. Crayon pieces may be melted in muffin trays in a warm oven. These pieces, when cooled, are nice for rubbings or drawings. Crayola® makes a unit that is designed specifically for melting crayons safely.

5. Printing with tempera is easier if the tray is lined with a sponge or a paper towel.

6. A card file for art activities helps organize the program

7. *Clay containers*. Airtight coffee cans and plastic food containers are excellent ways to keep clay moist and always ready for use.

8. *Paper scrap boxes*. By keeping two or more boxes of scrap paper of different sizes, children will be able to choose the size paper they want more easily.

9. Cover a wall area with pegboard and suspend heavy shopping bags or transparent plastic bags from hooks inserted in the pegboard to hold miscellaneous art supplies. Hang smocks in the same way on the pegboard (at child level, of course).

10. Use the back of a piano or bookcase to hang a shoe bag. Its pockets can hold many small items.

11. Use divided frozen food trays or a revolving lazy Susan to hold miscellaneous small items.

(From Mayesky, Mary. *Creative Activites for Young Children*, 7th ed., Clifton Park, NY: Delmar Learning.)

The ACMI provides an extensive list of materials and manufacturers of safe materials for all young children. This information is available on the ACMI Web site at http://www.acminet.org or by writing to 715 Boylston Street, Boston, MA 02116.

Some basic safety hints for art activities are:

- Always use products that are appropriate for the child. Use nontoxic materials for children in grades 6 and lower.

- Never use products for skin painting or food preparation unless the products are intended for those uses.

- Do not transfer art materials to other containers. You will lose the valuable safety information on the product packages.

- Do not eat or drink while using art and craft materials. Wash after use. Clean yourself and your supplies.

- Be sure that your work area is well ventilated.

Potentially unsafe art supplies for clay and play dough activities include:

- *Powdered clay.* Powdered clay is easily inhaled and contains silica, which harms the lungs. Instead, use wet clay, which cannot be inhaled.

- *Instant papier-mâché.* Instant papier-mâché may contain lead or asbestos. Use only black-and-white newspaper and library paste or liquid starch.

- *Epoxy, instant glues, or other solvent-based glues.* Use only water-based, white glue.

- *Paints that require solvents like turpentine to clean.* Use only water-based paints.

- *Cold water or commercial dyes that contain chemical additives.* Use only natural vegetable dyes made from beets, onion skins, and so on.

- *Permanent markers.* Permanent makers may contain toxic solvents. Use only water-based markers.

Be aware of all children's allergies. Children with allergies to wheat, for example, may be irritated by the wheat paste used in papier-mâché. Children allergic to peanuts must taste nothing with peanut butter. In fact, some centers make it a rule to avoid all peanut butter use in food or art activities. Other art materials that may cause allergic reactions include chalk or other dusty substances, water-based clay, and any material that contains petroleum products.

In addition to children's allergies, be aware of children's habits. Some young children put everything in their mouths. (This can be the case at any age.) Others may be shy and slow to accept new materials. Use your knowledge of children's tendencies to help you plan art activities that are safe for all children.

Creating a Child-Friendly Environment

It is difficult to be creative when you have to worry about keeping yourself and your work area clean. Remember to cover the children. Some good cover-ups are men's shirts (with the sleeves cut off), aprons, pillowcases with holes cut for the head and arms, and smocks. Some fun alternatives are sets of old clothes or shoes that can be worn as "art clothes." These old clothes could become "art journals" as they became covered with the traces of various art projects.

Creating a Child's Art Environment

Encourage young artists by displaying appropriate art prints and other works of art. Do not make the mistake of thinking young children do not enjoy "grownup" art. Children are never too young to enjoy the colors, lines, patterns, and designs of artists' work. Art posters from a local museum, for example, can brighten an art area. Such posters also get children looking at and talking about art, which encourages the children's creative work.

Display pieces of pottery, shells and rocks, and other beautiful objects from nature to encourage children's appreciation of the lines, symmetries, and colors of nature. These design concepts will be part of the children's clay and play dough experiences. Even the youngest child can enjoy the look and feel of smooth, colored rocks or the colors of fall leaves. All these are natural parts of a child's world that can be talked about with young children as they create art. Enjoying the beautiful objects you display in the room can only encourage the creativity of young children.

Understanding Clay and Play Dough Basics

Working with clay and play dough requires some planning. Without planning and basic information, you may have to constantly remind the children about the proper uses of clay.

Following are some tips for clay and play dough setup:

- Place surfaces for working with clay away from things like wheel and climbing toys. Cover the surfaces with linoleum or formica to make cleaning easier. When tables have formica tops, they usually require no additional covering.

- Young children enjoy working with clay on vinyl placemats, Masonite® boards, burlap squares, or brown-paper grocery bags. Newspaper does not work well, because when it gets wet, bits of paper may mix with the clay.

- For clay that is meant to be hardened and possibly painted later, set up a good drying place. Because clay objects may take a few days to dry, set up this place away from frequently used areas.

- Give each child a lump of clay or play dough at least the size of a large apple or a small grapefruit.

- Do not allow children to throw clay on the floor or to interfere with other children's work.

- As an adult, you may sit at the table and play with clay, too, but avoid making objects for the child to copy. This discourages the child's creative use of clay.

- When the children are done with activities, they must store clay and dough until the materials' next use. Form clay into balls, each about the size of an apple. A hole filled with water in each ball helps keep the clay just right for use the next time. Keep clay in a container with a wet cloth or a sponge over the clay. Cover the container with a tight-fitting lid. (Margarine tubs with plastic lids work well.)

- Clay will grow mold when it is too wet and too hard to handle when it becomes very dry. When clay dries, restore it to proper consistency by placing it in a cloth bag and pounding it with a hammer until it breaks into small pieces. After soaking the pieces in water, knead them to the proper consistency again.

- Clay that has grown mold is salvageable. Simply scrape off the moldy area and drain off any water in the bottom of the container.

- Store play dough in a tightly covered container. No water is needed to keep the dough at proper consistency.

Using Potter's Clay

Potter's clay, which you may purchase at any art supply store in moist form, is much easier to work with than dry powder. Potter's clay is available in two colors: gray and terra-cotta. (Terra-cotta looks pretty but stains clothing and is harder to clean). When oilcloth table covers are used with potter's clay, the covers can simply be hung up to dry, shaken well, and put away until next use.

Making Play Dough

Let the children participate in dough making whenever possible. Through making dough, children learn about measuring and blending and cause and effect, and they have the chance to work together.

Doughs that require no cooking are best mixed two batches at a time in separate deep dishpans. Deep pans keep the flour of the dough within bounds. Making two batches at a time relieves congestion and gives the children a better chance to participate.

Tempera powder is the most effective dough coloring agent, because it makes intense shades. For the best results, add it to the flour before pouring in into the liquid.

Dough can be refrigerated and reused several times. Remove the dough at the beginning of the day to allow it to reach room temperature before use. Otherwise, it can be discouragingly stiff and unappealing. It is usually necessary to add flour or cornstarch on the second day to reduce stickiness.

Cleaning Up

For clay cleanup, sponge off tables, mats, and boards. Burlap squares can be stacked and shaken when dry, and grocery bags can be thrown away. Clay-caked hands and tools should never be washed in the sink, because clay can clog the drain. Instead, have the children wipe off their tools and hands with paper towels, then wash them in a basin filled with soapy water. When the clay particles settle, you can let the soapy water down the drain and throw the pieces of clay in the trashcan. Children may then rinse their hands in the sink. The tools may be left to dry on paper towels.

Cooked-cornstarch recipes are particularly difficult to clean up after because they leave a hard, dry film on the pan during cooking. However, an hour or two of soaking in cold water converts this film to a jellylike material that is easily scrubbed off with a plastic pot-scrubbing pad. You might even have one or two of the children work on scrubbing the pot clean!

Exploring Other Ideas

Working with clay and play dough is considered a modeling or sculpture activity. Sculpture is a three-dimensional art form, which means it is "in the round,"or seen on all sides. You will find sculpture activities in this book that include such materials as natural objects, spools, and foil. These activities are included to expand on the traditional sculpture activities with clay and play dough.

Now, prepared with all the preceding information, you can start sharing and enjoying the activities in this book with the children. Enjoy!

5

Years Old and Up

Apple Sculptures

MATERIALS

- ☐ apples
- ☐ toothpicks
- ☐ marshmallows
- ☐ raisins

 **HELPFUL HINT**

- Be prepared for young artists who would rather eat the "details" rather than use them to decorate. This is part of the fun!

DEVELOPMENTAL GOALS

Develop creativity, small motor development, and hand-eye coordination and explore a new kind of sculpture material.

PREPARATION

Instruct children to wash their hands. Break the toothpicks into small pieces.

PROCESS

1. Give each child an apple.
2. Use tiny bits of toothpicks for attaching to the apple.
3. Attach raisins and marshmallows for details.
4. Use whole toothpicks for arms and legs.
5. Display the apple creations until snack time.
6. Enjoy the apple creation for snack!

VARIATIONS

- Make an orange or a pear creation.
- Make favorite animals or storybook characters from apples or other fruit.
- Older children can create a group of apple characters for a short play or story presentation.
- Children under 3 years can add details to the apples with cream cheese or peanut butter instead of toothpicks.

NOTES FOR NEXT TIME: _____

_____

_____

_____

_____

Baker's Dough

All Ages

CLAY

MATERIALS

- ☐ 4 cups flour
- ☐ 1 to 1-1/2 cups water
- ☐ 1 cup salt
- ☐ bowl, spoon for stirring
- ☐ measuring cups

💡 HELPFUL HINTS

- This activity is suitable for dried objects.
- Be careful that children do not touch the warm oven. Have constant adult supervision during the baking process.
- The dough will brown slightly, but baking at lower temperatures is not as successful.
- The children can safely taste this dough, but it is not very yummy!

DEVELOPMENTAL GOALS

Develop creativity, small motor development, and hand-eye coordination; explore a new kind of dough; and reinforce physical changes in materials during mixing.

PREPARATION

Have the children help measure all the ingredients.

PROCESS

1. Mix all ingredients.
2. Mix until the dough is easy to handle.
3. If the dough is sticky, add more flour.
4. If the dough is too dry, add more water.
5. Knead the dough.
6. Roll, punch, and shape the dough as desired.
7. Bake the dough at 350 degrees for 50 to 60 minutes.

VARIATIONS

- Add food coloring to the dough for variety.
- Sprinkle colored sugar on the dough for color before baking.
- Shape the dough into letters, numbers, and shapes.

NOTES FOR NEXT TIME: _____

_____

_____

_____

CLAY, PLAY DOUGH, AND MODELING MATERIALS   Copyright © 2005, Thomson Delmar Learning

All Ages

Basic Clay Modeling

MATERIALS

- ☐ potter's clay (moist clay)
- ☐ plastic garbage bag
- ☐ tape
- ☐ modeling tools (plastic knives, cookie cutters, spatula, tooth-picks, spools, garlic press)

💡 **HELPFUL HINT**

- Notice the different ways children work with the clay. One child may pull, pinch, or squeeze the material into a desired shape. Another may make each part separately, then put them together into a whole figure. Some children may combine these two ways of working. Encourage all children in every way they work with clay.

DEVELOPMENTAL GOALS

Develop creativity, small motor development, and hand-eye coordination and explore new ways to use potter's clay.

PREPARATION

Tape down large plastic garbage bag split at the seams to cover work area. **Be sure to never have loose plastic bags around young children.**

PROCESS

1. Give each child a grapefruit-sized piece of clay.
2. Roll, pound, squeeze, pull, and press clay in any way desired.
3. Use tools to make designs, cut out clay parts, and shape in any way.
4. Leave objects to dry or place clay in airtight container to use again.

VARIATIONS

- Add sticks, tongue depressors, toothpicks, Popsicle sticks, paper clips, nails, and combs for interesting modeling tools.
- For very young clay artists, be sure tools small enough to put in the mouth are not available! All young preschoolers must be supervised in their use of clay and modeling tools.

NOTES FOR NEXT TIME: _____

_____

_____

_____

Box Sculptures

MATERIALS

- ☐ boxes of different sizes and shapes
- ☐ paste
- ☐ tempera paint
- ☐ brushes
- ☐ construction paper
- ☐ scraps of fabric and trim

HELPFUL HINT

- Add powdered detergent to the paint so it will stick to a wax-coated box.

DEVELOPMENTAL GOALS

Develop creativity, small motor development, and hand-eye coordination; explore a new use for a familiar object; and explore a new type of three-dimensional artwork.

PREPARATION

Have children bring in an assortment of boxes. Be sure to include cereal boxes as they make great bases for box sculpture.

PROCESS

1. Use one box as a base.
2. Glue smaller boxes on to make a sculpture design.
3. Glue on cut-construction paper details.
4. Add fabric and trim scraps for more design details.

VARIATIONS

- Make a city of box sculpture buildings.
- Paint the sculpture.
- Create box robots, imaginary animals, and anything else imagined.

NOTES FOR NEXT TIME: _____

_____

_____

_____

_____

Bread-Dough Sculptures

All Ages

MATERIALS

- ☐ 3 tablespoons white glue
- ☐ bread
- ☐ one or two drops of lemon juice
- ☐ paint
- ☐ brushes
- ☐ plastic bag
- ☐ mixing bowl and spoon

 **HELPFUL HINTS**

- While this is not an edible dough, some young artists may taste the dough. If this does happen, rinse the children's mouths with clear water to get rid of the pasty taste.
- Bread-dough clay can be preserved for modeling by putting it in a plastic bag and placing it in a refrigerator.
- Be sure to talk about the physical changes children will see as they make this dough!

DEVELOPMENTAL GOALS

Develop creativity, small motor development, and hand-eye coordination and explore a new form of modeling dough.

PREPARATION

Remove the crusts from four slices of bread. Tear the bread into small pieces. Children love to do this!

PROCESS

1. Mix the pieces of bread thoroughly with white glue and one or two drops of lemon juice.
2. Model or shape as desired.
3. Allow 1 or 2 days for complete drying.

VARIATIONS

- Pieces may be painted with tempera paint.
- Add details with buttons, sequins, and so on before the bread dough dries.

NOTES FOR NEXT TIME: _____

_____

_____

_____

_____

Cheerio™ Sculptures

MATERIALS

- ☐ 3 tablespoons butter
- ☐ 3 cups miniature marshmallows
- ☐ 1/2 teaspoon vanilla
- ☐ 1/2 teaspoon food coloring
- ☐ 4 cups Cheerios™
- ☐ wax paper
- ☐ large pan
- ☐ mixing spoon

💡 HELPFUL HINTS

- Be sure to cool mixture well before shaping!
- Wash the hands before mixing the recipe and before shaping the dough.
- Be sure the children stay well away from the stove during the cooking process.

DEVELOPMENTAL GOALS

Develop creativity, small motor development, and hand-eye coordination and explore a new kind of three-dimensional material.

PREPARATION

Instruct the children to wash their hands. Have the children measure all ingredients.

PROCESS

1. Melt the butter and marshmallows in a large pan over low heat.
2. Remove the mixture from the heat and add vanilla and food coloring of your choice.
3. Fold in the Cheerios™. Allow to cool.
4. Butter the hands.
5. Give each child a lump of the mixture to shape and mold on a piece of wax paper.
6. Let the sculpture set before eating.

VARIATIONS

- Separate the mixture and make two colors of sculpture dough.
- Decorate the design or shape with raisins or gumdrops.

NOTES FOR NEXT TIME: _____

_____

_____

_____

3

Cinnamon Ornament Dough

MATERIALS

- ☐ 1 cup ground cinnamon
- ☐ 4 tablespoons white glue
- ☐ 3/4 cup water
- ☐ mixing bowl and spoon
- ☐ measuring cups
- ☐ cutting board
- ☐ cookie cutters
- ☐ Popsicle sticks
- ☐ straw or pencil for poking holes

💡 HELPFUL HINTS

- This is a non-edible dough. It has a very spicy, unpleasant taste.
- Unused dough can be stored in a covered container in the refrigerator for a day or two.

CLAY

DEVELOPMENTAL GOALS

Develop creativity, small motor development, and hand-eye coordination; explore a new kind of play dough; and reinforce the science concepts of changing materials through mixing the dough.

PREPARATION

Have the children measure all ingredients. Discuss how each ingredient looks, feels, and tastes.

PROCESS

1. Mix all ingredients until they form a cookie-dough.
2. Add more water if the dough is too stiff.
3. Sprinkle some cinnamon on a cutting board.
4. Knead the dough on the cutting board.
5. Roll out to 1/4" thickness.
6. Use cookie cutters, Popsicle sticks, or plastic knives to cut shapes from the dough.
7. Punch a hole in the top with a straw or pencil before drying (to string a ribbon through later for hanging.)
8. Bake in 350 degree oven for 30 minutes or until firm.
9. Cool, then decorate.

VARIATIONS

- Make cinnamon-dough storybook characters. Hang them near the book corner to enjoy.
- Make name in cinnamon-dough letters. Hang them near cubby holes.
- Children can make any object they desire, not only ornaments!
- Decorate with raisins and pieces of nuts before cooking.

NOTES FOR NEXT TIME: _____

_____

CLAY, PLAY DOUGH, AND MODELING MATERIALS

Clay-Coil Pots

MATERIALS

☐ potter's clay

☐ large plastic garbage bag

☐ tape

HELPFUL HINTS

- Older children often enjoy making "something" out of clay. This is a good activity for that purpose.

- Coil pots make nice gifts. And they are functional as well as artwork!

- Oil-based clay cannot be painted but may be exhibited when finished (away from the sun).

- Unfinished clay work may be wrapped in plastic bags or aluminum foil or placed in covered cans with child's name attached.

- Potter's clay may be painted. Use a mixture of fairly thick tempera paint so it will stick to the clay and be bright and bold in color.

DEVELOPMENTAL GOALS

Develop creativity, small motor development, and hand-eye coordination; and explore a new use for clay.

PREPARATION

Tape garbage bag split at the seams to top of work area.

PROCESS

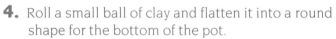

1. Give each child a grapefruit-sized ball of potter's clay.

2. Show the child how to make snakes by rolling out pieces of clay into coils.

3. Make several coils or one very long coil.

4. Roll a small ball of clay and flatten it into a round shape for the bottom of the pot.

5. Moisten the edges of the round bottom piece with water.

6. Wrap the coils around the round bottom piece.

7. Continue wrapping the coil around and around, putting coil upon coil.

8. Moisten the pieces together as you coil.

9. Let the pot dry before painting or decorating.

VARIATIONS

- Make coils into a square-shaped box. This takes more skill and is appropriate for children over 6 years of age.

- Make free-form coil sculptures.

NOTES FOR NEXT TIME: _____

_____

Clay or Dough Crawlers

MATERIALS

- ☐ clay or play dough
- ☐ buttons
- ☐ pipe cleaners
- ☐ toothpicks
- ☐ sequins
- ☐ plastic
- ☐ knives
- ☐ Popsicle sticks

💡 HELPFUL HINTS

- Potter's clay can be painted when dry. Use a fairly thick tempera paint so it will stick to the clay.

- Unfinished clay work may be wrapped in plastic bags or aluminum foil or placed in covered cans with child's name attached.

- Children do not have to make insects with their clay. They can make anything that comes to mind as they work with clay.

- Have a science or picture book with pictures or insects for the children to see.

DEVELOPMENTAL GOALS

Develop creativity, small motor development, and hand-eye coordination and explore new ways to play with clay or dough.

PREPARATION

Give each child an apple-sized ball of potter's clay or play dough. Talk about bugs—real and imagined. Discuss details on bugs such as feelers, eyes, legs, etc. Have the children think about what kind of bugs they could make with clay.

PROCESS

1. Break the clay into small pieces.
2. Roll the clay into round balls for bug bodies.
3. Add pieces of pipe cleaners for feelers.
4. Toothpicks can become legs.
5. Stick on buttons for eyes.
6. Poke in sequins for other details.
7. Leave to dry.

VARIATIONS

- Make clay butterflies, caterpillars, or worms.
- Make a bug family.
- Older children can make models of insects from a science book.

NOTES FOR NEXT TIME: _____

_____

_____

_____

CLAY, PLAY DOUGH, AND MODELING MATERIALS

A

CLAY

Clay Play with Tools

MATERIALS

- ☐ potter's clay
- ☐ rolling pins
- ☐ plastic knives
- ☐ forks
- ☐ cookie cutters
- ☐ garlic press (optional)
- ☐ wooden clay hammers
- ☐ plastic garbage bag
- ☐ tape

 **HELPFUL HINTS**

- A small lump of clay can be used as a magnet to pick up crumbs at cleanup time.

- Unfinished clay work may be wrapped in plastic bags or aluminum foil or placed in covered cans with the child's name attached.

- Oil-base clay cannot be painted but may be exhibited when finished (away from the sun).

- Some children will enjoy manipulating clay without making anything, which is acceptable. Others may want to give names to objects. Encourage all children whatever their approach to clay activities.

DEVELOPMENTAL GOALS

Develop creativity, small motor development, and hand-eye coordination and explore clay as a three-dimensional material.

PREPARATION

Cover work area with garbage bag taped to work surface.

PROCESS

1. Give each child a grapefruit-sized ball of clay.

2. Pat or roll the clay as desired.

3. Encourage the child to squeeze, pinch, or pull the clay into desired shapes.

4. Roll the clay into snakes and little balls.

5. Cut out the clay with cookie cutters or plastic knives.

6. Squeeze the clay through a garlic press.

7. Create texture using fingernails.

VARIATIONS

- For permanent clay sculptures, allow the clay shapes to dry.
- Moisten parts of the clay to join pieces of clay.

NOTES FOR NEXT TIME: _____

_____

_____

_____

A

Cornstarch!

MATERIALS

- ☐ 3 cups cornstarch
- ☐ 2 cups warm water
- ☐ mixing bowl and spoon

 **HELPFUL HINTS**

- Cornstarch works well in a baby bathtub set on a table, with a limit of two or three children making the recipe.

- This is a clean sort of play: the white, powdery mess on the floor can be cleaned easily with a dustpan and a brush or vacuum cleaner.

- Children come back to this cornstarch and water mix again and again, because it feels good and behaves in an interesting way.

DEVELOPMENTAL GOALS

Develop creativity, small motor development, and hand-eye coordination and explore a new kind of manipulative material.

PREPARATION

Have the children measure all ingredients.

PROCESS

1. Put the ingredients in a bowl and mix with the hands.

2. The mixture will solidify when left alone, but it turns to liquid from the heat of the hands. Magic!

3. Wet cornstarch forms an unstable material, which is fun because it exhibits unexpected behavior. It breaks, but it also melts.

VARIATIONS

- Rest the fingers lightly on the surface of the cornstarch-water mix. Let your fingers drift down to the bottom of the container. If you try to punch your way to the bottom, it will resist.

- Leave the cornstarch-water mixture in the container overnight. By morning it is dry. Add some water, and it becomes that wonderful "stuff" again. Be sure to invite the children to watch this event!

NOTES FOR NEXT TIME: _____

_____

_____

_____

_____

A

All Ages

Creative Clay

MATERIALS

- ☐ 1 cup cornstarch
- ☐ 2 cups baking soda (1-pound package)
- ☐ 1-1/4 cups cold water
- ☐ measuring cups
- ☐ mixing bowl and spoon
- ☐ plate
- ☐ damp cloth

💡 HELPFUL HINTS

- Creative clay dries at room temperature in about 3 days.
- It can be dried in a 200 degree oven.
- Use the clay immediately or store it in an air-tight container.
- Be sure the children are well away from the heat source during this activity!

DEVELOPMENTAL GOALS

Develop creativity, small motor development, and hand-eye coordination; explore a new modeling material; and reinforce the science concepts of changing materials through making the recipe.

PREPARATION

Have the children measure all ingredients. Talk about how each looks, feels, tastes, and smells.

PROCESS

1. Stir the starch and soda together.
2. Mix in cold water.
3. Stir over medium heat until the mixture has the consistency of mashed potatoes.
4. Turn the mixture onto a plate and cover it with a damp cloth until cool enough to handle.
5. Knead when cool enough to touch.

VARIATIONS

- Add food coloring for colored clay.
- This clay has a smooth consistency and is great for modeling or making ornaments or even pottery.
- Cut out creative clay with cookie cutters.
- Cut out numbers and letters from creative clay.

NOTES FOR NEXT TIME: _____

_____

_____

_____

CLAY

Crepe-Paper Clay

MATERIALS

- ☐ crepe paper
- ☐ 1 cup flour
- ☐ 1 cup salt
- ☐ large container
- ☐ water

💡 HELPFUL HINTS

- It is best to use one color of crepe paper at a time to produce a clear solid color clay. Crepe paper colors do not mix well.

- Store crepe paper clay in a covered container in the refrigerator.

DEVELOPMENTAL GOALS

Develop creativity, small motor development, and hand-eye coordination; explore a new use for a familiar material; and explore a new kind of modeling material.

PREPARATION

Place crepe paper in a large container and add enough water to cover the paper. Soak for about 1 hour until most of water absorbs into the paper.

PROCESS

1. Pour off excess water.
2. Add small amounts of flour and salt until mixture is clay-like.
3. Mold and form shapes by hand with crepe paper clay.
4. Let the forms dry.

VARIATIONS

- Apply a clear coat of varnish to dried forms to seal.
- Apply a mixture of glue and water to seal the crepe paper clay forms.

NOTES FOR NEXT TIME: _____

_____

_____

_____

Cube Sculptures

MATERIALS

- ☐ boxes of sugar cubes
- ☐ white craft glue
- ☐ toothpicks
- ☐ scrap pieces of fabric and trim
- ☐ beads
- ☐ buttons
- ☐ construction paper

💡 HELPFUL HINTS

- You will probably have a lot of tasting experiences in this activity. Be sure children wash their hands before the activity and keep the tasting experiences to their own artwork!

- Because sugar cubes are small, this activity is most appropriate for children who have fairly good small muscle development in their fingers and hands. It is not easy for very young children to manipulate an item as small as a sugar cube.

- The 2s and 3s may confuse the edible sugar cube with the nonedible glue. For this reason, this activity is not recommended for this age group.

DEVELOPMENTAL GOALS

Develop creativity, small motor development, and hand-eye coordination; and explore new kinds of three-dimensional materials.

PREPARATION

Give each child a good supply of sugar cubes.

PROCESS

1. Glue the sugar cubes together to make forms and shapes.

2. Add details by gluing on buttons, pieces of trim, beads, and so on.

3. Glue the cube sculpture to a construction paper base for display.

VARIATIONS

- Include marshmallows in the cube sculpture.
- Add flavoring such as lemon or maple extract to some sugar cubes. Let them dry and harden before using in this activity.

NOTES FOR NEXT TIME: _____

_____

_____

_____

All Ages

Easy Dough

MATERIALS

- ☐ 1 cup flour
- ☐ 1 cup salt
- ☐ 1 tablespoon salad oil
- ☐ food coloring
- ☐ water
- ☐ mixing bowl and spoon
- ☐ measuring cups

 **HELPFUL HINTS**

- Because this is such an easy recipe, older children may be able to make it themselves after the first couple of tries.
- Because of the very pliable nature of easy dough, it is a great material for young children just beginning to work with clay.

DEVELOPMENTAL GOALS

Develop creativity, small motor development, and hand-eye coordination; explore a new kind of play dough; and reinforce the science concepts of changing materials through making the dough.

PREPARATION

Have the children measure all ingredients.

PROCESS

1. Mix the flour and salt.
2. Add oil.
3. Slowly add water until the mixture is pliable.
4. The dough will be spongy and clay-like.

VARIATIONS

- Add food coloring for colored easy dough.
- Divide the dough and make two colors of dough.
- Add lemon or vanilla extract for a nice smell.
- Add cinnamon or clove powder for another pleasant smell.

NOTES FOR NEXT TIME: _____

_____

_____

_____

A

CLAY

Easy Fudge Dough

MATERIALS

- ☐ 1/4 cup butter
- ☐ 1/4 cup sweet-ened condensed milk
- ☐ 1 teaspoon vanilla
- ☐ 1 pound confec-tioner's sugar
- ☐ 3/4 cup cocoa
- ☐ 1/4 teaspoon salt
- ☐ mixing bowl and spoon
- ☐ measuring cups and spoons
- ☐ wax paper

💡 HELPFUL HINTS

- Wrap a few pieces in aluminum foil for a nice gift for special occasions.
- Be sure to keep children a safe distance from the stove during the cooking part of the recipe.
- Remember to point out the changes in materi-als when they are mixed.

DEVELOPMENTAL GOALS

Develop creativity, small motor development, and hand-eye coordination; explore a new kind of modeling material and reinforce the science concept of material as it changes during mixing.

PREPARATION

Instruct the children to wash their hands. Have the children help measure all ingredients. Talk about the look, feel, smell, and taste of each ingredient.

PROCESS

1. Melt the butter in a saucepan or in the microwave for 10 seconds on high.

2. Stir in the milk and vanilla.

3. Gradually add the mixture of sugar, cocoa, and salt.

4. Mix until soft and creamy.

5. Give each child a spoonful of fudge to mold with the hands.

6. Put the molded fudge on a piece of wax paper and chill.

7. Eat and enjoy!

VARIATIONS

- Use Popsicle sticks to cut and shape the fudge.
- Press the fudge into a buttered pan. Chill and cut into squares.
- For children over 3, top each piece with a piece of walnut or pecan half.
- Do not use nuts if any child has a food allergy.

NOTES FOR NEXT TIME: _____

_____

_____

_____

Favorite Play Dough

MATERIALS

- ☐ 2 cups flour
- ☐ 1 cup salt
- ☐ 4 teaspoons cream of tartar
- ☐ 2 cups water
- ☐ 2 tablespoons salad oil
- ☐ food coloring
- ☐ measuring spoons and cups
- ☐ pot
- ☐ mixing spoon

💡 HELPFUL HINTS

- Dough can be frozen and refrozen several times.
- Be very careful that children stand well away from the stove during the cooking process.

DEVELOPMENTAL GOALS

Develop creativity, small motor development, and hand-eye coordination; explore a new kind of play dough; and reinforce the science concepts of changing materials.

PREPARATION

Have children measure all ingredients. Talk about how each ingredient looks, feels, smells, and tastes.

PROCESS

1. Mix all ingredients in a pot.
2. Cook over medium heat until soft, lumpy ball forms. It happens quickly!
3. Knead for a few minutes until the dough is smooth.
4. Store in an airtight container.

VARIATIONS

- Add food coloring for colored play dough.
- Add spices and extracts such as cinnamon and lemon extract for a yummy-smelling play dough.

NOTES FOR NEXT TIME: _____

_____

_____

_____

CLAY

Feather and Pipe-Cleaner Sculptures

3 Years Old and Up

MATERIALS

- ☐ small paper plates
- ☐ play dough
- ☐ feathers
- ☐ pipe cleaners
- ☐ beads
- ☐ doughnut-shaped cereal (Cheerios™)

💡 HELPFUL HINTS

- You may have to show the children how to make spirals with the pipe cleaners. Give a simple demonstration, then let the children do it themselves.

- Do the same with threading beads or cereal on the pipe cleaners. Give one demonstration, then let the children experiment.

- Have a good supply of doughnut-shaped cereal on hand. Little artists get hungry!

- With 2s and 3s, do not mix beads with cereal pieces, because they are choking hazards.

- If you lack enough feathers for this activity, the pipe cleaners and cereal work well without them.

DEVELOPMENTAL GOALS

Develop creativity, small motor development, and hand-eye coordination and explore a new kind of three-dimensional sculpture.

PREPARATION

Give each child a small paper plate containing a ball of play dough about the size of a golf ball.

PROCESS

1. Flatten the ball just a bit.

2. Wrap the pipe cleaners around pencils or the children's fingers to make spirals.

3. Thread the beads or cereal pieces onto the pipe cleaners.

4. Stick the feathers and pipe cleaners into the play dough.

VARIATION

- Add other details, such as twigs, dried weeds, flowers, or buttons.

NOTES FOR NEXT TIME: _____

_____

_____

_____

_____

Foil Sculptures

MATERIALS

- ☐ foil
- ☐ gummed or transparent tape
- ☐ brush
- ☐ liquid detergent
- ☐ tempera paint
- ☐ cardboard
- ☐ paintbrushes
- ☐ tacky glue

💡 HELPFUL HINTS

- This is a good activity for recycling aluminum foil.
- An adult may help attach the foil sculpture to the cardboard base with a glue gun.

DEVELOPMENTAL GOALS

Develop creativity, small motor development, and hand-eye coordination and explore a new use of foil as a three-dimensional material.

PREPARATION

Crumple the foil into all kinds of forms.

PROCESS

1. Use pieces of crumpled foil to create an object or a design.
2. Join these forms with tape or tacky glue.
3. Glue the forms to a piece of cardboard for a base.
4. After the glue sets, paint the forms with a drop or two of liquid detergent mixed in tempera paint.

VARIATIONS

- Add fabric and trim scraps, feathers, and buttons for fun details.
- Create foil animals, flowers, trees, or even people!

NOTES FOR NEXT TIME: _____

_____

_____

_____

_____

Fun Decorations

MATERIALS

- ☐ play clay (see recipe on page 34)
- ☐ rolling pin
- ☐ cookie cutters of all sizes
- ☐ bottle tops
- ☐ plastic knife
- ☐ needle
- ☐ string or yarn
- ☐ wax paper

💡 HELPFUL HINTS

- Play clay may take up to 36 hours to dry. Be sure to store the drying objects in a safe place away from accidents!

- To speed drying, heat the oven to 350 degrees, then turn the oven off and place the objects on a wire rack or in a cardboard box on the rack. Leave in the oven until the oven is cool.

DEVELOPMENTAL GOALS

Develop creativity, small motor development, and hand-eye coordination; explore a new kind of play dough; and reinforce the science concept of change in materials while mixing the dough.

PREPARATION

Make play clay using the "Play Clay" recipe in this book. Let the children measure and mix the ingredients. Talk about the physical changes in materials when wet and dry materials are mixed.

PROCESS

1. Roll out the play clay to 1/4 inch thickness on wax paper.
2. Cut out shapes with cookie cutters.
3. Cut out free-form shapes, too.
4. Poke a hole in the top of the cut-out object.
5. Let the object dry before inserting yarn in the hole.

VARIATIONS

- Objects may be left white or painted when dry.
- Sprinkle with glitter when the play clay is wet for a glittery effect.

NOTES FOR NEXT TIME: _____

_____

_____

_____

A

All Ages

Gloop

MATERIALS

- ☐ 8 oz. white craft glue
- ☐ 1 cup water
- ☐ 1 cup warm water
- ☐ 1-1/2 teaspoon borax powder
- ☐ tempera paint
- ☐ one large and one small mixing bowl
- ☐ spoon
- ☐ measuring cups and spoons

💡 HELPFUL HINTS

- Elmer's Glue™ works well in this recipe.
- Store the gloop in an airtight container.
- Gloop is very much like silly putty—stretchy and fun to play with!
- Press gloop over colored comic strips. Then, press the gloop on a piece of paper to make a print of the drawing.

DEVELOPMENTAL GOALS

Develop creativity, small motor development, and hand-eye coordination and explore a new kind of modeling material.

PREPARATION

Have the children measure all ingredients. Talk about how each material looks, feels, and smells.

PROCESS

1. Pour the glue into a large bowl.
2. Add water and stir until blended.
3. Add a few drops of paint and stir until mixed well.
4. Set this mixture aside.
5. In a small bowl, stir together the warm water and borax powder until the powder dissolves.
6. Slowly pour this mixture into the glue mixture, stirring constantly for 2 minutes.
7. Knead the mixture with the hands until it is smooth and stretchy.

VARIATION

- Leave out the tempera paint and make white gloop.

NOTES FOR NEXT TIME: _____

_____

_____

_____

A

All Ages

Homemade Glitter Clay

MATERIALS

- ☐ 3 cups flour
- ☐ 1-1/2 cups salt
- ☐ 6 teaspoons cream of tartar
- ☐ 4 tablespoons vegetable oil
- ☐ 3 cups water
- ☐ food coloring
- ☐ glitter (you will need at least 5 containers)
- ☐ large pot
- ☐ mixing spoon
- ☐ measuring cups and spoons

💡 HELPFUL HINTS

- This clay is very salty. Do not let children eat it!

- Be sure children stay well away from the stove top during the cooking process.

- When not in use, store the glitter clay in a plastic bag or plastic container.

DEVELOPMENTAL GOALS

Develop creativity, small motor development, and hand-eye coordination and explore a new kind of play dough.

PREPARATION

Let the children measure all the ingredients.

PROCESS

1. In a pot, combine the flour, salt, and cream of tartar.
2. Add the oil, water, and food coloring.
3. Mix until there are no lumps and the color is uniform.
4. Have adult heat the mixture on medium heat, stirring constantly.
5. Heat the mixture until it forms a ball and pulls away from the sides of the pan.
6. Let the mixture cool.
7. Have the children knead the glitter into the clay by flattening the clay with the hands and pouring some glitter on it. Fold over the clay and knead it for a while.
8. Repeat until the clay looks glittery.
9. Use glitter clay to mold objects and designs.

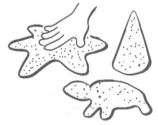

VARIATIONS

- Make two colors of glitter dough.
- Make glitter dough numbers, letters, and ornaments.

NOTES FOR NEXT TIME: _____

_____

All Ages

Honey Dough

MATERIALS

- ☐ 3 tablespoons honey
- ☐ 4 tablespoons peanut butter
- ☐ 1/2 cup nonfat dry milk
- ☐ 1/4 cup dry cereal flakes (crushed)
- ☐ mixing bowl and spoon
- ☐ measuring cups and spoons
- ☐ wax paper
- ☐ butter or margarine

💡 HELPFUL HINTS

- This recipe makes 18 1" balls.
- Be sure the children wash their hands well before mixing the recipe and again before shaping the honey dough.
- Always be sure to check for peanut allergies before using any edible-dough recipe with peanuts or peanut butter.

DEVELOPMENTAL GOALS

Develop creativity, small motor development, and hand-eye coordination; explore a new kind of play dough, relate the science concepts of changing materials to art activities.

PREPARATION

Instruct the children to wash their hands. Have the children measure all ingredients and crush the cereal flakes with a spoon on wax paper. Talk about the appearance, color, taste, and texture of each of the ingredients.

PROCESS

1. Mix the honey and peanut butter in a bowl.
2. Gradually add the nonfat dry milk. Mix well.
3. Give each child a pat of butter or margarine to grease the hands.
4. Give each child a lump of dough to shape into balls or any other desired form.
5. Roll the balls or shapes in dry cereal flakes.
6. Chill until firm.

VARIATIONS

- Roll honey-dough balls in graham cracker crumbs.
- Shape the dough in numbers or letters.
- A group of children can make the letters for a sign or a title for a party or special group project.

NOTES FOR NEXT TIME: _____
_____
_____
_____

Kool-Aid™ Play Dough

MATERIALS

- ☐ 2-1/2 cup flour
- ☐ 1/2 cup salt
- ☐ 2 packages unsweetened Kool-Aid™
- ☐ 2 cups boiling water
- ☐ 3 tablespoons vegetable oil
- ☐ measuring cups and spoons
- ☐ mixing bowl and spoon

💡 HELPFUL HINTS

- This recipe lasts for several months stored in an air-tight container between uses.
- Children will enjoy this different use of a familiar drink mix.
- Be sure to talk about how the ingredients change while they are being mixed.

DEVELOPMENTAL GOALS

Develop creativity, small motor development, and hand-eye coordination; explore a new kind of play dough; and reinforce the science concept of changing materials through mixing the dough.

PREPARATION

Have the children measure all ingredients.

PROCESS

1. Mix all dry ingredients.
2. Add water and oil and stir.
3. Knead with the hands when the mixture is cool.
4. Store the dough in an air-tight container.

VARIATIONS

- Mix dough in colors for holidays or special occasions.
- Add spices or extracts such as lemon, vanilla, and cinnamon for fun smells.

NOTES FOR NEXT TIME: _____

_____

_____

_____

Marshmallow Sculptures

MATERIALS

- ☐ Styrofoam plates or trays
- ☐ miniature and regular sized marshmallows
- ☐ toothpicks
- ☐ gum drops
- ☐ pieces of vegetables
- ☐ grapes

 **HELPFUL HINT**

- Be sure to have a good supply of marshmallows on hand for this activity. Little artists get hungry!

DEVELOPMENTAL GOALS

Develop creativity, small motor development, and hand-eye coordination; explore a new modeling material; and practice three-dimensional designs.

PREPARATION

Instruct the children to wash their hands. Cut up gum drops, grapes, and vegetables into small pieces.

PROCESS

1. Give each child a Styrofoam plate.
2. Use one marshmallow as the base.
3. Build a sculpture with other marshmallows and toothpicks.
4. Add details with bits of gumdrops, grapes, and vegetable pieces.

VARIATIONS

- Use colored marshmallows and regular white marshmallows.
- Make marshmallow animals, people, trees, flowers, and so on.
- Make marshmallow decorations for a special occasion.

NOTES FOR NEXT TIME: _____

_____

_____

_____

_____

All Ages

Mary's Dough

MATERIALS

- ☐ 1 egg
- ☐ 1-1/2 cups warm water
- ☐ 1 package yeast
- ☐ 1 teaspoon salt
- ☐ 1 tablespoon sugar
- ☐ 4 cups flour
- ☐ measuring cups and spoons
- ☐ large bowl
- ☐ mixing spoon
- ☐ cookie sheet
- ☐ grease
- ☐ pastry brush

💡 HELPFUL HINTS

- Be very careful that children do not stand too near the stove.
- Be sure to include such vocabulary words as *liquid*, *solids*, and *tart* when mixing play dough.
- Because this dough uses very little sugar, it is a healthy alternative to most cookie doughs.

DEVELOPMENTAL GOALS

Develop creativity, small motor development, and hand-eye coordination; explore a new kind of play dough; and reinforce the idea of changing materials when mixing the dough.

PREPARATION

Instruct the children to wash their hands. Have the children help measure and pour the ingredients into the bowl and mix. Talk about how materials look different when they are mixed. Let the children taste each of the ingredients. Talk about the tastes and how they differ.

PROCESS

1. Pour 1-1/2 cups warm water into the bowl.
2. Sprinkle the yeast into the water and stir until it is dissolved.
3. Add salt, sugar, and flour. Mix together to form a ball.
4. Sprinkle flour onto the work surface and place dough on it.
5. Let the children knead the dough until it is smooth and elastic.
6. Encourage the children to roll and twist the dough into shapes.
7. Place the dough sculptures on the cookie sheet and cover it with a clean towel. Place in warm area to rise.
8. After dough designs have doubled in size, brush each one with a beaten egg.
9. Cook dough in 350-degree oven for 12 to 15 minutes until they are firm and golden brown.
10. Remove from oven, cool, and enjoy!

VARIATIONS

- Sprinkle sugar or salt on shapes before baking.
- Make dough letters, numbers, animals, or people.

NOTES FOR NEXT TIME: _____

_____

4 Years Old and UP

Mobile Sculptures

MATERIALS

- ☐ tree branches
- ☐ string
- ☐ natural objects such as leaves, acorns, pinecones
- ☐ construction paper
- ☐ wax paper

💡 HELPFUL HINTS

- If the waxed paper does not stay attached to the leaves, the wax coating left by the heat application is enough to harden and preserve the leaves.

- Children may watch the ironing process, but it must be done by an adult. And children need to be closely supervised during the process.

- Adult may need to help child knot the string.

- An adult may need to help the child attach the string so the branch hangs horizontally. This is a good experiment in balance!

- This activity is most appropriate for children with good small motor development.

DEVELOPMENTAL GOALS

Develop creativity, small motor development, and hand-eye coordination; and explore a new three-dimensional activity.

PREPARATION

Go on an outdoor walk with the children. Instruct each child to find a branch about 12 inches long to use in this activity. Collect leaves and other items as well.

PROCESS

1. Adult presses the leaves between two sheets of wax paper, using an iron on the "low" setting. This preserves the leaves.

2. When the wax paper has cooled, cut around the leaves to separate them for the mobile.

3. Adult makes holes in the leaves with a blunt needle, hairpin, or pencil point.

4. Insert string or thin yarn into the holes in each of the leaves. Knot the string or yarn.

5. Attach a piece of string or yarn (about 12 inches long) to the branch, so that the branch hangs horizontally.

6. Tie the leaves on the branch in various places.

7. Leaf shapes cut out of red, yellow, orange and brown construction paper can also be attached to the branch with yarn.

8. Acorns, pinecones and berries may also be strung and attached for added color and variety.

VARIATIONS

- Make theme mobiles such as "All about Me" with cut-out pictures of favorite things.

- Make mobiles of "My Family" or "My Friends."

- Make mobiles with favorite storybook characters.

NOTES FOR NEXT TIME: _____

_____

Mud Bricks

MATERIALS

- ☐ dirt
- ☐ warm area or oven
- ☐ muffin tins
- ☐ plastic bucket
- ☐ newspaper
- ☐ mixing spoon

HELPFUL HINT

- Children usually love playing in the mud. Be prepared for a lot of side activities besides making bricks! Enjoy the slippery, cool feel of the mud yourself, too!

DEVELOPMENTAL GOALS

Develop creativity, small motor development, and hand-eye coordination and explore a new clay technique.

PREPARATION

Dig up dirt outdoors. This is a fun thing for children to do, so you will not lack the dirt you need!

PROCESS

1. Put the dirt in the bucket.
2. Make mud by mixing in a little water at a time.
3. Make it a thick mud.
4. Press the mud into muffin tin cups.
5. It takes about 10 days to set, or bake at 250 degrees for 15 minutes.
6. Spread newspaper on the floor.
7. Create a design using mud bricks.

VARIATIONS

- Add plaster of paris to the mud mixture to help it stick together better.
- Add pieces of twigs, stones, and bits of wood to the design.
- Dig up dirt from different areas of soil. Compare the colors, feel, and texture. Talk about how different the bricks look from each type of soil.

NOTES FOR NEXT TIME: _____

_____

Natural Object Sculptures

MATERIALS

- ☐ clay or play dough
- ☐ natural objects of various sizes and colors (e.g., seeds, twigs, pine cones, seed pods, stones, driftwood, leaves)
- ☐ quick-drying glue
- ☐ construction paper
- ☐ felt
- ☐ fabric and trim scraps

💡 HELPFUL HINTS

- Encourage the children to arrange and rearrange the objects until they are satisfied with the sculpture before gluing it down.

- The younger the child, the shorter the attention span, so expect that very young children will probably use only a few items for this sculpture activity.

- Older children will enjoy adding more details. Be prepared with a wider variety of materials for this age group.

DEVELOPMENTAL GOALS

Develop creativity, small motor development, and hand-eye coordination; explore a new three-dimensional technique; and relate science to art activities.

PREPARATION

Talk about the collection of natural items. Discuss how they can be put together to make a design. Include a discussion on the lines, shapes, sizes, and other details of the natural objects.

PROCESS

1. Use a lump of play dough as a base.
2. Flatten the lump for the base.
3. Poke several natural items into the dough base.
4. When satisfied with the creation, leave it to dry.

VARIATIONS

- Paint or colored paper can be added to enhance the sculpture.
- Use a piece of driftwood or a large twig as the base. Glue objects to it.
- Use toothpicks to attach other interesting items, such as buttons or sequins.

NOTES FOR NEXT TIME: _____
_____
_____
_____
_____

A

All Ages

Ornamental Dough

MATERIALS

- ☐ 1 cup cornstarch
- ☐ 1-1/4 cups water
- ☐ 2 cups baking soda
- ☐ measuring cups
- ☐ spoon for stirring
- ☐ cooking pot (double boiler/ optional)

💡 HELPFUL HINTS

- This activity is suitable for dried objects.
- Let the children measure all ingredients.
- Be very careful with children around the hot stove and pan.
- This dough does not store well. It is best used for making dried objects.
- This dough does not taste good, but it will not harm the children if they taste it.

DEVELOPMENTAL GOALS

Develop creativity, small motor development, and hand-eye coordination; explore a new kind of play dough; and reinforce the science concepts of change in materials while mixing the dough.

PREPARATION

Have the children help measure the ingredients. Mix the ingredients in a pan. Discuss how different the materials look when they are dry and when they are wet and mixed. Use such proper measuring terms such as 1 *cup*. Talk about how materials taste, too.

PROCESS

1. An adult cooks the ingredients until thickened, either in a double boiler or over direct heat. Stir constantly.
2. Cool the mixure.
3. Have the children knead the dough.
4. Have the children make dough into whatever they wish.
5. If the dough is to be used for ornaments, make a hole for hanging the ornament while the dough is still moist.

VARIATIONS

- Add dry tempera paint for vivid colors.
- Sprinkle glitter on wet dough objects for a shiny effect.

NOTES FOR NEXT TIME: _____

_____

_____

Painted-Clay Sculptures

MATERIALS

- [ ] non–oil-based clay (potter's clay), sometimes called "moist clay"
- [ ] rolling pin
- [ ] plastic knives
- [ ] tools such as spatula, cookie cutters, garlic press, forks
- [ ] tempera paint
- [ ] brushes
- [ ] clear gloss enamel (optional)
- [ ] plastic garbage bag
- [ ] tape

💡 HELPFUL HINTS

- After the paint is dry, an adult may apply clear gloss over the clay creation for a shiny effect.
- Store the clay in an airtight container.

DEVELOPMENTAL GOALS

Develop creativity, small motor development, and hand-eye coordination and explore new ways to use clay.

PREPARATION

Tape garbage bag to top of work area.

PROCESS

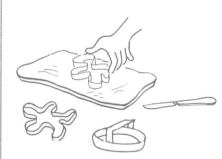

1. Give each child a grape-fruit-sized ball of moist clay.
2. Roll out the clay with a rolling pin.
3. Roll out to about 1/2" thick.
4. Cut out shapes with cookie cutters.
5. Alternatively, cut out shapes with plastic knives.
6. Allow the clay design to dry.
7. Paint the designs with tempera paint.

VARIATIONS

- Add buttons, tiny stones, sequins, and other decorative details.
- Older children can create a group of clay characters, animals, or people to illustrate a favorite story or character.
- Make clay letters and numbers.

NOTES FOR NEXT TIME: _____

_____

_____

_____

CLAY

Paper-Pulp Sculptures

MATERIALS

- ☐ newspaper
- ☐ powder wallpaper paste
- ☐ wintergreen oil
- ☐ bowl
- ☐ wax paper

💡 HELPFUL HINTS

- Let the children tear up the newspaper for this activity. They will love it, and it is good exercise for the small muscles in the fingers and hands.

- Dried paper-pulp objects can be painted with tempera paint or decorated with markers.

DEVELOPMENTAL GOALS

Develop creativity, small motor development, and hand-eye coordination and explore a new three-dimensional material.

PREPARATION

Tear newspaper into tiny pieces and strips. Soak overnight in water.

PROCESS

1. Squeeze excess water from the newspaper pieces.
2. Add powder wallpaper paste and few drops of oil of wintergreen to prevent mold.
3. Keep adding wallpaper paste until a doughy consistency is reached.
4. Knead the mixture until it is smooth and pliable.
5. Mold into shapes or designs on piece of wax paper.
6. Let dry for several days before painting.

VARIATIONS

- Add food coloring to the mixture for colored paper pulp.
- Use buttons, beads, pinecones, and tiny stones for added details. Poke them into the wet paper pulp before drying.

NOTES FOR NEXT TIME: _____

_____

_____

_____

A

All Ages

Peanut-Butter No-Cook Dough

MATERIALS

- ☐ mixing bowl and spoon
- ☐ 1 cup peanut butter
- ☐ 1 cup Karo® syrup
- ☐ 1-1/4 cups nonfat dry milk solids
- ☐ 1 cup sifted confectioner's sugar

💡 HELPFUL HINTS

- Be sure the children wash their hands well before this activity, as well as before shaping their peanut-butter objects—especially if they will be eating them later!
- If the dough is too sticky, add more dry milk.
- Always be sure that the children are not allergic to peanuts before conducting this activity.

DEVELOPMENTAL GOALS

Develop creativity, small motor development, and hand-eye coordination; explore a new type of play dough; and reinforce science concepts through mixing of materials.

PREPARATION

Instruct the children to wash their hands. Have the children sift the confectioner's sugar and measure all ingredients. Discuss each of the materials, its texture, its appearance, and its taste.

PROCESS

1. Blend the peanut butter and syrup in a large mixing bowl.
2. Mix the dry milk and sifted confectioner's sugar.
3. Mix all ingredients—first with a spoon, then with the hands.
4. Turn the mixture onto board and continue kneading until the mixture is well blended and smooth.
5. Give the child a ball of dough to knead and shape.
6. To make cut-out cookies, roll the dough to 1/2" thickness.

VARIATIONS

- Top the mixture with raisins or nuts.
- Make peanut-butter animals to eat at snack time.

NOTES FOR NEXT TIME: _____

_____

_____

_____

CLAY, PLAY DOUGH, AND MODELING MATERIALS

3 Years Old and Up

Play Clay

MATERIALS

- ☐ 1 cup cornstarch
- ☐ 2 cups baking soda (1-pound package)
- ☐ 1-1/4 cups water
- ☐ saucepan
- ☐ measuring cups
- ☐ spoon

💡 HELPFUL HINTS

- For solid-colored play clay, add a few drops of food coloring or tempera paint powder to water before it is mixed with the starch and soda.

- Be sure to talk about the physical changes the children can see during the mixing and making of the dough.

- Be ever watchful of children when working at the stove. Adult supervision must be constant when at the stove.

DEVELOPMENTAL GOALS

Develop creativity, small motor development, and hand-eye coordination; explore a new kind of dough; and reinforce the science concept of change in materials during mixing.

PREPARATION

Let the children measure all ingredients.

PROCESS

1. Mix the cornstarch and baking soda thoroughly in a saucepan.
2. Mix in water.
3. Bring to a boil over medium heat, stirring constantly, until the mixture reaches a moist, mashed-potato consistency.
4. Remove the mixture immediately from heat.
5. Turn the mixture out on a plate and cover it with a damp cloth until cool.
6. When the mixture is easy to handle, the children can knead it like dough.
7. Shape the clay as desired or store it in a tightly closed plastic bag for later use.

VARIATIONS

- Objects may be left white or painted when dry.
- Sprinkle glitter onto the wet play clay. The object will dry even more sparkly!
- Play clay can be shaped into small balls or ovals for beads. Have a adult use a long pin or needle to make a hole for string or yarn to hang the ornament.

NOTES FOR NEXT TIME: _____

_____

Play Clay Pins and Buttons

MATERIALS

- ☐ play clay (see the preceding "Play Clay" activity)
- ☐ rolling pin
- ☐ plastic knife
- ☐ tempera paint
- ☐ sparkle
- ☐ glue
- ☐ wax paper
- ☐ blunt-tipped needle

 **HELPFUL HINTS**

- Dough thicker than 1/4" will make the objects too heavy to wear.

- Play-clay objects will dry and harden at room temperature in approximately 36 hours, depending on thickness.

- To speed drying, heat the oven to 350 degrees. Turn the oven off and place the objects on a wire rack or in a cardboard box on the rack. Leave the play clay in the oven until the oven is cool.

DEVELOPMENTAL GOALS

Develop creativity, small motor development, and hand-eye coordination; explore a new use for play dough; and reinforce the design concepts of line, pattern, and balance.

PREPARATION

Prepare play clay according to the "Play Clay" activity in this book. Let the children measure and mix the ingredients.

PROCESS

1. Roll out the play clay to 1/4 inch thickness on wax paper.
2. Cut the play clay into circles or other designs.
3. Moisten each piece slightly so the pieces stick together.
4. Alternatively, glue the pieces in place when dry.
5. Use the blunt-tipped needle to make holes for buttons. For pins, glue a safety pin to the back when dry.

VARIATIONS

- Paint pins and buttons with tempera paint after the play clay has dried.
- Sprinkle on glitter before drying for a sparkly effect.
- Dried play clay can be decorated with felt-tip markers.
- Dry play clay can also be sprayed with clear plastic, dipped into shellac, or coated with clear nail polish for a permanent finish. Be sure to use any spray in a well-ventilated area!

NOTES FOR NEXT TIME: _____

_____

Play Dough Beads and Such

4 Years Old and Up

MATERIALS

- ☐ 1/2 cup flour
- ☐ 1/3 cup cornstarch
- ☐ 1/2 cup salt
- ☐ 1/3 cup warm water
- ☐ mixing bowl and spoon
- ☐ measuring cups
- ☐ paint
- ☐ paint brushes
- ☐ thread
- ☐ needle

HELPFUL HINTS

- To dry beads, stick toothpicks into a ball of play dough. Then, place a bead on each toothpick.
- As the beads dry, twist the beads on the toothpicks to keep them from sticking to the toothpicks.
- Children can make any other kind of object with the dough if they are not interested in making beads.

DEVELOPMENTAL GOALS

Develop creativity, small motor development, and hand-eye coordination and explore a new kind of modeling material.

PREPARATION

Have the children measure all ingredients.

PROCESS

1. Mix the dry ingredients.
2. Add warm water gradually until the mixture can be kneaded into a stiff dough.
3. If the dough is sticky, dust it with dry flour.
4. Roll the play clay into 1/2-inch balls.
5. Make holes in the balls with toothpick.
6. When dry, paint the beads and string on thread.

VARIATIONS

- Add food coloring or dry tempera paint to the dough for colored play-dough beads.
- Roll out the dough and cut out shapes with cookie cutters. Make a hole in the top for hanging.
- Encourage the children to make original shapes and designs with the dough.

NOTES FOR NEXT TIME: _____

_____

_____

_____

CLAY

3
Years Old and Up

Play Dough Seed Collage

MATERIALS

- ☐ ball of play dough or clay
- ☐ plastic lids
- ☐ seeds, beans, other grains

💡 HELPFUL HINTS

- These dough objects do not have to be left to dry. They can be disassembled, if preferred.
- Clay works well with this activity, as well.
- Talk about what a pattern is: repeating a shape or design. Discuss how a pattern can be used in this activity.
- Introduce the idea of contrast: how different things can be placed near each other to make them stand out. For example, discuss placing a large, shiny stone next to a small, green one.

DEVELOPMENTAL GOALS

Develop creativity, small motor development, and hand-eye coordination; explore a new use for play dough; and practice such design concepts as balance, line, and pattern.

PREPARATION

Give each child a ball of play dough large enough to fit inside the plastic lid.

PROCESS

1. Roll the play dough into a ball.
2. Press the dough into the plastic lid.
3. Arrange seeds, beans, and other grains on the dough.
4. Press the materials into the dough.
5. Allow the dough to dry.

VARIATIONS

- Add other details, such as feathers, small stones, and twigs.
- Press an assortment of buttons into the play dough.

NOTES FOR NEXT TIME: _____
_____
_____
_____

Potato Dough

MATERIALS

- ☐ 1/3 cup mashed potatoes
- ☐ 1-3/4 cups powdered sugar
- ☐ 1 teaspoon vanilla
- ☐ 2 cups flaked coconut
- ☐ measuring cups and spoons
- ☐ mixing bowl and spoon

💡 HELPFUL HINTS

- Be sure the children wash their hands before mixing the recipe and again before shaping the dough.

- This is a fun recipe for young children, because it uses something they think of as a vegetable in a sweet way!

- Because this activity involves no heating, it is a good recipe for very young cooking-artists. It is edible, too!

DEVELOPMENTAL GOALS

Develop creativity, small motor development, and hand-eye coordination and explore a new kind of play dough.

PREPARATION

Instruct children to wash their hands. Prepare the mashed potatoes, either from potatoes or from dry, flaked potatoes. Have the children measure all ingredients.

PROCESS

1. Mix the ingredients in a bowl thoroughly.
2. Give each child a lump of potato dough on a piece of wax paper.
3. Shape the dough into desired shapes.
4. Place the dough in the refrigerator until very cool.

VARIATIONS

- Add details with bits of raisins, nuts, or semisweet chocolate pieces.
- Shape the dough into numbers or letters.

NOTES FOR NEXT TIME: _____

_____

_____

_____

3
Years Old and UP

Rock Sculptures

MATERIALS

- ☐ rocks of various sizes
- ☐ glue
- ☐ markers
- ☐ paint
- ☐ scraps of fabric, trim

💡 HELPFUL HINTS

- Be sure to be watchful of very young children who put everything in their mouth during this activity.

- Be sure rocks are too large to be swallowed.

DEVELOPMENTAL GOALS

Develop creativity, small motor development, and hand-eye coordination; explore a new use for a familiar object; and explore a new form of sculpture design.

PREPARATION

Go outside and collect the rocks for this activity. Talk with the children about the rocks—their colors, shapes, sizes, lines and other details. Ask them to think about what they would like to make with the rocks. Wash and dry the rocks thoroughly.

PROCESS

1. Use one rock for a base.
2. Glue on a rock for a head or simply for another part of the sculpture.
3. Glue on other details with bits of trim and fabric.
4. Draw on details with markers or paint.

VARIATIONS

- Make a family of rock people.
- Make a zoo filled with rock animals.
- Make abstract sculptures out of rocks.
- Glue small pebbles onto paper boxes for unusual gifts.

NOTES FOR NEXT TIME: _____

_____

_____

_____

3 Years Old and Up

Salt Dough

CLAY

MATERIALS

- ☐ 3/4 cup water
- ☐ 1 cup salt
- ☐ 1/2 cup cornstarch
- ☐ mixing spoon
- ☐ measuring cups
- ☐ aluminum foil
- ☐ pan
- ☐ stove or hot plate

💡 HELPFUL HINTS

- Constant adult supervision is necessary when cooking the dough. Keep children a safe watching distance from the stove top.

- Store leftover salt dough in a plastic bag. It will keep for a few days. Knead the dough before using it to make it pliable again.

DEVELOPMENTAL GOALS

Develop creativity, small motor development, and hand-eye coordination and explore a new use for crayons.

PREPARATION

Have the children help measure all ingredients. Let the the children taste the dry ingredients. Talk about how the ingredients taste.

PROCESS

1. Mix 1 cup salt, 3/4 cup water, and 1/2 cup cornstarch in a pan.
2. Cook over medium heat, stirring constantly until the mixture thickens into a doughy consistency.
3. Remove the mixture from the heat and cool on a piece of foil.
4. Have the child knead the dough thoroughly until it is soft and pliable.
5. Shape the dough into forms or objects.
6. The dough will dry hard without baking.

VARIATIONS

- Make decorations, pins, play fruit, beads, and letters from the salt dough.
- An adult or older children can brush on a coat of clear nail polish for a shiny finish.
- Add food coloring or liquid tempera for colored salt dough.

NOTES FOR NEXT TIME: _____

_____

_____

48 **CLAY, PLAY DOUGH, AND MODELING MATERIALS**

A

All Ages

Sawdust Sculptures

MATERIALS

- ☐ wallpaper paste
- ☐ water
- ☐ large mixing bowl
- ☐ mixing spoon
- ☐ sawdust

💡 HELPFUL HINTS

- The sawdust sculpture takes 2 or 3 days to dry.
- Store drying pieces in a safe place where they will not get knocked down during the drying period.
- Ask folks at a local lumber-yard or home-decorating store to save sawdust for this activity.

DEVELOPMENTAL GOALS

Develop creativity, small motor development, and hand-eye coordination; explore a new kind of dough; and reinforce the recycling of sawdust for an art activity.

PREPARATION

Have at least 2 cups of sawdust for this recipe. Ask parents or friends to help accumulate it for this activity.

PROCESS

1. Mix the wallpaper paste and water to a thick, doughy consistency.
2. Add sawdust until the mixture can be formed into a ball.
3. Give each child a lump of the mixture to mold into any shape or form.
4. Dry the shapes for 2 or 3 days.

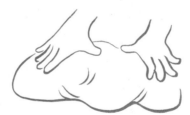

VARIATIONS

- Paint the dried shapes with tempera paint.
- Add toothpicks, buttons, and sequins for added details.

NOTES FOR NEXT TIME: _____

_____

_____

_____

Sculpture Bouquets

MATERIALS

☐ container to hold play dough (e.g., tin can, old vase, paper cup, margarine tub)

☐ play dough or clay

💡 HELPFUL HINTS

• Start by poking in the tallest pieces first; then use the short ones.

• Objects can be added later to the bouquet. It can be an ongoing display reflecting the seasons!

DEVELOPMENTAL GOALS

Develop creativity, small motor development, and hand-eye coordination; explore a new kind of three-dimensional sculpture material; and discuss such design concepts as size, shape, texture, and placement.

PREPARATION

Collect such natural objects as dried flowers, weeds, twigs, and leaves. Take the children on an outdoor walk for the fun of collecting objects for their sculpture bouquets.

PROCESS

1. Select a container in which to put the natural objects.

2. Put a lump of clay or play dough in the bottom of the container.

3. Squish down the clay or dough so it fills the bottom (or most of the bottom) of the container.

4. Begin the arrangement by poking one object into the dough.

5. Put in other pieces, one by one.

6. Try placing objects at various heights and angles.

7. Turn the sculpture around and look at it from all sides. Fill open spots.

VARIATIONS

• Use objects with different textures, colors, and shapes.

• Look for interesting objects, such as feathers and pine cones on pieces of branches, to add to the bouquet.

NOTES FOR NEXT TIME: _____

_____

_____

_____

Soap-Ball Sculptures

MATERIALS

- ☐ box of soap flakes
- ☐ bowl
- ☐ mixing spoon
- ☐ water
- ☐ wax paper

💡 HELPFUL HINT

- The sculpture can be taken apart and used as soap later.

DEVELOPMENTAL GOALS

Develop creativity, small motor development, and hand-eye coordination and explore a new kind of modeling material.

PREPARATION

Pour whole box of soap flakes into a large bowl.

PROCESS

1. Add water to the soap flakes until the mixture is the consistency of paste.
2. Working on a piece of wax paper, roll the mixture into balls.
3. Put the balls together for designs or objects.
4. Toothpicks help hold balls together.
5. Let the sculpture dry on a piece of wax paper.

VARIATIONS

- Use pipe cleaners or toothpicks for arms.
- Use buttons, sequins, and beads for other details.
- Make soap balls to give as gifts.
- Make soap animals, flowers, and people.
- Add tempera paint for colorful soap balls.

NOTES FOR NEXT TIME: _____

_____

_____

A

All Ages

Soapy Sculpture Dough

MATERIALS

- ☐ 2 cups soap flakes
- ☐ 2 tablespoons water
- ☐ large bowl
- ☐ mixing spoon
- ☐ measuring spoons and cups

💡 HELPFUL HINTS

- This dough is white and very pliable. Because it is very easy to manipulate, it is good for very young children just starting to use modeling materials.

- If a child accidentally gets a taste of the soap dough, help rinse the child's mouth with water until the taste is gone. If soap gets into the child's eye, flood the eye with clear water.

- This is a good material to carve with a spoon, a Popsicle stick, a toothpick or another tool.

- Be sure to talk about the physical changes children can see during the mixing and making of this dough.

DEVELOPMENTAL GOALS

Develop creativity, small motor development, and hand-eye coordination; explore a new kind of dough and reinforce the science concept of change in materials during mixing.

PREPARATION

Let children measure all ingredients.

PROCESS

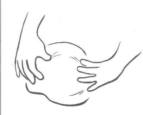

1. Add water slowly to the soap flakes until the mixture is the consistency of paste.
2. Let the children mix the materials to this consistency.
3. Form grapefruit-sized balls with lumps of the mixture.
4. Use the modeling soap to make any dough creation desired.

VARIATIONS

- Decorate soap-dough creations with toothpicks, pipe cleaners, buttons, and sequins.
- Add this soap-dough mixture to your modeling materials in the wintertime.
- Add food coloring for colored soap dough.
- Make the dough into soap balls or shapes to use at home or school, or give them as gifts.
- Make fragrant soap balls by adding vanilla or lemon extract or spices like cinnamon.

NOTES FOR NEXT TIME: _____

_____

_____

A

All Ages

Spicy Cinnamon Apple Dough

MATERIALS

- ☐ 1 cup ground cinnamon
- ☐ 1 cup applesauce
- ☐ 1/4 cup white glue
- ☐ bowl
- ☐ measuring cups
- ☐ spoon
- ☐ cutting board
- ☐ rolling pin
- ☐ cookie cutters
- ☐ Popsicle sticks
- ☐ plastic knives

 **HELPFUL HINT**

- Store the dough in a bowl covered with plastic wrap.

DEVELOPMENTAL GOALS

Develop creativity, small motor development, and hand-eye coordination; explore a new kind of play dough; and reinforce the science concepts of changes in materials through making the recipe.

PREPARATION

Remind the children that this dough is not edible! Have children measure out all ingredients. They can taste the materials before mixing them together.

PROCESS

1. Add cinnamon to applesauce until it is a clay-like consistency.
2. Add glue to thicken the mixture.
3. Mix until smooth and pliable.
4. Give each child a ball of dough to mold and shape.
5. Let the dough dry.

VARIATIONS

- Add glitter for a sparkly dough.
- Cut out letters, numbers, and shapes with Popsicle sticks or plastic knives.
- Cut out dough with cookie cutters.
- Decorate dough with buttons, sequins, and tiny rocks before setting out to dry.

NOTES FOR NEXT TIME: _____

_____

_____

_____

Clay

CLAY

Spool Sculptures

MATERIALS

- ☐ spools (a variety of sizes)
- ☐ assorted fabric pieces
- ☐ markers
- ☐ glue
- ☐ sequins
- ☐ buttons
- ☐ feathers
- ☐ anything that will stimulate children's imaginations as decorations

💡 HELPFUL HINTS

- Ask a local tailor or dry cleaner to save spools for this activity.
- Remember that the younger the child, the larger the spools required.

DEVELOPMENTAL GOALS

Develop creativity, small motor development, and hand-eye coordination and explore a new use of spools as three-dimensional materials.

PREPARATION

Talk about the various spools. Discuss what they could become. ("What do their shapes remind you of?") Encourage all kinds of replies.

PROCESS

1. Use the spool as a body.
2. Glue on materials for clothes.
3. Alternatively, use the spool purely as a base of a decoration.
4. Draw details on the spool with markers.
5. Glue on bits and pieces of yarn and ribbon for other details.

VARIATIONS

- Make a spool family.
- Older children can create a group of characters from a favorite story or fairy tale.
- Make spool buildings, cars, or animals.

NOTES FOR NEXT TIME: _____

_____

_____

_____

4
Years Old and Up

String and Glue Sculptures

MATERIALS

- ☐ heavy string
- ☐ glue
- ☐ wax paper
- ☐ bowl

💡 HELPFUL HINTS

- The longer the piece of string, the more fun it will be to make a string sculpture. If you conduct this activity with children under age 4, however, use a string no longer than 12 inches.

- Because this activity involves waiting to see how the product turns out, it is most suitable for children aged 4 and up. Younger children will simply enjoy manipulating the string!

DEVELOPMENTAL GOALS

Develop creativity, small motor development, and hand-eye coordination and explore new kinds of sculpture materials.

PREPARATION

Dip the heavy string into a bowl of glue. Be sure the string is completely covered with glue.

PROCESS

1. Give each child a glue-soaked piece of string.
2. Form a shape with the string on wax paper.
3. Let the glue dry completely.
4. Remove the string sculpture from the wax paper.

VARIATIONS

- Add food color to the glue for a colorful string sculpture.
- Add glitter to the glue for a sparkly string sculpture.
- Hang on a string for a string sculpture mobile.
- Use different kinds of heavy string for different textures.
- Use small, medium, and long pieces of glue-soaked string.

NOTES FOR NEXT TIME: _____

_____

_____

_____

CLAY, PLAY DOUGH, AND MODELING MATERIALS

Years Old and Up

CLAY

Stuffed Paper-Bag Sculptures

MATERIALS

- ☐ paper bags of various sizes
- ☐ newspaper
- ☐ tempera paint
- ☐ paintbrushes
- ☐ markers
- ☐ string or rubber bands
- ☐ wallpaper paste
- ☐ mixing bowl and spoon

💡 HELPFUL HINTS

- Be sure to tell the children that this is a two-step process. Remind the children they will have to wait until the bags are completely dry before painting.

- Very young children enjoy simply stuffing the bag with paper and possibly doing a little bit of decorating, as well.

DEVELOPMENTAL GOALS

Develop creativity, small motor development, and hand-eye coordination and explore a new three-dimensional media.

PREPARATION

Wad newspapers into balls. Tear other pieces of newspaper into strips. Mix wallpaper paste according to directions on package.

PROCESS

1. Fill a paper bag with wads of newspaper.
2. Close the bag with piece of string or rubber band.
3. Dip strips of newspaper into the wallpaper paste.
4. Pull the newspaper strip between two fingers to remove excess paste.
5. Wrap the strip around the paper bag
6. Continue adding strips, forming such details as arms, a nose, ears, and a tail.
7. Let the bag dry completely before painting or decorating it with markers or crayons.

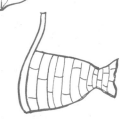
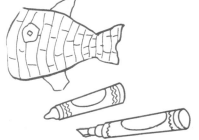

VARIATIONS

- Cover milk cartons, tissue boxes, oatmeal boxes, and other containers with paper strips. Dry and then paint.
- Glue on yarn for hair, buttons for eyes, and fabric and trim scraps for clothing details.

NOTES FOR NEXT TIME: _____

_____

Styrofoam Sculptures

MATERIALS

- ☐ Styrofoam of various sizes and shapes, such as sheets, broken parts of packaging materials, "peanuts," etc.
- ☐ white glue
- ☐ pieces of cardboard (optional)
- ☐ toothpicks
- ☐ scraps of fabric, trim
- ☐ ribbon
- ☐ markers
- ☐ tempera paint
- ☐ brushes

💡 HELPFUL HINT

- Some children may insist on making "something" out of the Styrofoam rather than an abstract design. This is perfectly okay. Try to encourage them to make a "creative something!"

DEVELOPMENTAL GOALS

Develop creativity, small motor development, and hand-eye coordination and explore a new three-dimensional material.

PREPARATION

Talk with the children about the collection of Styrofoam. Discuss size and shape of the pieces. Ask the children to think about what they would like to create with these pieces.

PROCESS

1. Use a piece of cardboard or sheet of Styrofoam as a base.
2. Glue pieces of Styrofoam onto the base.
3. Use toothpicks to add small pieces to the design.
4. Continue gluing on pieces until satisfied with the design.

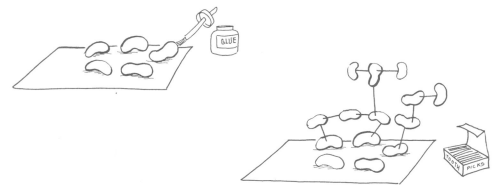

VARIATIONS

- Use markers to draw details on the sculpture.
- Paint the sculpture with tempera paint.
- Glue on pieces of fabric, trim, and ribbon for interesting effects.

NOTES FOR NEXT TIME: _____

_____

_____

_____

CLAY

A

All Ages

Uncooked Play Dough

MATERIALS

- ☐ 3 cups flour
- ☐ 1 cup water
- ☐ 1/4 cup salt
- ☐ 1 tablespoon oil
- ☐ coloring
- ☐ spoon for mixing
- ☐ measuring cups and spoons

💡 HELPFUL HINTS

- The deeper the dishpan, the less mess.
- Store dough in the refrigerator in a closed container.
- Take the play dough out early in the day so it is at room temperature when used. It is more pliable and fun to work with at room temperature.

Clay

DEVELOPMENTAL GOALS

Develop creativity, small motor development, and hand-eye coordination and explore science concepts while making play dough.

PREPARATION

Gather all materials. Have a deep plastic dishpan available for mixing ingredients. Let the children help with the measuring and mixing. Talk about the changes in materials as they are mixed. Talk about how the flour looks dry, then how it looks mixed with the water and with the oil. Use words like *dry* and *liquid*, as well as the correct words for the measurements of materials.

PROCESS

1. Mix the flour and salt.
2. Add water with coloring and oil gradually.
3. Add more water if too stiff.
4. Add more flour if too sticky.
5. Store the dough in plastic bags or a covered container.

VARIATIONS

- Prepare two recipes in two dishpans. Make each a different color.
- Shake in cinnamon, ground cloves, or peppermint extract for interesting smells.
- Divide the recipe into several smaller bowls to make several colors of dough.

NOTES FOR NEXT TIME: _____

_____

Yummy Play Dough

MATERIALS

- ☐ creamy peanut butter
- ☐ marshmallow crème
- ☐ graham cracker crumbs
- ☐ wax paper
- ☐ bowls
- ☐ spoons
- ☐ plastic knives

HELPFUL HINTS

- Check for peanut allergies before conducting this activity.
- Be sure children wash hands before mixing the recipe and before shaping the dough.
- Because this is such a simple recipe, it is great for very young artists!
- Remember to talk about each of the ingredients—its smell, texture, color, and taste before, during, and after mixing.

DEVELOPMENTAL GOALS

Develop creativity, small motor development, and hand-eye coordination; explore a new kind of play dough; and reinforce the science concepts of changing materials through mixing the dough.

PREPARATION

Instruct the children to wash their hands. Let the children feel the smoothness of both the peanut butter and the marshmallow crème.

PROCESS

1. Mix equal parts of peanut butter and marshmallow crème in a bowl.
2. Stir until smooth and pliable. Children can help do this.
3. With clean hands, mold into shapes or designs on wax paper surface.
4. Roll in graham-cracker crumbs.
5. Let set for an hour or so.
6. Enjoy!

VARIATIONS

- Use chunky peanut butter. Talk about the difference it makes in the dough.
- Use tools to cut out the dough into shapes, letters, and numbers.

NOTES FOR NEXT TIME: _____

_____

_____

_____

Edible Doughs

PEANUT-BUTTER NO-COOK DOUGH

1 cup peanut butter

1 cup Karo syrup

1-1/4 cups nonfat dry milk solids

1 cup sifted confectioners sugar

1. Blend peanut butter and syrup in large mixing bowl.
2. Mix dry milk and sifted confectioners sugar together.
3. Mix all together—first with a spoon and then with the hands.
4. Turn onto board and continue kneading until mixture is well blended and smooth.
5. Give each child a ball of dough to knead and shape.
6. To make cut-out cookies, roll dough to 1/2 inch thickness.

HONEY DOUGH

3 tablespoons honey

4 tablespoons peanut butter

1/2 cup nonfat dry milk

1/4 cup dry cereal flakes (crushed)

1. Mix honey and peanut butter in bowl.
2. Gradually add nonfat dry milk. Mix well.
3. Give each child a pat of butter or margarine to grease their hands.
4. Give child a lump of dough to shape into balls or any other desired form.
5. Roll balls or shapes in dry cereal flakes.
6. Chill until firm.

EASY FUDGE DOUGH

CLAY

1/4 cup butter

1/4 cup sweetened condensed milk

1 teaspoon vanilla,

1 pound confectioners' sugar

3/4 cup cocoa

1/4 teaspoon salt

1. Melt butter in a saucepan (or in the microwave for 10 seconds on HIGH).
2. Stir in milk and vanilla.
3. Gradually add mixture of sugar, cocoa, and salt.
4. Mix until soft and creamy.
5. Give each child a spoonful of fudge to mold with hands.
6. Put molded fudge on piece of wax paper and chill.
7. Eat and enjoy!

MARY'S DOUGH

1 egg

1-1/2 cups cups warm water

1 package yeast

1 teaspoon salt

1 tablespoon sugar

4 cups flour

1. Pour 1-1/2 cups warm water into the bowl.
2. Sprinkle the yeast into the water and stir until it is dissolved.
3. Add salt, sugar, and flour. Mix together to form a ball.
4. Sprinkle flour onto the work surface and place dough on it.
5. Let the children knead the dough until it is smooth and elastic.
6. Encourage the children to roll and twist the dough into shapes.
7. Place the dough sculptures on the cookie sheet and cover it with a clean towel. Place in warm area to rise.
8. After dough designs have doubled in size, brush each one with beaten egg.
9. Cook dough in 350-degree oven for 12 to 15 minutes until they are firm and golden brown.
10. Remove from oven, cool, and enjoy!

POTATO DOUGH

1/3 cup mashed potatoes

1-3/4 cups powdered sugar

1 teaspoon vanilla

2 cups flaked coconut

1. Mix ingredients in a bowl thoroughly.
2. Give each child a lump of potato dough on a piece of wax paper.
3. Shape into desired shape.
4. Place in refrigerator until very cool.

YUMMY PLAY DOUGH

creamy peanut butter

marshmallow crème

graham cracker crumbs

1. Mix equal parts of peanut butter and marshmallow crème together in bowl.
2. Stir until smooth and pliable. Children can help do this.
3. With clean hands, mold into shapes or designs on wax paper surface.
4. Roll in graham cracker crumbs.
5. Let set for an hour or so.
6. Enjoy!

Index by Ages

CLAY

PART II

Crayons, Chalk, and Markers

Fun with Crayons, Chalk, and Markers

Welcome to the world of crayons, chalk, and markers! As the activities in this book show, these are more than just traditional art materials. Crayons, chalk, and markers are art materials full of creative possibilities!

Crayons are the most basic, most familiar, and easiest tool for young children to use. Large crayons are easy to hold and can make attractive marks on paper. Crayon drawing is an excellent opportunity for creative picture marking. Using crayons, children can tell stories visually, as they feel them. Most young children have crayons, but they often only use them to draw on paper. As this book shows, crayons can engage children's interest in many other ways. The creative uses of crayons in this book inspire many other unique uses for them.

Like crayons, chalk has endless creative possibilities. It is inexpensive and comes in various colors. Most people think of using chalk only on a chalkboard, but, as this book shows, chalkboard is but one of the many surfaces on which to use chalk. As you use the activities in this book, you will surely develop new and different surfaces for chalk creations.

Felt-tip markers are excellent tools for creative activities. They provide clear, quick, easily made, and nice-looking marks. Because felt-tip markers require little pressure to make bold marks, they are excellent tools for the youngest artists. Though this book emphasizes crayons and chalk, many activities include markers, as well.

The activities in this book are designed for children aged 2 through 8. An icon representing a suggested age for the activity is listed at the top of each activity. However, use your knowledge of the child's abilities to guide you in choosing and using the activities in this book. Wherever appropriate, information is provided on how to adapt the activity for children over age 8.

The focus of this book is a creative approach to using crayons, chalk, and markers. The activities are meant to be starting points for exploring this art form. Both you and the children are encouraged to explore, experiment, and enjoy the world of crayons, chalk, and markers.

GETTING STARTED

Process vs. Product

The focus of this book and all early childhood art activities is the process, not the product. This means that the process of creating, not the product, is the main reason for the activity. The joys of creating, exploring materials, and discovering how things look and work are all part of the creative process. How the product looks, what it is "supposed to be," is unimportant to the child, and it should be unimportant to the adult.

Young children delight in the experience, the exploration, and the experimentation of art activities. The adult's role is to provide interesting materials and an environment that encourages children's creativity. Stand back when you are tempted to "help" children in their art activities. Instead, encourage all children to discover their own unique abilities.

Starting with Crayons, Chalk, and Markers

In their first attempts at using crayons, young children usually work randomly. This first step is normally called "scribbling." At the very beginning, early scribblers scribble for the sheer joy of the movement. There is little concern for making scribbles in any particular direction or shape.

As children become more and more involved with crayoning, they gradually develop the physical skills to control their scribbles. As this stage, they scribble purposefully in one direction or another.

As children develop motor control and hand-eye coordination, and when they have a chance to use crayons regularly, they are gradually able to make simple forms: lines, circles, ovals, squares, and rectangles. As their motor control and hand-eye coordination continue to develop, children can combine these simple forms into figures, such as stick figures, trees, and houses. Combining these simple figures, a child can make a picture. This is an important step, because children can express their feelings and ideas visually on the paper. It is a long way from those first random scribbles!

The process is much the same with chalk and markers—from random scribbling through controlled scribbles to basic forms and finally to picture making. Of the two, young artists use chalk less commonly, perhaps because chalk is brittle and easily broken. It is also impermanent, smearing very easily. However, there are some effective ways to incorporate chalk into young children's artwork. These ideas are covered in later sections.

Considering the Child

Young children find it hard to wait patiently to use materials in an activity. Often, the excitement of creativity and patience do not mix. In addition, it is sometimes difficult for young children to share. With young children, plan to have enough crayons, markers, and chalk for each child's use. For example, have a good supply of markers so that each child can use colors without waiting. Ample supplies encourage creative activities.

Gathering Materials

Each activity in this book includes a list of required materials. It is important to gather all materials before starting an activity with children. Children's creative experiences are easily discouraged when they must sit and wait while the adult looks for the tape, extra scissors, or colored paper. Be sure to gather materials in a place children can easily access.

Storing and Making Materials Available

Having the appropriate crayons and markers for artwork is not enough. These materials must be stored and readily accessible to the children. For example, jumbling crayons, markers, and chalk together in a basket is not ideal. Instead, place the materials in separate boxes so that each child has an individual, complete set. This system reduces arguments and ensures that all colors are available to all children as needed.

Another option is to store the materials in a clear-plastic box that is shallow enough for children to easily search. Some teachers find clear-plastic shoeboxes invaluable for storing children's chalk, crayons, and markers. Such containers, which are available at economy stores, are great for storing and stacking all kinds of art materials. Yet another alternative is to store crayons or markers in wide-mouth containers according to color: all red crayons in one container, all blue in another, and so on.

Be creative when thinking about how to store and make available materials for your little artists. Storing supplies in handy boxes and other containers makes creating art, and cleaning up afterward, more fun! **Figure 1** gives some added hints for storing materials.

Using Food Products

Several activities involve the use of different kinds of foods. There are long-standing arguments for and against food use in art activities. For example, many teachers have long used potato printing as a traditional printing activity for young children. These teachers feel that potatoes are an economical way to prepare printing objects for children. Using potatoes beyond their shelf life is an alternative to throwing them away. On the other hand, many teachers feel that food is for eating and should be used for nothing else.

This book has many activities that do not use food so that there will be options for teachers who oppose food use in art activities. Also, where possible, alternatives to food items are suggested. Whatever your opinion, creative activities in printing are provided for your and the children's exploration and enjoyment.

Employing Safe Materials

For all the activities in this book and in any art activities for young children, be sure to use safe art supplies. Read labels on all art materials. Check materials for age appropriateness. The Art and Creative Materials Institute (ACMI) labels art materials AP (approved product) and CL (certified label). Products with these labels are certified safe for use by young children. The ACMI provides an extensive list of materials and manufacturers of safe materials for all young children. This information is available on the ACMI Web site at http://www.acminet.org or by writing to 715 Boylston Street, Boston, MA 02116.

Some basic safety hints for art activities are:

- Always use products that are appropriate for the child. Use nontoxic materials for children in Grades 6 and lower.
- Never use products for skin painting or food preparation unless the products are intended for those uses.
- Keep art materials in their original containers. Do not transfer art materials to other containers. You will lose the valuable safety information on the product packages.
- Do not eat or drink while using art and craft materials. Wash after use. Clean yourself and your supplies.
- Be sure that your work area is well ventilated.

FIGURE 1 · TIPS FOR STORING ART MATERIALS

The ways materials, supplies, and space are arranged can make or break children's and teachers' art experiences. Following are suggestions for arranging supplies for art experiences:

1. *Scissor holders*. Holders can be made from gallon milk or bleach containers. Simply punch holes in the containers and place scissors in the holes with the scissor points to the inside. Egg cartons turned upside down with slits in each mound also make excellent holders.

2. *Paint containers*. Containers can range from muffin tins and plastic egg cartons to plastic soft-drink cartons with baby food jars in them. These work especially well outdoors as well as indoors, because they are large and not easily tipped. Place one brush in each container. This prevents colors from mixing and makes cleanup easier.

3. *Crayon containers*. Juice and vegetable cans painted or covered with contact paper work very well.

4. Crayon pieces may be melted in muffin trays in a warm oven. These pieces, when cooled, are nice for rubbings or drawings. Crayola® makes a unit that is designed specifically for melting crayons safely.

5. Printing with tempera is easier if the tray is lined with a sponge or a paper towel.

6. A card file for art activities helps organize the program.

7. *Clay containers*. Airtight coffee cans and plastic food containers are excellent ways to keep clay moist and always ready for use.

8. *Paper scrap boxes*. By keeping two or more boxes of scrap paper of different sizes, children will be able to choose the size paper they want more easily.

9. Cover a wall area with pegboard and suspend heavy shopping bags or transparent plastic bags from hooks inserted in the pegboard to hold miscellaneous art supplies. Hang smocks in the same way on the pegboard (at child level, of course).

10. Use the back of a piano or bookcase to hang a shoe bag. Its pockets can hold many small items.

11. Use divided frozen food trays or a revolving lazy Susan to hold miscellaneous small items.

(From Mayesky, Mary. *Creative Activites for Young Children*, 7th ed., Clifton Park, NY: Delmar Learning.)

Potentially unsafe paper-art supplies include the following:

- *Epoxy, instant glues, or other solvent-based glues*. Use only water-based white glue.
- *Paints that require solvents like turpentine to clean*. Use only water-based paints.
- *Cold water or commercial dyes that contain chemical additives*. Use only natural vegetable dyes made from beets, onion skins, and so on.

- *Permanent markers.* Permanent markers may contain toxic solvents. Use only water-based markers.

Be aware of all children's allergies. Children with allergies to wheat, for example, may be irritated by the wheat paste used in papier-mâché. Children allergic to peanuts must taste nothing with peanut butter. In fact, some centers make it a rule to avoid peanut butter use in food or art activities. Other art materials that may cause allergic reactions include chalk or other dusty substances, water-based clay, and any material that contains petroleum products.

Also be aware of children's habits. Some young children put everything in their mouths. (This can be the case at any age.) Others may be shy and slow to accept new materials. Use your knowledge of children's tendencies to help you plan art activities that are safe for all children.

Take the time to talk with the children about which things they may taste and which they may not. For example, when making anything mixed with glue, remind the children that glue is not to be tasted. You may find it helpful to use a large cutout of a smiley face with a tongue at the end of the smile to indicate an "edible activity." Make a copy of the smiley face and place a large black X over it to show a "no-taste activity."

Using Crayons—Basics

Crayons are an ideal medium for children: They are bold, colorful, clean, and inexpensive. They consist of an oily or a waxy binder mixed with color pigments. They are of various types; some are soft, some are semihard, and some (kindergarten or "fat" crayons) are for general use with young children. Crayons work well on most papers, but they do not blend well. Attempts to blend crayon often tear the paper.

Many different types of crayons are available. There are special crayons for use on construction paper, there are washable crayons, and there are fabric crayons, to name just a few. All these crayons are great to try with children, but if you have a limited budget, traditional wax crayons work well for most activities. However, be sure to buy good-quality, wax crayons. Good-quality crayons like Crayola® crayons hold up to children's frequent and hard use. Inexpensive crayons create less successful crayon experiences for children.

Children may use crayons on a wide assortment of surfaces, including newsprint, wrapping paper, newspaper, construction paper, corrugated cardboard, cloth, and wood. Crayons work well on most papers. Crayons can be applied thinly to produce semitransparent layers of subtle color, and they can be coated with black paint and scratched through for crayon etching.

Understanding Crayons at Different Stages

Toddlers and children just beginning to scribble need crayons that are safe and easy to hold and use. Large, nontoxic crayons are good tools for young scribblers. A good-grade, kindergarten-type crayon is the best tool for this stage. The crayon should be large and unwrapped so it can be used on both the sides and the ends. Good-quality crayons are strong enough to hold up to rough first scribbles. They also make bright, clear colors, which appeal to children.

Young artists use their whole arms, as well as their hands and fingers, when using crayons or markers. For this reason, early scribblers should use large, white paper.

Crayon scribbles show better on white paper, so children can see more easily the results of their scribbling. The want-ad section of the newspaper is also appropriate paper for beginning artists. The advertisements' small print makes a neutral, nonintrusive background for scribbling. In addition, this section of the paper provides a generous supply of material for young scribblers. This, in turn, encourages children to scribble more often.

Young scribblers need only a few crayons at a time. Too many crayons may distract children during scribbling. At this point, the process of scribbling, not the color of the crayon, is the main point of the activity. A box of 32 crayons, for example, could become an object of exploration and thus a distraction from scribbling. A new color may be added when a new drawing is started.

As preschool children develop more motor skills and can scribble purposefully, they hold their tools more like adults and have growing control of their materials. Preschool children at this point can now control their scribbles, making loops, circles, and lines that are distinguishable and can be repeated at will.

Preschool children in this stage have enough motor control and hand-eye coordination to use smaller crayons. A variety of papers can be used, from newsprint to construction paper. It is not as necessary to have the largest paper, because the child can now control the crayon on a smaller surface. Papers of many sizes, shapes, and colors are appropriate for children at this stage.

When children can make pictures with crayons, the larger the variety of paper and crayons, the better! A box of 32 crayons is perfect for a young artist at this stage. Challenge the children with new and different colors of paper and crayons. Make some crayons of your own using the Crayon Cupcakes activity. There are limitless creative possibilities with crayons.

School-age children also benefit from using crayons. The fact that crayons were introduced to these children at a younger age may lead the children to think that crayons are beneath the dignity of older artists, but this is not the case. Examples abound of distinguished drawings made in this medium, as far back as the nineteenth century. Miro and Picasso used crayons in their work, so, do not neglect this material with your more "grown-up" artists!

Using Crayons—Processes

Encourage the children to experiment with crayons and to use different parts of the crayon. Through these experiments, the children will discover new methods that satisfy their needs for expression. The wax crayon has great versatility and can be used in many different ways:

- Make thin lines with the point of the crayon, heavy lines with the blunt end or the side.
- Vary the pressure to create subtle tints or solid, brilliant colors.
- Make rough texture by using broken lines, dots, jabs, dashes, and other strokes with the point.
- Create smooth texture by using the flat side or by drawing lines close together in the same direction with the point.

- Twist, turn, and swing the crayon in arcs, and move it in various ways to achieve different effects.

- Repeat motions to create a rhythm or pattern.

Avoid small pieces of paper and patterned artwork or coloring books. Asking children to color patterned artwork undermines the children's creativity. Children who are frequently given patterns to cut out or outlines to color are in fact being told that their own artwork is inadequate. For example, a pattern of a dog for children to color in or cut out says to them—more clearly than words could—that, "This is what your drawing should look like; this is the *right* way to make a dog. You and the way you might draw a dog aren't good enough."

Using Chalk—Basics

Children are often given chalk with a blackboard, but young children seem to use it ineffectively there. Young children do better when they can mark on the sidewalk with chalk, perhaps because the rougher texture of the cement more easily pulls the color off the chalk stick. The children seem more able to tell what they are doing as they squat and draw. It is, of course, necessary to explain to the children that they may draw with chalk only on special places.

Some young artists apply chalk in separate strokes, letting the color blend in the viewer's eye. Others are not reluctant to blend the colors and do so successfully, although the colors may get muddied. Of course, there is no need to caution children against this. They should be encouraged to explore by rubbing with the fingers, cotton swabs, or anything available. Most children will select and use chalk easily, However, chalk is too brittle for toddlers' early scribbling.

Chalk is inexpensive and available in several forms. Typical blackboard chalk is appropriate for using on blackboards and in art projects. Some chalk, made specifically for chalk drawings, is more expensive but worth the cost because it produces rich and vibrant colors. Another form of chalk is sidewalk chalk.

This chalk is commonly available during summer months at most commodity stores. Sidewalk chalk, which is designed to wash away with water, usually has a detergent component. It is also larger than regular chalk, which makes it easier to use on cement. Sidewalk chalk is inexpensive and is available in a good range of colors. Crayola makes a liquid sidewalk chalk that can be brushed directly onto cement.

Using Chalk—Processes

The following basic information can help you successfully incorporate chalk into art activities for young children:

- Chalk drawing is best done on a paper with a slightly coarse, abrasive surface. This texture helps the paper trap and hold the chalk particles. Many papers have this quality, including inexpensive manila paper.

- Chalks are brittle and break easily. They are also impermanent, smearing very easily. The teacher, with proper ventilation, should spray completed works with a "fixative" (ordinary hairspray works well).

- Chalk strokes can be strengthened by wetting the chalk or paper.

- Various liquids can be used with chalks for interesting results. These include dipping the chalk sticks in buttermilk, starch, and sugar water.

- Liquid tends to seal the chalk, so you must occasionally rub a piece of old sandpaper on the end of the chalk to break this seal and allow the color to come off again.

Using Markers—Basics

Markers are popular tools for young artists. They are especially good for children who have progressed through the scribble stage and can make basic shapes. Markers require little pressure to make bold marks and basic shapes. They should be nontoxic and water soluble so that most spots can be washed out of the children's clothes. One drawback of markers is lost tops. A marker will dry out fairly quickly without its top. See **Figure 2**, Marker Maintenance, for some suggestions on how to prolong the life of colored markers.

As with crayon use, children's progression from random scribbling through controlled scribbling to basic forms and then picture making applies to marker use. However, markers are not suggested for beginning scribblers, because they can only be used one way. Unlike crayons, which can be used on the sides, top, and bottom, markers are a one-way (top-only) tool.

Once children can control their scribbles, markers are an appropriate tool. Markers produce attractive lines and shapes. Children enjoy seeing their marks come out as desired and in such a colorful way. Markers make great tools for picture making, as well. Be sure to have colored markers in many colors and tip widths for picture making. Also, be sure the markers are not permanent.

Using Markers—Processes

Colored markers come in beautiful, clear colors. Some markers even have scents! Glittery markers are another treat for young artists. Compared with paint, markers have the additional advantage of staying bright and clear until the children exhaust them.

Some basic materials to use with markers are:

- *Sturdy sheets of paper (manila or newsprint, 8" × 12" or 12" × 18")*. Spread the paper on a table or on the floor, or pin it to a wall or an easel. Paper of different shapes and colors may be used for variety.

- A *basket of colored markers in many colors and tip widths*. See the preceding "Storing Tips for Art Materials" section for ways to organize markers effectively.

- *Colored pens and pencils for older children to incorporate with their marker drawings*.

Creating a Child-Friendly Environment

It is difficult to be creative when you have to worry about keeping yourself and your work area clean. Cover all artwork areas with newspaper. It is best to tape the paper to the surface to avoid having markers or other materials seep through the spaces. In addition, picking up a messy newspaper and throwing it away is so much easier than cleaning up a tabletop! Other coverups that work well are shower curtains and plastic tablecloths.

Remember to cover the children, too! Some good child coverups are men's shirts (with the sleeves cut off), aprons, pillowcases with holes cut for the head and arms, and

FIGURE 2 · MARKER MAINTENANCE

Markers are wonderful for young artists. But busy artists frequently lose caps from these markers, often resulting in dried-out markers. Replacing dried-out markers can be expensive, so here are a few hints on "marker maintenance" to help preserve them as long as possible.

- Solve the lost cap/dry-out problem by setting the caps with *open ends up* in a margarine or whipped topping container filled with plaster of Paris. Make sure the plaster does not cover the holes in the caps. When the plaster dries, the markers can be put into the caps and will stand upright until ready for use again.

- Give new life to old, dry felt markers by storing them *tips down with the caps on*. When the markers become dried out, remove the caps and put in a few drops of water. This usually helps "revive" them.

- Recycle dried-out markers by having children dip them in paint and use them for drawing.

- Make your own pastel markers by adding dry tempera paint (or food color) to bottles of white shoe polish that come with sponge applicator tops.

- Use empty plastic shoe polish bottles or roll-on deodorant bottles to make your own markers. Wash the tops and bottles thoroughly and fill them with watery tempera paint.

(From Mayesky, Mary. *Creative Activites for Young Children*, 7th ed., Clifton Park, NY: Delmar Learning.)

smocks. Some fun alternatives to these are sets of old clothes or shoes that can be worn as "art clothes." These old clothes could become "art journals" as they became covered with the traces of various art projects.

Creating a Child's Art Environment

Encourage young artists by displaying appropriate art prints and other works of art. Do not make the mistake of thinking young children do not enjoy "grown-up" art. Children are never too young to enjoy the colors, lines, patterns, and designs of artists' work. Art posters from a local museum, for example, can brighten an art area. Such posters also get children looking and talking about art, which encourages their creativity.

Display pieces of pottery, shells and rocks, and other beautiful objects from nature to encourage children's appreciation of the lines, symmetries, and colors of nature. These design concepts are part of the drawing experience. Even the youngest child can enjoy the look and feel of smooth, colored rocks and the beauty of fall leaves. All these are natural parts of a child's world that can be talked about with young children as those children create artwork. Beautiful objects encourage creativity.

Now, enter the world of crayons, chalk, and markers in the pages that follow. Enjoy the trip!

A

All Ages

Basic Crayon Rubbings

MATERIALS

- ☐ newsprint or other light-type paper
- ☐ unwrapped crayons
- ☐ objects to rub over (e.g., paper clips, leaves, coins, rickrack)

HELPFUL HINTS

- Rubbings are a good activity, even for very young artists, because they require a lesser degree of small motor development in the fingers and hands.
- For 2-year-olds, the objects rubbed over need to be large and too big to put in the mouth.

DEVELOPMENTAL GOALS

Develop creativity, small motor development, and hand-eye coordination and explore a new crayoning technique.

PREPARATION

Talk about the collection of objects for this activity. Discuss shape and size.

PROCESS

1. Place the paper over an object.
2. Color hard over the object with the side of the crayon.
3. Repeat the process with other objects.

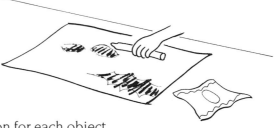

VARIATIONS

- Use a different color crayon for each object.
- Do a rubbing with items that are related (e.g., items all from nature, items all from the hardware store).
- Go on a walk with the children. Gather objects to use in crayon rubbings.
- Have the children bring in items from home to use in crayon rubbings.

NOTES FOR NEXT TIME: _____

_____

_____

_____

CRAYONS, CHALK, AND MARKERS

Basic Crayon Shavings

CRAYONS

MATERIALS

- ☐ unwrapped crayons
- ☐ pencil sharpener
- ☐ glue
- ☐ paper

HELPFUL HINTS

- Children will enjoy shredding the crayons. It is also a good small motor exercise.
- This activity makes great use of broken crayons.

DEVELOPMENTAL GOALS

Develop creativity, small motor development, and hand-eye coordination and explore another use for crayons.

PREPARATION

Peel off the jackets of various colored crayons. The children enjoy doing this. Insert the crayons in a pencil sharpener to make shavings.

PROCESS

1. Spread glue over a sheet of paper.
2. Press the crayon shavings into an interesting design or picture.
3. Let the glue dry thoroughly.

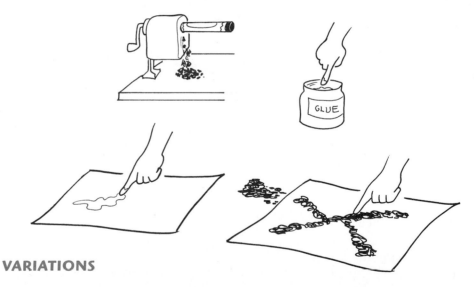

VARIATIONS

- Moisten the sticky side of a length of paper tape and glue the crayon shavings to the tape.
- Spread glue on parts of a crayon drawing and sprinkle crayon shavings on it for an interesting effect.

NOTES FOR NEXT TIME: _____

_____

_____

_____

Carton Creatures

MATERIALS

- ☐ recycled boxes
- ☐ cardboard rolls from paper towels or gift wrap
- ☐ collage materials
- ☐ construction paper
- ☐ markers
- ☐ glue
- ☐ blunt-tip scissors
- ☐ clean paper
- ☐ plastic milk cartons

💡 HELPFUL HINTS

- While children are creating their animals, talk about the art elements you see in their work (e.g., line, shape, form, color, texture) and principles of visual organization (e.g., unity, variety, balance repetition/rhythm/pattern).
- Younger children (3 years and under) may tear the paper to fit the carton. Children 4 years and older may be better able to cut the paper with scissors.

DEVELOPMENTAL GOALS

Develop creativity, small motor development, and hand-eye coordination; encourage recycling and focus on art elements of line, shape, form, color, and texture.

PREPARATION

Discuss the animals the children would like to invent. Talk about the animal's size, shape, color, and texture.

PROCESS

1. Create an animal with milk cartons, cardboard tubes, and other materials.
2. Glue the animal together. Let it dry overnight.
3. If desired, cover the creature with construction paper.
4. Decorate it with markers.
5. Add cloth and trim scraps and any other collage materials for details.
6. Let the glue dry overnight.

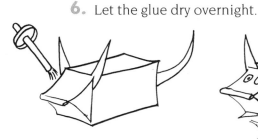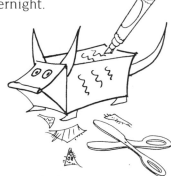

VARIATIONS

- Make enough animals for a play zoo, farm, or pet store.
- Include the imaginary animals in the block or housekeeping area.
- Ask children which sounds their imaginary animals make. What do the animals eat? Where do they live? What is it like there?

NOTES FOR NEXT TIME: _____

_____

_____

_____

A

All Ages

Chalk-Texture Experiences

MATERIALS

- ☐ thin paper (e.g., copy or tracing paper)
- ☐ sandpaper
- ☐ bricks
- ☐ corrugated cardboard
- ☐ chalk

 **HELPFUL HINT**

- This is a good activity even for the very young artist because it involves simple hand movements.

DEVELOPMENTAL GOALS

Develop creativity, small motor development, and hand-eye coordination and explore new chalk experiences.

PREPARATION

Collect objects with interesting textures. Discuss the textures. Use words like *coarse, bumpy, rough,* and any other descriptive words.

PROCESS

1. Place thin paper over a surface with a unique texture.

2. Rub over the paper with the side of the chalk.

3. The texture of the object appears on the paper.

4. Use several objects for many interesting effects.

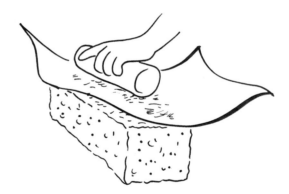

VARIATIONS

- Use a different color of chalk for each object.
- Add details with crayons or markers.
- Go outside and make chalk rubbings on the bark of trees, on the sidewalk, or on the grass.

NOTES FOR NEXT TIME: _____

_____

_____

Chalk ABCs

CRAYONS

MATERIALS

☐ sidewalk chalk in several colors

 **HELPFUL HINT**

- This activity is appropriate for children who know the alphabet.

DEVELOPMENTAL GOALS

Develop creativity, small motor development, and hand-eye coordination and emphasize letter and number recognition and patterning.

PREPARATION

Have the children practice writing their names or some words before going outside for this activity. Give each letter of the alphabet a color. For example, the first letter A is red, the second letter B is blue, the third letter is yellow, the fourth letter is red (again), and so on. Make an alphabet chart showing the color sequence.

PROCESS

1. Take the children, color alphabet chart, and sidewalk chalk outside.

2. Have the children use colored chalk to write their names and words following the color chart.

3. Numbers can be any color the children want.

4. Let the children repeat the process as many times as time allows.

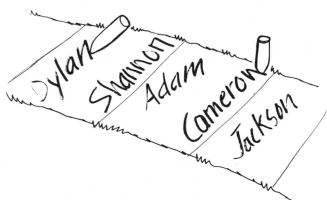

VARIATIONS

- Write spelling words outside using the color sequence.
- Do the same activity inside using chalk and paper.

NOTES FOR NEXT TIME: _____

_____

_____

_____

4 Years Old and Up

Chalk and Tempera Paint

CRAYONS

MATERIALS

- ☐ chalk
- ☐ tempera paint
- ☐ shallow container for paint
- ☐ paper
- ☐ pencils

💡 HELPFUL HINTS

- After the paint is dry, an adult sprays the drawing with hairspray. Be sure to spray in a well-ventilated area.

- This activity is suitable for children able to use pencils and chalk.

DEVELOPMENTAL GOALS

Develop creativity, small motor development, and hand-eye coordination and explore chalk and tempera technique.

PREPARATION

Discuss with the children which kind of pencil drawing or design they would like to make. Explain that they will be using tempera paint and chalk with this drawing.

PROCESS

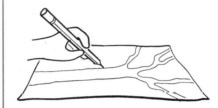

1. Make a light pencil outline drawing on paper.

2. Mix tempera paint to the consistency of cream.

3. Dip the end of colored chalk into chosen color paint.

4. Apply paint with chalk stick in brush-like strokes.

5. Continue until the picture is completed.

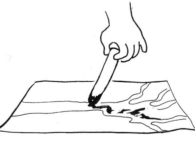

VARIATIONS

- Add details with plain chalk.
- Try light colors on dark paper and vice versa.

NOTES FOR NEXT TIME: _____

_____

_____

_____

Chalk and Tempera Print

MATERIALS

- ☐ colored chalk
- ☐ white tempera paint
- ☐ paper
- ☐ large brush

 **HELPFUL HINT**

- Some children may lack the attention span for the two-step process. It is perfectly acceptable for these children to complete just one of the steps if they so choose.

DEVELOPMENTAL GOALS

Develop creativity, small motor development, and hand-eye coordination and explore chalk and tempera technique.

PREPARATION

Discuss with the children the kind of picture or design they would like to make. Explain that they will be making a print of this picture.

PROCESS

1. Make a design or drawing with colored chalk on a piece of good-quality paper. Be sure to use the chalk heavily.

2. Coat another piece of paper of the same size with white tempera paint

3. Use a large brush and paint in both directions to smooth the paint over one entire side of the paper.

4. While the tempera is still wet, place the chalk drawing face down in the tempera paint.

5. Rub firmly over the paper with the fingers and/or the hand.

6. Separate the two papers before they are dry.

7. Two prints will result—the chalk will have merged with the paint on both prints.

VARIATION

- Experiment with different colors of chalk and tempera paint to produce many interesting effects.

NOTES FOR NEXT TIME: _____

_____

_____

_____

CRAYONS

Chalk Body Tracing

MATERIALS

- ☐ outdoor chalk (extra-large chalk)
- ☐ concrete area for chalk drawing

HELPFUL HINTS

- This is a great activity for a sunny, warm day, but it could also be done on a cooler day when the children are wearing jackets. Note how different these body outlines are from those on a sunny day.

- This activity can be used with toddlers as they can scribble inside, outside, or anywhere near their body outlines. Details are unneeded for this age group.

DEVELOPMENTAL GOALS

Develop creativity, small motor development, and hand-eye coordination and explore the outdoor use of chalk.

PREPARATION

Check out a concrete area that is appropriate for chalk drawings.

PROCESS

1. Have a child lie down face-up on the cement.
2. Have another child or an adult trace around the child's body with chalk.
3. Have the child color in the body outline.
4. Add details such as clothing, hair and eye color, and so on.

VARIATIONS

- Let the children color and add detail to each others' chalk body outlines.
- Write descriptive words or statements near the outline, as dictated by the child. This is a good way to tie language arts to this activity.

NOTES FOR NEXT TIME: _____

_____

_____

_____

A

Chalk-Sand Painting

MATERIALS

- ☐ sawdust or sand
- ☐ old pieces of broken chalk
- ☐ dry tempera paint
- ☐ water
- ☐ bowl
- ☐ construction paper
- ☐ glue

 **HELPFUL HINT**

- Even the youngest artists will enjoy sprinkling this colorful sand on the glue-covered paper. They probably will enjoy spreading on the glue just as much!

DEVELOPMENTAL GOALS

Develop creativity, small motor development, and hand-eye coordination and explore more chalk techniques.

PREPARATION

Shave chalk with a knife (adults only). Put sawdust or sand with chalk shavings mixed with tempera paint (dry) in a bowl of water (just enough water to cover). Stir and allow to dry overnight. This will make a colorful sand (or sawdust) material.

PROCESS

1. Apply glue or paste to a piece of construction paper.

2. Sprinkle colored sand or sawdust over the glued area to create a sand painting.

VARIATIONS

- Outline the details of the picture with crayons or markers.
- Make a sand painting on posterboard or cardboard.

NOTES FOR NEXT TIME: _____

_____

_____

_____

CRAYONS

CRAYONS, CHALK, AND MARKERS

Chalk Shape Rubbings

CRAYONS

MATERIALS

- ☐ chalk
- ☐ thin paper (e.g., copy paper)
- ☐ scissors
- ☐ shapes cut out of sandpaper
- ☐ pieces of screen
- ☐ corrugated cardboard
- ☐ any other materials with obvious texture

💡 HELPFUL HINTS

- This is a good activity for encouraging vocabulary development by talking about shapes, size, number, and so on.
- With toddlers, use only one or two shapes for this activity.

DEVELOPMENTAL GOALS

Develop creativity, small motor development, and hand-eye coordination and reinforce shapes, sizes, and object placement.

PREPARATION

Discuss shapes with the children. Talk about how shapes are all around, such as in round plates, rectangular books, and triangular blocks. Allow children to choose a shape.

PROCESS

1. Place paper over the shape.
2. Make a chalk rubbing of the shape with the side of the chalk.
3. Choose another shape.
4. Make another chalk rubbing of this shape.
5. Continue until satisfied with the design.

VARIATIONS

- Use other flat shapes, such as puzzle or game pieces, buttons, or parquetry blocks for chalk rubbings.
- Let the children find interesting shapes for chalk rubbings.
- Do chalk rubbings of numbers and letters cut out of sandpaper or other textured materials.

NOTES FOR NEXT TIME: _____

_____

_____

Years Old and UP

Chalk Stenciling

MATERIALS

- ☐ drawing paper
- ☐ scissors
- ☐ facial tissue
- ☐ small piece of cotton or patch of cloth
- ☐ colored chalk

HELPFUL HINTS

- This activity is appropriate for children who can use scissors.
- When rubbing with tissue, it works best to make strokes from the stencil paper toward the center of the opening. Continue this around the edge of the opening until the paper under the stencil has a clear print.

DEVELOPMENTAL GOALS

Develop creativity, small motor development, and hand-eye coordination and explore a new chalking technique.

PREPARATION

Cut the drawing paper into pieces about 4" square. Give each child four or five pieces of paper.

PROCESS

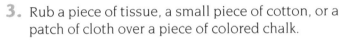
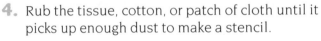

1. With scissors, cut holes or shapes of various sizes and shapes in the center of each piece. This is the stencil.

2. Cut more than one hole or shape in each piece for more interesting stencils.

3. Rub a piece of tissue, a small piece of cotton, or a patch of cloth over a piece of colored chalk.

4. Rub the tissue, cotton, or patch of cloth until it picks up enough dust to make a stencil.

5. Place the cut-out stencil over another piece of paper.

6. Rub the chalk dust over the stencil, covering the entire shape with chalk dust.

7. Continue using the same stencil again over the paper or use another stencil.

VARIATIONS

- Use a combination of several stencils on one piece of paper for visual rhythms.
- Cut stencils of objects, such as trees, ornaments, and animals.
- Holiday cards, programs, and decorations may be made from stencils.
- The same technique can be used with wax crayons.

NOTES FOR NEXT TIME: _____

_____

CRAYONS

CRAYONS, CHALK, AND MARKERS

4

Chalk, Tempera, and Starch Print

MATERIALS

- ☐ liquid starch
- ☐ powdered tempera paint
- ☐ brushes
- ☐ a scratching instrument (e.g., a stick, a spoon)
- ☐ colored chalk
- ☐ two sheets of paper per child

💡 HELPFUL HINTS

- Young artists who have had experience painting with a brush should be able to enjoy this activity.

- Liquid starch is available in the grocery store where laundry products are sold.

DEVELOPMENTAL GOALS

Develop creativity, small motor development, and hand-eye coordination and explore the use of chalk in printing.

PREPARATION

Mix the liquid starch and tempera paint to produce a dripless paint.

PROCESS

1. Brush the paint and starch mixture on a sheet of paper.
2. Scratch a design in the wet paint.
3. Coat another sheet of paper with colored chalk.
4. Place the second sheet, chalk side down, over the wet paint surface.
5. Lightly rub the back of the top sheet.
6. Pull off the top sheet.

VARIATIONS

- Use different kinds of paper and colors.
- After the prints are dry, add details with crayons and markers.
- These prints make attractive wrapping paper.
- Cover the prints with clear Contac® paper and use them for placemats.

NOTES FOR NEXT TIME: _____

_____

_____

Crayons and Wax-Paper Creations

MATERIALS

- ☐ autumn leaves or other natural objects (e.g., dried weeds or flowers)
- ☐ wax paper
- ☐ crayon shavings
- ☐ iron
- ☐ pieces of cardboard (to press on)

💡 HELPFUL HINTS

- Be very careful when using an iron around the children! Caution the children to stay well away from the iron during the pressing.
- This activity can be used with many other themes by using cut-out construction paper objects. For example, a Valentine's Day theme would involve cut-out paper hearts and crayon shavings. A birthday theme could be cut-out paper candles and cake and crayon shavings. A "Me" theme could include cut-out magazine pictures of favorite things with crayon shavings scattered for effect.

DEVELOPMENTAL GOALS

Develop creativity, small motor development, and hand-eye coordination and explore a different use for crayon shavings.

PREPARATION

Go on a walk to collect interesting natural objects for this activity. Have the children choose their favorite leaves, flowers, or weeds for their original creations. Shave crayons by putting them through a pencil sharpener.

PROCESS

1. Place leaves, weeds, or dried flowers on a sheet of waxed paper.
2. Arrange and rearrange the items until satisfied with the design.
3. Sprinkle crayon shavings around the arrangement.
4. Place another piece of waxed paper on top.
5. The adult presses with a warm iron, sealing the artwork between the pieces of waxed paper.

VARIATIONS

- If leaves are not available, cut leaf shapes from colored construction paper.
- Use several colors of crayon shavings.
- Hang these nature pictures on a window. The light will shine through them.
- These nature pictures also make nice placemats.

NOTES FOR NEXT TIME:

_____

_____

CRAYONS

3

Years Old and Up

Crayon Batik

MATERIALS

- ☐ crayons
- ☐ paper
- ☐ water
- ☐ container for water
- ☐ thin solution of tempera paint
- ☐ brushes
- ☐ paper towels

💡 HELPFUL HINTS

- Because the color will be more intense in the creased area, the finished drawing will have dramatic contrasts.
- This activity is appropriate for children who have lots of experience using crayons.
- Bring in some samples of batik fabric for the children to see. These can be found in most fabric stores in the cotton-fabric section. Many ethnic fabrics are also made with batik designs.

DEVELOPMENTAL GOALS

Develop creativity, small motor development, and hand-eye coordination and explore a new crayoning technique.

PREPARATION

Discuss that the term *batik* is a design with wrinkles in the paper. This is part of the design. Talk about which kind of picture or design the children would like to make in this activity.

PROCESS

1. Make a drawing or design with the crayons on paper.
2. Soak the paper in water.
3. Crumple the paper into a ball.
4. Uncrumple the paper.
5. Flatten it.
6. Blot off excess water with paper towels.
7. Flow diluted tempera paint over the surface with a wet brush.
8. Let the batik dry thoroughly.

VARIATIONS

- Draw with light-colored crayons and cover the drawing with dark tempera paint.
- Draw with dark-colored crayons and cover the drawing with light tempera paint.
- After the painting has dried, add more design elements or details with markers.

NOTES FOR NEXT TIME: _____

_____

_____

A

Crayon Cupcakes

MATERIALS

- ☐ broken crayons of various sizes and colors
- ☐ muffin tins
- ☐ oven

💡 HELPFUL HINTS

- Adult supervision is always required when working around an oven.

- Let the children unwrap the crayons. They love to do it, and it is great exercise for the small muscles in the fingers and hands.

DEVELOPMENTAL GOALS

Develop creativity, small motor development, and hand-eye coordination and encourage crayon recycling.

PREPARATION

Unwrap all crayons.

PROCESS

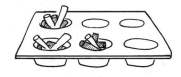

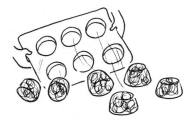

1. Sort the crayons by color.
2. Fill the muffin tins loosely with different colors.
3. Mix colors, if desired. Try white and red for pink, for example.
4. Put the filled muffin tins in a 250 degree oven for about 20 minutes.
5. Let the tins cool completely after baking.
6. Place the tins in the refrigerator, or put them outside if it is cool.
7. Pop the cupcakes out, and they are ready to go.

VARIATIONS

- Put several colors of crayons in one muffin tin cup. See how it comes out!
- Sprinkle in some glitter with the crayons before baking to create a sparkly recycled crayon!
- Mix primary colors. See what happens!

NOTES FOR NEXT TIME: _____

_____

_____

CRAYONS

A

All Ages

Crayon Explorations

MATERIALS

- ☐ crayons
- ☐ construction paper
- ☐ chalk
- ☐ various surfaces (see the following)

 **HELPFUL HINT**

- Be open to all suggestions. Children may come up with some amazing and funny suggestions.

DEVELOPMENTAL GOALS

Develop creativity, small motor development, and hand-eye coordination and explore different crayoning techniques.

PREPARATION

Collect corrugated cardboard, cloth, wood, paper rolls, sandpaper, and other interesting items for crayoning activities.

PROCESS

1. Encourage the children to explore the various items and to choose one or two for crayoning.

2. Challenge the children to use crayon and white chalk on colored construction paper.

3. Try drawing or scribbling with crayons on cardboard or sandpaper.

4. Consider drawing or scribbling with crayons on pieces of wood.

5. Find out how crayons work on pieces of cloth.

VARIATIONS

- Let the children come up with new and different surfaces for their crayon drawings.
- Keep examples of some of these crayon explorations to help you and the children remember them for next time.

NOTES FOR NEXT TIME: _____

_____

_____

_____

A

Crayon Feeling Pictures

MATERIALS

☐ crayons
☐ paper

HELPFUL HINT

- This activity is appropriate for even the youngest child, because it is free-form and encourages spontaneous drawing.

NOTES FOR NEXT TIME:

_____

_____

_____

_____

_____

_____

_____

DEVELOPMENTAL GOALS

Develop creativity, small motor development, and hand-eye coordination and express feelings through crayoning.

PREPARATION

Discuss the variety of lines with the children. Use words like *fat, wavy, textured, thin,* and *zig-zag.*

PROCESS

1. The adult takes a crayon and draws randomly on the paper while describing a feeling the adult had that morning (e.g., "First, I got out of bed" while drawing a line that shows the movement getting out of bed).

2. "Then I went to the shower" while making scribble lines to mimic water falling.

3. "Then I dried myself off with a fluffy towel" while making zig-zag lines to mimic the movement of the towel.

4. Have the children do their own feeling drawings, going through what they did in the morning or throughout the day.

5. Encourage the children to fill the page with lines showing their activities.

6. Encourage the children to change colors frequently.

7. Use the crayon on the side to make fat lines.

VARIATIONS

- The more motion, the better. The more variety of line, the better.
- Fill spaces between lines with crayons or markers.
- Let the children tell about their feelings while pointing to the lines they made on the page.

CRAYONS

4

Crayon Leaf Designs

CRAYONS

MATERIALS

- ☐ crayons
- ☐ paper
- ☐ a variety of leaves

 **HELPFUL HINT**

- Go on a walk out-doors and collect the leaves for this activity.

DEVELOPMENTAL GOALS

Develop creativity, small motor development, and hand-eye coordination and develop an appreciation for lines and shapes in nature.

PREPARATION

Unwrap the crayons so they can be used on their sides as well as on their tips. Discuss with the children the lines, shapes, sizes, and details of the leaves collected for this activity. Use such words as *vertical*, *horizontal* and even *swerved* when discussing the types of lines seen in the leaves.

PROCESS

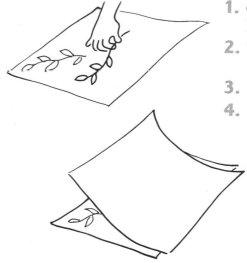

1. On a sheet of paper, arrange the leaves in a design.
2. When satisfied with the design, cover it with a thin sheet of paper.
3. Rub over the paper with crayon.
4. Make an overall design by moving the objects several times and repeating the rubbing.

VARIATIONS

- Colors may be overlapped and blended to create interesting effects.
- Add details to the leaf rubbing with colored markers or crayons.
- Older children may want to label the leaves on their designs. They could look them up in an encyclopedia (book or even online!) to help identify each leaf.

NOTES FOR NEXT TIME: _____

_____

_____

_____

Crayon over Tempera Paint

MATERIALS

- ☐ tempera paints and brushes
- ☐ wax crayons
- ☐ paper
- ☐ sponge
- ☐ water
- ☐ container for water

💡 HELPFUL HINTS

- The degree of flaking may be sped up by brushing or, if it has gone too far, retouching may be done with the crayons.
- This is an excellent activity for older children who think using crayons is "boring."

DEVELOPMENTAL GOALS

Develop creativity, small motor development, and hand-eye coordination and explore a new crayoning technique.

PREPARATION

Children make pictures or designs of their choice with tempera paint on paper. Let the pictures dry thoroughly.

PROCESS

1. Work a contrasting color crayon over each area, using moderate pressure.
2. Immerse the sponge in water.
3. "Wash" the painting until the underlying tempera paint begins flaking off.
4. The result will be a picture of mottled, textured quality. The crayon left on will accent the varied tempera tones that remain.

VARIATION

- This technique may be modified by applying the crayons more heavily, then holding the drawing under water that is just hot enough to melt the crayons. Be very careful if you choose this variation. The teacher should hold the drawing under the hot water.

NOTES FOR NEXT TIME: _____

_____

_____

CRAYONS, CHALK, AND MARKERS

CRAYONS

Crayon Resist

MATERIALS

- ☐ wax crayons
- ☐ paper
- ☐ brush
- ☐ tempera paint
- ☐ water container

 **HELPFUL HINT**

- Be sure the mixture of tempera paint is thin. A too-thick mix will darken too much of the crayon drawing.

DEVELOPMENTAL GOALS

Develop creativity, small motor development, and hand-eye coordination and explore a new crayoning technique.

PREPARATION

Discuss with the children the designs or pictures they might like to make for this activity. Explain that the design will be covered with paint and will look different when painted over.

PROCESS

1. Make a design or picture with crayons. Press very hard with the crayon to make it thick on the paper.
2. Leave some areas of the paper uncolored.
3. Cover the entire surface of the paper with tempera paint.
4. The paint will be absorbed by the uncolored paper.
5. The paint will be "resisted" by the wax crayons.

VARIATIONS

- Use light-colored or white crayons with dark tempera paint for an interesting effect.
- Crayon resist can make dramatic effects in special holiday pictures.
- Instead of crayons, use a candle stub to draw a picture. Then, paint over the design with thin tempera paint.

NOTES FOR NEXT TIME: _____

_____

_____

_____

Crayon-Rubbing Pictures

CRAYONS

MATERIALS

- ☐ crayons
- ☐ textured surfaces (e.g., sandpaper, pieces of screen, cardboard)
- ☐ newsprint or another thin-type paper

💡 **HELPFUL HINT**

- This activity is appropriate for children who are already using crayons.

DEVELOPMENTAL GOALS

Develop creativity, small motor development, and hand-eye coordination and explore a new approach to crayon rubbing.

PREPARATION

Discuss the pieces of textured surfaces with the children. Use descriptive words like *coarse*, *bumpy*, and *criss-cross*.

PROCESS

1. Make an outline drawing with a pencil on thin paper.
2. Hold the drawing against a surface that has a definite texture.
3. Rub the crayon over all areas of the drawing, filling the area with an interesting texture pattern.
4. The texture will transfer to the paper.
5. Place the paper against another texture and transfer this texture to another part of the drawing.
6. Textures may be repeated or overlapped.
7. Continue until all areas are filled with texture rubbings.

VARIATIONS

- Unusual effects can be obtained by using several colors of crayons.
- Make the outline drawing in crayon and markers. Do the rubbings for texture effects on them.

NOTES FOR NEXT TIME: _____

_____

_____

_____

Crayon Scratchings

MATERIALS

- ☐ paper
- ☐ crayons
- ☐ black tempera paint
- ☐ a drop of liquid soap (dishwashing liquid soap)
- ☐ paintbrush
- ☐ paper clips

💡 **HELPFUL HINT**

- This activity is appropriate for children who have a lot of experience using crayons.

DEVELOPMENTAL GOALS

Develop creativity, small motor development, and hand-eye coordination and explore a new crayoning technique.

PREPARATION

Give each child a piece of heavy paper. Manila paper works well for this activity.

PROCESS

1. Color a sheet of paper with bright crayons.
2. Make stripes, blotches, or any pattern.
3. Press hard to make a thick layer of crayon all over the paper.
4. Paint a coat of black tempera paint all over the top of the crayon.
5. Add a drop of liquid soap to the black paint so it will stick to crayon wax.
6. Let the paint dry thoroughly.
7. Scratch a design or picture into the black surface with a bent paper clip. The bright crayon color will show beautifully through the black.

VARIATIONS

- Scratch letters or numbers into the crayon.
- Make a group scratch project. Use a large piece of paper and divide it up for each student to fill with crayon. Make a group decision about what to scratch into the crayon.

NOTES FOR NEXT TIME: _____

_____

_____

_____

CRAYONS (side tab)

4

Crayon Shavings— The Hot Way!

MATERIALS

☐ old electric iron
☐ heavy cardboard box close to size of the iron
☐ old, broken wax crayons
☐ paper
☐ cardboard
☐ pencil sharpener
☐ tape

HELPFUL HINTS

- Be very careful when using an iron around the children. Be sure the children maintain a safe distance from it. An adult should always be the one to handle the iron.

- Heat sources other than the iron may be used to melt the shavings. The drawing may be placed in direct sunlight, on a radiator, or over a lightbulb. Take care to avoid too much exposure, which will make the wax run.

DEVELOPMENTAL GOALS

Develop creativity, small motor development, and hand-eye coordination and explore a new crayon-shaving use.

PREPARATION

Shave the wax crayons in the pencil sharpener. The adult must place the iron in the cardboard box with the ironing surface up. Plug in and turn on the iron to the "low" setting.

PROCESS

1. Tape the edges of the paper to a piece of cardboard.
2. Drop some crayon shavings onto the paper.
3. Push the shavings around until the design or picture is created.
4. Pass the paper above the heated iron until the crayon shavings begin to melt. (Supervise closely.)
5. Continue this process with additional crayon until the desired pattern is created.

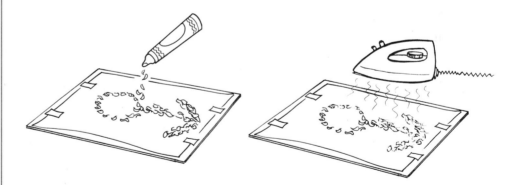

VARIATION

- Add details to the picture or design with tempera paint, crayons, or markers.

NOTES FOR NEXT TIME: _____

_____

_____

_____

CRAYONS, CHALK, AND MARKERS

CRAYONS

Crayon-Transfer Print

MATERIALS

- ☐ paper
- ☐ colored chalk
- ☐ crayons
- ☐ pencil or ball-point pen

💡 HELPFUL HINTS

- Some children may lack the attention span to complete the two-step process. Allow these children to complete just one step.

- The simpler the drawing or the design, the better the results with the crayon-transfer print.

- You may want to introduce the words *positive* and *reverse* when doing the crayon-transfer print.

DEVELOPMENTAL GOALS

Develop creativity, small motor development, and hand-eye coordination and explore a new crayoning technique.

PREPARATION

Discuss with the children which kind of design or picture they would like to make. Explain that the children will be making more than one copy of this artwork by making a "transfer print."

PROCESS

1. Completely cover a sheet of white paper with a heavy coating of light-colored chalk.

2. Cover the coating of chalk with a very heavy layer of darker colored crayon.

3. Make a design or drawing on another piece of white paper.

4. Place the drawing over the crayon and chalk-covered paper.

5. Using a dull pencil or ball-point pen and using pressure, trace over the drawing.

6. The pressure causes the crayon to adhere to the underside of the drawing. It creates a separate drawing on the crayon and chalk-covered paper.

VARIATION

- Use different colors of chalk and crayons and repeat this activity.

NOTES FOR NEXT TIME: _____

_____

_____

4 Years Old and Up

Disappearing Line Drawings

MATERIALS

- ☐ hard soap (the type from hotels works well)
- ☐ black construction paper
- ☐ crayons
- ☐ water
- ☐ sink or large tub of water

💡 HELPFUL HINT

- Through this activity children should see how important lines are to a drawing. Some lines outline shapes or forms and can still be seen, but, in many cases, the lines are the artwork.

DEVELOPMENTAL GOALS

Develop creativity, small motor development, and hand-eye coordination and appreciate the importance of lines in drawings.

PREPARATION

Talk about lines in drawings and how they can be straight, curvy, horizontal, vertical, zigzag, and so on. This project is messy, so you may want rubber gloves and a newspaper-covered drying area.

PROCESS

1. Give each child a piece of black paper.
2. Do a line drawing with the soap.
3. The drawing should have lots of outlined areas in which to color.
4. Note that the soap will not work for areas the children want white; for these areas the children must use white crayon.
5. Color in the drawing. Light colors work best.
6. Rinse the drawing until the soap lines disappear.
7. Allow to dry.

VARIATION

- Draw a design using only shapes. Repeat the process.

NOTES FOR NEXT TIME: _____

_____

_____

Fantastic Plants

MATERIALS

- ☐ scissors
- ☐ crayons
- ☐ glue
- ☐ construction paper
- ☐ scrap pieces of trim and fabric

 **HELPFUL HINT**

- Children aged 3 and younger may be most interested exploring glue texture in this activity. This is appropriate, because they are learning how these materials work.

DEVELOPMENTAL GOALS

Develop creativity, small motor development, and hand-eye coordination and tie science to art activities.

PREPARATION

Talk with the children about plants. Observe the plants outdoors. Discuss the differences in stems, bark, leaves, flowers, and other plant parts.

PROCESS

1. Choose a favorite plant, such as a fruit tree, a pine tree, or a prickly cactus.
2. Think about how special you can make this plant.
3. Create the plant with crayons.
4. Glue on cut-out construction pieces for details.
5. Add pieces of trim or fabric scraps for more detail.

VARIATIONS

- Make crayon rubbings of tree bark or dried leaves. Cut out the rubbings and include them in the plant picture.
- Glue on real leaves and twigs for details.
- Do this activity outdoors with nature all around for inspiration!
- Create imaginary plants with fantastic colors and details.

NOTES FOR NEXT TIME: _____

_____

_____

_____

First Chalk Experiences

MATERIALS

- ☐ fat, soft chalk of different colors
- ☐ brown paper bag
- ☐ water
- ☐ container for water

 **HELPFUL HINT**

- Cover each piece of chalk with a piece of aluminum foil, leaving about half an inch of the chalk exposed. This prevents smearing colors on the hands and fingers. It also prevents the transferring of colors from one piece of chalk to another while they are stored.

DEVELOPMENTAL GOALS

Develop creativity, small motor development, and hand-eye coordination and introduce the medium of chalk.

PREPARATION

Cut open the brown paper bags so they are flat.

PROCESS

1. Dip the brown paper in water.
2. Draw with dry chalk on the wet brown paper.
3. Colors will be bright and almost fluorescent.

VARIATIONS

- Use white or manila paper and repeat the process.
- Try using light colors of chalk on dark paper and dark chalk on light paper.

NOTES FOR NEXT TIME: _____

_____

_____

_____

3
Years Old and UP

Line Dancing

MATERIALS

☐ a variety of instruments (e.g., rattles, drums, bells, kazoos, recorders, tambourines)

☐ paper

☐ markers

💡 HELPFUL HINT

• There is no single or right answer to the kind of lines that go with each instrument. A child may make one line for a triangle on the first hearing and another type of line the next time it is played. In that way, music is very much like art.

DEVELOPMENTAL GOALS

Develop creativity, small motor development, and hand-eye coordination and explore line and movement to tie music to art.

PREPARATION

Discuss the instruments gathered for this activity. Let the children hold, touch, and use them. Talk about the sounds each makes.

PROCESS

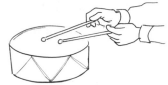

1. Play one of the instruments.
2. Talk about the kind of line the instrument sounds like. For example, a triangle can be a dotted line, a kazoo a straight line, or a tambourine zigzag lines.
3. Draw a line for each of the instrument's sounds.
4. Keep playing the instruments to see if new lines come to mind for the sound.
5. Fill the paper with different kinds of lines for the various instruments.

VARIATIONS

• Decide which type of movement goes with the lines (e.g., a sliding step for a straight line, hopping on one foot for a dotted line, waving your arms for a wavy line). Have fun acting out these lines!

• Play "Simon Says" using the steps above for the commands. For example, "Simon Says to be a dotted line." The children would hop on one foot to be a dotted line.

• Play classical, pop, or any other type of music. Have the children draw lines to go with the music. For example, in fast parts of the music, make spiral lines. In the slower parts, make slow, curvy lines. Fill the paper with lines representing the piece of music.

NOTES FOR NEXT TIME: _____

_____

_____

A

All Ages

Markers and Wet Paper

MATERIALS

- ☐ paper
- ☐ markers
- ☐ brush
- ☐ water
- ☐ container for water

HELPFUL HINT

- Use watercolor markers, not permanent markers, for this activity.

DEVELOPMENTAL GOALS

Develop creativity, small motor development, and hand-eye coordination and explore a new technique with colored markers.

PREPARATION

Paint an entire sheet of paper with water.

PROCESS

1. While paper is still wet, draw on it with markers.
2. Watch the colors run.
3. See how the shapes and lines soften.

VARIATION

- Draw with marker, then squirt with water. You will get the same softening and running of colors.

NOTES FOR NEXT TIME: _____

_____

_____

_____

Outdoor Chalk Fun

Years Old and Up

MATERIALS

- ☐ sidewalk chalk (extra-large chalk)
- ☐ toy cars, trucks, trains

💡 **HELPFUL HINT**

- Be sure you check that it is all right to draw on the concrete area before starting this activity!

CRAYONS

DEVELOPMENTAL GOALS

Develop creativity, small motor development, and hand-eye coordination and explore a new chalk technique.

PREPARATION

Talk about the toy vehicles and where they can be found. Discuss the neighborhood and where the cars, trucks, and trains are found.

PROCESS

1. Go outside and choose a concrete area for chalk drawings.
2. Let the children draw roads for the toy vehicles.
3. Draw buildings and houses.
4. Include people, pets, trees, and other details.

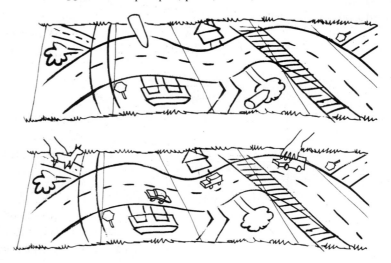

VARIATION

- Use a long piece of paper (butcher paper is a good choice) to repeat this activity indoors. Draw the roads, houses, buildings, and so on on the paper with chalk, crayons, or markers.

NOTES FOR NEXT TIME: _____

_____

_____

_____

Paper Quilts

MATERIALS

- ☐ blunt-tip scissors
- ☐ markers
- ☐ construction paper
- ☐ white paper
- ☐ glue
- ☐ glitter (optional)
- ☐ wallpaper samples

HELPFUL HINTS

- Cut a square template out of sturdy paper (gift box material or even cardboard). This will help the children make their squares. The children simply trace around the template onto the wallpaper with a crayon or pencil. Then, they can simply cut along these lines.

- You may have to precut the squares for children not yet able to use scissors.

DEVELOPMENTAL GOALS

Develop creativity, small motor development, and hand-eye coordination and explore a new use for markers to reinforce the design elements of rhythm, repetition unity, balance, and pattern.

PREPARATION

Find quilts or books with pictures of quilts made with square patches. Discuss the patterns in the quilts. Talk about the rhythm or repetition of certain lines in the quilts. Discuss the shapes the children see in the quilts. Talk about how the square patches are put together to make a harmonious design or pattern.

PROCESS

1. Choose several pieces of wallpaper.
2. Cut squares out of the wallpaper.
3. Arrange the wallpaper squares on a piece of white paper.
4. When satisfied with the arrangement, glue the pieces to the paper.
5. Use markers to outline areas of interest.

VARIATIONS

- Put the children's quilts together to make a class quilt.
- Read stories about quilt making in several cultures.
- Ask a family member to demonstrate quilting. Watch the quilter at work.

NOTES FOR NEXT TIME: _____
_____
_____
_____

CRAYONS

Poetry and Chalk Art

MATERIALS

- ☐ white and pastel colored chalk
- ☐ dark construction paper

 **HELPFUL HINT**

- If some children have trouble seeing mind pictures, ask them to draw a picture of the season. Anything they want to draw is acceptable.

DEVELOPMENTAL GOALS

Develop creativity, small motor development, and hand-eye coordination and encourage the appreciation of poetry that ties art and language arts.

PREPARATION

Read the poem "Snowstorm" to the children once.

Snowstorm

I love to see the snowflakes fall,
And cover everything in sight.
The lawn and trees and orchard wall
With spotless white.

PROCESS

1. Ask what the children saw in their minds when they heard the poem.

2. Read the poem again, and ask how many childen saw pictures of the scene in their minds.

3. Have a discussion. Let the children share their mind pictures of the poem.

4. Give each child a piece of dark construction paper.

5. With white and pastel chalk, have the children draw what comes to mind when they hear the poem.

VARIATIONS

- Use other poems about different seasons.
- Use a CD or tape of classical, rock, or other kinds of music. Ask the children to draw mind pictures of the music.

NOTES FOR NEXT TIME: _____

_____

_____

_____

Pressed-Plant Designs

MATERIALS

- ☐ cardboard
- ☐ construction paper
- ☐ recycled newspapers
- ☐ leaves
- ☐ flowers
- ☐ markers
- ☐ glue
- ☐ paper towels

HELPFUL HINT

- Very young children will have a hard time waiting for the plants and flowers to dry. It may help to let them peek every day to see how it is going.

NOTES FOR NEXT TIME:

_____

_____

_____

_____

_____

DEVELOPMENTAL GOALS

Develop creativity, small motor development, and hand-eye coordination and tie science to art activities.

PREPARATION

On an outdoor walk, collect fallen leaves and flowers. Cut cardboard into two pieces approximately 12" × 18". Each child will need two pieces of cardboard.

PROCESS

1. Collect nonpoisonous fallen leaves and such flowers as dandelions or clover.

2. Make a plant press. On top of cardboard, layer two or three paper towels. Spread leaves or flowers flat on the paper towels.

3. Place several sheets of newspaper over the leaves or flowers.

4. Have a child write his or her name with markers on the newspaper. (An adult may do this for younger children.)

5. Put heavy books or bricks on the plant press. Dry the press overnight.

6. Change the newspaper each day until the plants/flowers are dry.

7. Arrange the dried plant on construction paper in a design.

8. Glue on cut-out pieces of construction paper for details.

9. Complete the design with markers for decorative details.

VARIATIONS

- Have the children predict what they think will happen to the color and shape of plants as they dry. Measure sizes. Draw before and after pictures.

- Talk about other dried things, like raisins, prunes, and apricots. Have these dried fruits available to taste.

- Mix dried milk. Try making gelatin or pudding as another example of a dried food.

CRAYONS

Rubbing Chalk Experiences

MATERIALS

- ☐ chalk in many colors
- ☐ cotton swabs
- ☐ cotton balls
- ☐ paper

 **HELPFUL HINT**

- This activity is appropriate for children who have had some experience using chalk.

DEVELOPMENTAL GOALS

Develop creativity, small motor development, and hand-eye coordination and explore new chalk techniques.

PREPARATION

Give the children a chance to experience using chalk on different kinds of papers. Note if some apply chalk in separate strokes. See if some blend the colors. Encourage the children to talk about their work with chalk.

PROCESS

1. Draw a picture or make a design with the chalk on paper.

2. Use a cotton swab or cotton ball to rub the chalk drawing to soften and blend the colors.

3. Expect that some colors may get muddied. This is a natural part of the process.

VARIATIONS

- Use different textures of paper.
- Use scraps of cloth for blending.
- Rub only certain sections of the picture or design. Talk about the differences.

NOTES FOR NEXT TIME: _____

_____

_____

_____

Salty Crayon Fun

MATERIALS

- ☐ dark construction paper
- ☐ crayons
- ☐ container for water
- ☐ salt
- ☐ brush
- ☐ water

 **HELPFUL HINT**

- Be prepared for a bit more of a mess when you mix glitter into the thinned white glue. Considering the sparkly effects of this mixture, it is worth the mess!

DEVELOPMENTAL GOALS

Develop creativity, small motor development, and hand-eye coordination and explore a new use for crayons.

PREPARATION

Mix the salt and water, using twice the amount of salt as water (e.g., 2 cups salt to 1 cup water).

PROCESS

1. Draw with crayons on dark construction paper.
2. Paint the entire picture or design with the salt and water mixture.
3. When the water dries, the picture will sparkle.

VARIATIONS

- Thin white glue with water. Mix in glitter. Paint this mixture over a crayon drawing on light-colored construction paper. It will be another sparkly drawing!
- Make greeting cards and wrapping paper using this crayon technique.

NOTES FOR NEXT TIME: _____

_____

_____

_____

CRAYONS

Sandy Chalk Work

MATERIALS

☐ colored chalk

☐ sandpaper
(rough grade)

💡 HELPFUL HINTS

- Spray the drawing with hairspray to help keep it from smearing. Be sure to spray in a well-ventilated area.

- This activity is appropriate for even the very young artist who is in the controlled scribble stage.

DEVELOPMENTAL GOALS

Develop creativity, small motor development, and hand-eye coordination and explore another chalking technique.

PREPARATION

Cover the ends of chalk with foil. This helps make them easier to hold when working on rough surfaces.

PROCESS

1. Draw with chalk on the sandpaper.
2. The rough surface of the sandpaper helps make rich and vivid texture effects.

VARIATIONS

- Richer color can be achieved if the sandpaper is moist. It will also attract and hold greater amounts of rich chalk color.

- Use other grades of sandpaper for different effects.

NOTES FOR NEXT TIME: _____

_____

_____

_____

4 Years Old and Up

Scribbles

MATERIALS

- ☐ crayons
- ☐ paper
- ☐ markers

 **HELPFUL HINT**

- This activity can be adapted to the very young artist and for the most "grown-up" one, as well. The younger the artist, the simpler the scribble activity. Older children will enjoy trying some of the variations.

DEVELOPMENTAL GOALS

Develop creativity, small motor development, and hand-eye coordination and explore a new crayoning technique.

PREPARATION

Discuss scribbling, how it looks, and how much fun it is to do. Explain that this activity begins with scribbling.

PROCESS

1. Make a large scribble on the paper.
2. Outline with a marker parts of the scribble.
3. Fill the outline areas with crayons.
4. Leave some areas uncolored.

VARIATIONS

- Make rules for filling the scribbles (e.g., "You can't put the same colors next to each other," "You can only use primary colors," "Use only complementary colors.").
- Challenge the children to make scribbles using straight lines and angles.
- Have a group of children make a scribble picture mural.
- Scribble using crayon, then paint the spaces using tempera paint.

NOTES FOR NEXT TIME: _____

_____

_____

_____

Shading with Chalk Dust

MATERIALS

- ☐ chalk
- ☐ flat, hard tool for scraping chalk into dust (e.g., knife, screwdriver)
- ☐ paper
- ☐ cotton balls
- ☐ facial tissue
- ☐ cotton swabs

💡 HELPFUL HINTS

- Chalk is easily smeared and the completed drawing should have some protection. An adult may use hairspray for a fixative. Be sure to use it in a well-ventilated area.

- This activity requires experience with chalk drawing.

DEVELOPMENTAL GOALS

Develop creativity, small motor development, and hand-eye coordination and explore chalk as an expressive technique.

PREPARATION

An adult scrapes the tool along the side of the chalk to produce chalk dust. Collect the chalk dust in a jar lid or another small, shallow container.

PROCESS

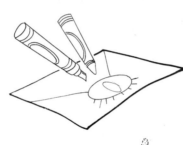

1. Discuss shadows, light, and dark.
2. Talk about how chalk can be rubbed into drawings to make shadows or to make things look softer.
3. Make a chalk, crayon, or marker drawing/design.
4. Use the fingers or a cotton swab to sprinkle chalk dust into areas of a drawing or design.
5. Use tissue or a cotton ball to blend the dust in to make shadows and soft areas of color.

VARIATION

- The dust particles from the chalk may be scraped by the adult directly onto areas of the drawing.

NOTES FOR NEXT TIME: _____

_____

_____

_____

CRAYONS

Shape Game

MATERIALS

- ☐ markers
- ☐ construction paper
- ☐ music
- ☐ music player
- ☐ ruler
- ☐ blunt scissors
- ☐ double-stick tape

💡 HELPFUL HINTS

- Children under age 4 will need help cutting out the shape.
- The younger the child, the fewer and more basic the shapes must be.
- For very young children, you will need to precut the large shapes. Let the children decorate the shapes with markers for the game.
- Using a ruler may be a new skill for children. You might give them time to practice using it before beginning this activity.

DEVELOPMENTAL GOALS

Develop creativity, small motor development, and hand-eye coordination and explore different uses for markers to tie shape recognition to art.

PREPARATION

Talk about shapes. Begin with the most basic, such as the circle, square, and rectangle. Add more shapes as children learn the basic ones.

PROCESS

1. On construction paper, draw a big shape with markers. Use a ruler to draw straight lines.
2. Cut out the shape.
3. Draw designs and borders on the shape with markers.
4. Place a small piece of double-stick tape on the back of the shape.
5. Stick the shape on the floor.
6. Play "Name That Shape " game.
7. In this game, a leader starts the music. Walk around the room, stepping on different shapes. When the music stops, the leader asks a child to name the shape. That child becomes the next leader.

VARIATIONS

- Use colors, animals, letters, names, or any other concept the children are learning about for this game.
- Add instruments to play during the game.
- Add listening and motor-skill challenges. The children make up directions in advance and write them on cards (e.g., "If you are on a red square, put your hand on your head").

NOTES FOR NEXT TIME: _____

_____

Shape Tracing

MATERIALS

- ☐ common objects (e.g., a fork, a spoon, cup, dish)
- ☐ construction paper
- ☐ markers
- ☐ oak tag or poster board
- ☐ glue
- ☐ clear contact paper (optional)

HELPFUL HINT

- Matching games are good individual activities for children. Sometimes even young children need some alone time.

DEVELOPMENTAL GOALS

Develop creativity, small motor development, and hand-eye coordination and practice grouping and sorting skills.

PREPARATION

Talk about the items collected for this activity. Let the children see and hold the items. Talk about how the items go together. For example, the items are all used at the table when we eat.

PROCESS

1. Place one object on a piece of construction paper and trace around it with a marker.
2. Place another object on the construction paper and trace around it.
3. Continue until all objects have been traced.
4. Use the sheets with the traced objects for a matching game.
5. Have a child select an object from a box and match it to the outline on the paper.
6. Glue the sheet to poster board and cover it with clear contact paper for durability.

VARIATIONS

- Trace around the cardboard shapes or letters. Use them in a matching game.
- Make placemats for lunch or snack time with outlines for cups, napkins, and so on.

NOTES FOR NEXT TIME: _____

_____

_____

Shoebox Crayon Creations

MATERIALS

- ☐ construction paper
- ☐ shoeboxes
- ☐ blunt-tip scissors
- ☐ glue
- ☐ crayons

💡 HELPFUL HINTS

- Expect older children to want to add many details to their shoebox structures. Be sure to have plenty of markers, crayons, and colored pencils available for this purpose.

- Younger children may need help in cutting out the doors and windows on their shoeboxes.

DEVELOPMENTAL GOALS

Develop creativity, small motor development, and hand-eye coordination and encourage recycling.

PREPARATION

Ask parents or friends to collect shoeboxes for this activity. Walk around the neighborhood to observe the kinds of places people live in, where they park their cars, and what kinds of stores can be seen.

PROCESS

1. Cut out construction paper to cover the shoebox.
2. Glue construction paper on the shoebox.
3. Draw windows, a roof, and other features on with crayons.
4. Cut out doors and windows with scissors.

VARIATIONS

- Make a neighborhood of shoebox houses, garages, and stores.
- Add toy cars to drive into the shoebox garages.
- Make shoebox "treasure boxes." Decorate with crayons and markers. Store found objects from walks and other goodies in them.

NOTES FOR NEXT TIME: _____

_____

_____

_____

Sidewalk Chalk

MATERIALS

- ☐ 4 to 5 eggshells
- ☐ 1 teaspoon flour
- ☐ 1 teaspoon very hot tap water
- ☐ food coloring
- ☐ mixing bowl
- ☐ spoon
- ☐ paper towels

💡 HELPFUL HINTS

- This chalk is for sidewalks only. Do not use this chalk on any other surface.
- Be sure to tell the children that the chalk must dry for 3 days before you start the activity. You might circle the day on the calendar when the chalk will be ready to use.
- This recipe makes one large piece of chalk or two smaller pieces.
- Have the children bring in the washed eggshells for this activity.

DEVELOPMENTAL GOALS

Develop creativity, small motor development, and hand-eye coordination and create a new type of chalk.

PREPARATION

Wash and dry the eggshells. Put them in a bowl and grind into a powder. A mortar and pestle works fine for this, or just use the bowl of a large spoon. Discard any large pieces.

PROCESS

1. Place the flour and hot water in another bowl.
2. Add 1 tablespoon eggshell powder and mix until a paste forms.
3. Add food coloring, if desired.
4. Shape and press the mixture firmly into the shape of a chalk stick.
5. Roll up tightly in a strip of paper towel.
6. Allow to dry approximately 3 days until hard.
7. Remove paper towel and you have chalk!

VARIATIONS

- Shape the chalk dough into a round or an oval shape.
- Make chalk with several different colors of food colorings.

NOTES FOR NEXT TIME: _____

_____

_____

Sleep-Time Friends

CRAYONS

MATERIALS

- ☐ markers
- ☐ glue
- ☐ blunt-tip scissors
- ☐ grocery bags
- ☐ newspaper
- ☐ yarn (optional)

💡 HELPFUL HINT

- Be sure to emphasize that sleeping is not always necessary at rest time. Just resting is acceptable.

NOTES FOR NEXT TIME:

_____

_____

_____

_____

_____

_____

DEVELOPMENTAL GOALS

Develop creativity, small motor development, and hand-eye coordination and explore a new use of markers.

PREPARATION

Discuss rest time. Ask about things that help the children rest. Talk about favorite blankets or cuddly stuffed animals. Have the children think about what they want to make to help them at rest time. To make grocery bags soft, soak them in water. Crumple the bags and squeeze water through them. Flatten them to dry. This may take a day or two.

PROCESS

1. With markers, draw the shape and size of your sleep-time friend.
2. Make the friend big enough to stuff.
3. Cut two pieces the same size: one for front, and one for back.
4. Decorate both sides with markers.
5. Crumple recycled newspaper for stuffing. Lay the stuffing on the bottom half of the sleep-time friend.
6. Put glue all around the outside edges. Place the top of the sleep-time friend on the stuffing and seal the edges.
7. Dry overnight.
8. Add details with markers or glue yarn around the edges.

VARIATIONS

- Small sleep-time friends can be stuffed with cotton balls or recycled, washed pantyhose.
- Make sleep-time friends out of flannel or muslin. Decorate the friends with fabric crayons. Fill with pillow stuffing.

Splatter Chalk Designs

MATERIALS

- ☐ colored chalk
- ☐ plastic pump bottles of different sizes

💡 HELPFUL HINT

- Be prepared for the possibility that some children will enjoy the spraying more than the chalk drawing. Make this a creative experience, too. Challenge the children to come up with different ways to spray water to create different effects on their chalk drawings.

DEVELOPMENTAL GOALS

Develop creativity, small motor development, and hand-eye coordination and explore a new chalk technique.

PREPARATION

Fill the plastic pump bottles with water.

PROCESS

1. Color the sidewalk with colored chalk.

2. Press the pump top and let the water splatter over the chalk on the sidewalk.

3. This makes a splatter design on the chalk.

VARIATIONS

- Use different-sized pump bottles, comparing the different water marks each bottle makes.

- Add food coloring to water in the pump bottles. See what different effects this makes on the chalk drawing.

- Do this activity indoors on sheets of paper with chalk drawings on them. Be sure to prepare the area for lots of water spraying!

NOTES FOR NEXT TIME: _____

_____

_____

_____

Squares

MATERIALS

- ☐ crayons
- ☐ paper

💡 HELPFUL HINT

- This activity is appropriate for children who can identify shapes.

DEVELOPMENTAL GOALS

Develop creativity, small motor development, and hand-eye coordination.

PREPARATION

Talk about squares and how we know things are square because they have four even sides. Discuss how squares are all over the place. Look at these square things.

PROCESS

1. On a piece of paper, draw squares.
2. Draw the squares in different sizes.
3. Try stacking the squares.
4. Draw a design or an object made totally of squares.
5. Color the squares different colors.

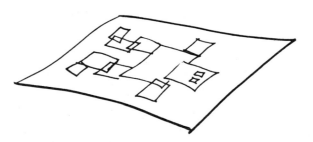

VARIATIONS

- Do the same activity using only circles, triangles, rectangles, ovals, and so on.
- Use markers to add details to the design.
- Glue on scraps of fabric or cloth for added effects.

NOTES FOR NEXT TIME: _____

_____

_____

_____

CRAYONS

Stained-Glass Chalk Designs

MATERIALS

- ☐ black construction paper
- ☐ white glue
- ☐ colored chalk
- ☐ examples of stained glass (pictures or the real thing)

 **HELPFUL HINT**

- This is a good activity for children in the basic forms stage of drawing.

DEVELOPMENTAL GOALS

Develop creativity, small motor development, and hand-eye coordination and explore a new chalking technique.

PREPARATION

Show the children pictures of stained glass (or the real thing). Discuss the colors. See how the colors are in separate sections. Talk about the colors and shapes the children see in the stained glass.

PROCESS

1. Create a stained glass design and draw it on the construction paper using white glue.

2. Experiment with different shapes and images.

3. When the glue is dry, color between the glue lines using colored chalks.

4. Adult sprays design with hairspray to prevent the chalk from smudging off the paper.

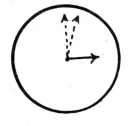

VARIATION

- Try light-colored construction paper and pastel-colored chalks for a very different kind of stained-glass effect.

NOTES FOR NEXT TIME: _____

_____

_____

_____

3
Years Old and Up

Starchy Chalk

MATERIALS

- ☐ liquid starch
- ☐ dry chalk
- ☐ paper
- ☐ brush for applying starch
- ☐ water

💡 HELPFUL HINTS

- There is less friction when using chalk on liquid starch. The paper is less likely to tear because of this.

- Liquid starch is available in the grocery store where laundry products are sold.

DEVELOPMENTAL GOALS

Develop creativity, small motor development, and hand-eye coordination and explore new chalk activities.

PREPARATION

Pour the starch into a shallow container. Provide each child with a brush and piece of paper.

PROCESS

1. Brush liquid starch onto the paper.
2. Apply dry chalk to the paper, making a picture or a design.
3. Allow to dry thoroughly.
4. Spray with a fixative to keep from smearing. (Ordinary hairspray works well.) Be sure to spray fixative in a well-ventilated area!

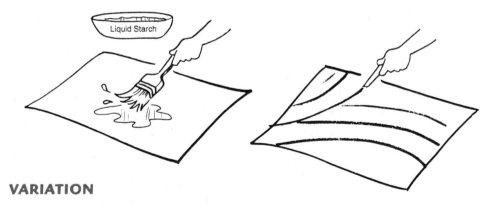

VARIATION

- Use different colors of chalk and different kinds of paper.

NOTES FOR NEXT TIME: _____

_____

_____

_____

All Ages

Sugar and Chalk

MATERIALS

- ☐ sugar
- ☐ water
- ☐ large pieces of chalk
- ☐ paper
- ☐ container for sugar-water mixture

 **HELPFUL HINT**

- Have the sugar-soaked chalk ready when you begin this activity. The children do not enjoy waiting 15 minutes to start this activity.

DEVELOPMENTAL GOALS

Develop creativity, small motor development, and hand-eye coordination and explore new chalk techniques.

PREPARATION

Mix one part sugar and two parts water (e.g., 1/2 cup sugar and 1 cup water).

PROCESS

1. Soak pieces of large chalk in the sugar-water mixture for about 15 minutes.
2. Use the chalk on dry paper.
3. Sugar gives the chalk a shiny look when dry.

VARIATIONS

- Use all light or all dark chalks.
- Use the sugar-soaked chalk on cardboard and recycled white gift boxes.
- Use sugar-soaked white chalk on black construction paper for "snowy" pictures.

NOTES FOR NEXT TIME: _____

_____

_____

_____

3 Years Old and Up

The Adventures of a Line

MATERIALS

☐ flip pad

☐ colored markers

☐ 8-1/2" × 11" sheets of white paper for each child

💡 HELPFUL HINT

- If you lack art books, have the children look for lines in the room or outdoors.

DEVELOPMENTAL GOALS

Develop creativity, small motor development, and hand-eye coordination and explore the concept of lines using markers.

PREPARATION

Review the types of lines with the children. Talk about wavy, straight, zigzag, vertical, horizontal, dotted, and spiral lines. Draw the lines on the flip pad as they are discussed.

PROCESS

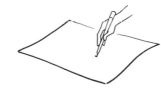

1. Using a colored marker, draw a dot on the paper.

2. Have a child make a type of line starting with that dot.

3. Have a child draw many kinds of lines, each starting with a dot.

4. Alternate colors of markers when making lines.

5. Use your favorite line to make a design or picture on another piece of paper.

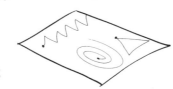

VARIATIONS

- Create a story using different types of lines (e.g., a line is a dot that went for a walk in the snow). Each set of subsequent lines can be different things (e.g., thin parallel lines are sled tracks, thin curvy lines are a bicycle track, parallel zigzags could be car tires, spiral lines could be a snake track).

- Older children may search art books for types of lines. This can be done as a group in front of a single painting, or the children can be given a card with a type of line and told to search the room for the best example of that type of line.

NOTES FOR NEXT TIME: _____

_____

_____

Years Old and UP

T-Shirt Crayon Designs

MATERIALS

- ☐ T-shirt (light-colored)
- ☐ wax crayons
- ☐ newspaper
- ☐ iron
- ☐ ironing board (or pieces of heavy cardboard)
- ☐ paper

💡 HELPFUL HINTS

- Be very careful when using an iron around the children. Be sure they stay well away from it during the pressing process.
- The color will last only if the fabric is washed in cool water with a non-detergent soap.

DEVELOPMENTAL GOALS

Develop creativity, small motor development, and hand-eye coordination and explore new uses for crayons.

PREPARATION

Discuss with the children what they would like to draw on their T-shirts. Explain that when they draw on the T-shirt, it will be permanent. They may want to practice their picture or design on paper before drawing it on the T-shirt.

PROCESS

1. Using wax crayons, draw a picture on a white or light-colored T-shirt.
2. The teacher uses an iron to press with newspaper over the picture and on an ironing board or a piece of heavy cardboard.
3. The picture will stay indefinitely.

VARIATIONS

- Fabric crayons are available for drawing on T-shirts. These work very well, but not everyone can afford these in addition to regular crayons!
- If you do have fabric crayons, use them to make designs on white tennis shoes.

NOTES FOR NEXT TIME: _____

_____

_____

_____

CRAYONS

Yarn and Marker Fun

MATERIALS

- ☐ recycled yarn
- ☐ markers
- ☐ glue
- ☐ construction paper
- ☐ ruler

💡 HELPFUL HINTS

- This is an appropriate activity for children who are learning their letters.
- For children who are not yet at letter recognition, use shapes instead.

DEVELOPMENTAL GOALS

Develop creativity, small motor development, and hand-eye coordination and explore a new use for markers while making letters.

PREPARATION

Cut the yarn into 24" pieces. (Older children may use a ruler to measure and cut their own yarn.)

PROCESS

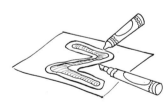

1. Choose a piece of yarn.
2. Shape the yarn into a letter. Make another letter.
3. Make a letter with glue on colored construction paper.
4. Glue the yarn to the paper. Dry overnight.
5. Trace around the yarn letter with markers. Trace several times with different colors.
6. Make other interesting designs around the letter.

VARIATIONS

- Use yarn with a flannel board. It sticks well and is fun for open-ended, creative designing.
- Lay the yarn on letters, such as on newspaper headlines or poster titles.
- Have the children work in pairs. One child names a letter and the other shapes it with yarn.

NOTES FOR NEXT TIME: _____

_____

_____

_____

CRAYONS

Index by Ages

PART III

Painting

Fun with Painting

Painting comes naturally to young children. It is a way children visually communicate their ideas and feelings about themselves and their world. Painting encourages the spontaneous use of color in the joyful process of creating.

Through painting, children can express their reactions about the world as they understand it. In this way, children discover and build their own styles of expression. Each child's painting differs from another child's, just as children's appearances and personalities differ.

The activities in this book are designed for children aged 2 through 8. An icon representing a suggested age for the activity is listed at the top of each activity. However, use your knowledge of the child's abilities to guide you in choosing and using the activities in this book. Wherever appropriate, information is provided on how to adapt the activities for children over age 8.

GETTING STARTED

Process vs. Product

The focus of this book and all early childhood art activities is on the process, not the product. This means that the process of creating, not the product, is the main reason for the activity. The joys of creating, exploring materials, and discovering how things look and work are all part of the creative process. How the product looks, what it is "supposed to be," is unimportant to the child, and it should be unimportant to the adult.

Young children delight in the experience, the exploration, and the experimentation of art activities. The adult's role is to provide interesting materials and an environment that encourages children's creativity. Stand back when you are tempted to "help" children with their artwork. Instead, encourage all children to discover their own unique abilities.

Considering the Child

Young children find it hard to wait patiently to use materials in an activity. Often, the excitement of creativity and patience do not mix. In addition, it is sometimes difficult for young children to share. With young children, plan to have enough materials for each child. For example, having a paintbrush and paint for each child to use makes the process of painting more fun and relaxed for young children.

Using Painting Materials and Equipment

The most basic materials you will need for painting activities are paint, brushes, and paper. Following are some hints for each of these painting materials.

• Paint

The most basic type of paint young children use is tempera paint. It comes in dry-powder and liquid forms. With liquid tempera, water is unneeded, although liquid tempera may be diluted with water to thin paint for different activities, like crayon-resist paintings. The dry form of tempera can be made very thick or very thin, depending on the amount of water added.

Watercolor paint sets are dehydrated tempera colors in concentrated cakes. They are easy and convenient for individual or group use.

Using Paints in Cakes: Place a few drops of water on the surface of each cake to moisten the paint. Dip the paintbrush in water, and brush the surface of the moistened cake of paint to obtain smooth, creamy paint.

Using Powder (Tempera) Paint: A surprising amount of dry tempera is needed relative to the quantity of water to make rich, bright, creamy paint. For this reason, it is best to put the tempera in the container first, then add water bit by bit. Fill a container one-quarter full of dry paint. Add water slowly, stirring constantly until the paint has the consistency of thin cream. Instead of water, some teachers prefer using liquid starch (found in the grocery store in the laundry aisle), because it thickens the paint mixture. It is also helpful to add a dash of liquid detergent, which eases cleaning.

For best results, prepare paint when needed. Large amounts of paint kept over time tend to sour. Good containers for use with tempera paint include milk cartons, juice cans, coffee cans, plastic cups, and cut-down plastic bottles. See **Figure 1** for more helpful hints for storing and handling painting materials.

• Brushes
Large, long-handled brushes are best for young children's painting. Those with 12" handles and 3/4" bristle length are easy for young children to use. Soft, floppy, camel-hair brushes allow the children to swoop about the paper most freely. The stiff, flat kind of brush makes it harder to produce such free movements. Many watercolor paint sets come with paintbrushes designed for watercolor use.

• Paper
Pieces of paper measuring 12" × 18" work well for painting, as do roll paper, manila paper, newspaper, wallpaper, newsprint, and freezer paper. More details on different types of materials for painting are provided in specific activities.

• Easels and Other Surfaces
An ideal way for children to paint is at child-level easels, but painting can still be an enjoyable, creative experience when easels are not available. Painting can be done on a tabletop. Simply cover the area with newspapers, place a piece of paper on top, and let the painting begin! Another way to paint is to cover a wall space with a large piece of plastic. Cover the area below the plastic with newspapers Tape pieces of paper (masking tape works best) to the plastic-covered wall.

Gathering Materials

Each activity in this book includes a list of required materials. It is important to gather all materials before starting the activity with children. Children's creative experiences are easily discouraged when they must sit and wait while the adult looks for the tape, extra scissors, or colored paper. Be sure to gather the materials in a place the children can easily access.

FIGURE 1 · TIPS FOR STORING ART MATERIALS

The ways materials, supplies, and space are arranged can make or break children's and teachers' art experiences. Following are suggestions for arranging supplies for art experiences:

1. *Scissor holders.* Holders can be made from gallon milk or bleach containers. Simply punch holes in the containers and place scissors in the holes with the scissor points to the inside. Egg cartons turned upside down with slits in each mound also make excellent holders.

2. *Paint containers.* Containers can range from muffin tins and plastic egg cartons to plastic soft-drink cartons with baby food jars in them. These work especially well outdoors as well as indoors, because they are large and not easily tipped. Place one brush in each container. This prevents colors from mixing and makes cleanup easier.

3. *Crayon containers.* Juice and vegetable cans painted or covered with contact paper work very well.

4. Crayon pieces may be melted in muffin trays in a warm oven. These pieces, when cooled, are nice for rubbings or drawings. Crayola® makes a unit that is designed specifically for melting crayons safely.

5. Printing with tempera is easier if the tray is lined with a sponge or a paper towel.

6. A card file for art activities helps organize the program.

7. *Clay containers.* Airtight coffee cans and plastic food containers are excellent ways to keep clay moist and always ready for use.

8. *Paper scrap boxes.* By keeping two or more boxes of scrap paper of different sizes, children will be able to choose the size paper they want more easily.

9. Cover a wall area with pegboard and suspend heavy shopping bags or transparent plastic bags from hooks inserted in the pegboard to hold miscellaneous art supplies. Hang smocks in the same way on the pegboard (at child level, of course).

10. Use the back of a piano or bookcase to hang a shoe bag. Its pockets can hold many small items.

11. Use divided frozen food trays or a revolving lazy Susan to hold miscellaneous small items.

(From Mayesky, Mary. *Creative Activites for Young Children*, 7th ed., Clifton Park, NY: Delmar Learning.)

PAINTING

Using Food Products

Several activities involve the use of different kinds of foods. There are long-standing arguments for and against food use in art activities. For example, many teachers have long used potato printing as a traditional printing activity for young children. These teachers feel they are an economical way to prepare printing objects for children. Using potatoes beyond their shelf life is an alternative to throwing them away. On the other hand, many teachers feel that food is for eating and should be used for nothing else.

This book has many activities that do not use food so that there will be options for teachers who oppose food use in art activities. Also, where possible, alternatives to food items are suggested. Whatever your opinion, creativities in painting are provided for your and the children's exploration and enjoyment.

Employing Safe Materials

For all activities in this book and in any art activities for young children, be sure to use safe art supplies. Read labels on all art materials. Check for age appropriateness. The Art and Creative Materials Institute (ACMI) labels art materials AP (approved product) and CL (certified label). Products with these labels are certified safe for use by young children.

The ACMI provides an extensive list of materials and manufacturers of safe materials for all young children. This information is available on the ACMI Web site at http://www.acminet.org by writing to 715 Boylston Street, Boston, MA 02116.

Some basic safety hints for art activities are:

- Always use products that are appropriate for the child. Use nontoxic materials for children in grades six and lower.

- Never use products for skin painting or food preparation unless the products are intended for those uses.

- Do not transfer art materials to other containers. You will lose the valuable safety information that is on the product packages.

- Do not eat or drink while using art and craft materials. Wash after use. Clean yourself and your supplies.

- Be sure that your work area is well ventilated.

Following are potentially unsafe painting supplies:

- *Epoxy, instant glues, or other solvent-based glues.* Use only water-based, white glue.

- *Paints that require solvents like turpentine to clean.* Use only water-based paints.

- *Cold water or commercial dyes that contain chemical additives.* Use only natural vegetable dyes made from beets, onion skins, and so on.

- *Permanent markers.* Permanent markers may contain toxic solvents. Use only water-based markers.

Be aware of all children's allergies. Children with allergies to wheat, for example, may be irritated by the wheat paste used in papier-mâché. Children allergic to peanuts must taste nothing with peanut butter. In fact, some centers make it a rule to avoid the use of peanuts or peanut butter in food or art activities. Other art materials that may cause allergic reactions include chalk or other dusty substances, water-based clay, and any material that contains petroleum products.

Also be aware of children's habits. Some young children put everything in their mouths. (This can be the case at any age.) Others may be shy and slow to accept new materials. Use your knowledge of children's tendencies to help you plan art activities that are safe for all children.

Take the time to talk with the children about which things they may taste and which they may not. For example, when making anything mixed with glue, remind the children that glue is not to be tasted. You may find it helpful to display a sign of a large smiley face with a tongue at the end of the smile to indicate an "edible activity." Use another sign with the same smiley face but a large black X over the tongue to show a "no-taste activity."

Creating a Child-Friendly Environment

It is difficult to be creative when you have to worry about keeping yourself and your work area clean. Cover all artwork areas with newspaper. It is best to tape the paper to the work surface to avoid having paint or other materials seep through the spaces. In addition, it is much easier to pick up and throw away paint-spattered newspaper than it is to clean a tabletop.

Other coverups that work well are shower curtains and plastic tablecloths. Remember to cover the children, too! Some good child coverups are men's shirts (with the sleeves cut off), aprons, pillowcases with holes cut for the head and arms, and smocks. Some fun alternative to these are sets of old clothes or shoes that can be worn as "art clothes." These old clothes could become "art journals" as they become covered with the traces of various art projects.

Other things to have on hand while painting are paper towels or scrap paper for blotting brushes. A bucket of child-sized, moist sponges is also handy to have on hand for cleanup.

Another hint to easier cleanup after painting is to cut and laminate both sides of a posterboard that fits the painting easel. Tape the laminated posterboard over the easel so that the children can easily wipe off the paint with a damp cloth, rag, or paper towel. Such a posterboard helps children learn how to clean up, keeps the easel clean, and develops more hand-eye coordination in a fun way.

The Painting Process—Some Basics

Following are some hints for making the painting process run smoothly:

- Thicken tempera paint with liquid starch to cut down on drips.

- To help paint stick better to such slick surfaces as foil, wax paper, Styrofoam, or plastic, mix dry tempera with liquid soap.

- To keep paints smelling fresh and sweet, add a few drops of mint extract or oil of wintergreen or cloves, which are available in the spices section of the grocery store.

- Lay paintings horizontally to dry before stacking. An unused floor space along the wall works well for this purpose, or use a stacking rack as **Figure 2** illustrates. See **Figure 3** for ideas on stretching painting-budget dollars.

Art Tool Holder

Heavy paper, folded several times, will make a holder that keeps tools from rolling.

Drying Rack

Drying racks for wet artwork are ideal when space is at a premium. A number of wooden sticks of the same size, tacked or stapled to pieces of corrugated cardboard of the same size, make a drying rack. When pieces of wood are unavailable, substitute two, three, or four pieces of corrugated cardboard taped together. Tape the stacked pieces to the cardboard base.

Paint Container

Paper milk cartons (with the tops removed) stapled together and with cardboard handles make ideal containers for colored paint and water.

Paint Dispensers

Plastic mustard or ketchup containers make good paint dispensers. An aluminum nail in the top of each will keep the paint fresh. In some cases, the plastic containers can be used for painting directly from the container. Syrup pitchers make good paint dispensers and are ideal for storing paint.

Plastic Spoons

Keep plastic spoons in cans of powdered tempera for easy paint dispensing.

(From Mayesky, Mary. *Creative Activites for Young Children*, 7th ed., Clifton Park, NY: Delmar Learning.)

- Wipe paint sets clean with paper towels. Store the sets in a cardboard carton.

- For tempera paint or watercolor, rinse brushes in clean water, blot, gently point bristles, and leave to dry standing upright in a container.

- Clean brushes after each use. Neglect causes brushes to lose their shape. Be sure to never rest a brush vertically on its bristles. Suspend it, if possible; if not, rest it on its side.

FIGURE 3 · CREATIVE BUDGETING

Painting supplies can eat up a large part of your budget. The following ideas may help your budget (and maybe your creativity, too):

1. Individual watercolor sets can be made by pouring leftover tempera paint into egg-carton cups. Set them aside to dry and harden. Use the paints with water and brushes, just as you would ordinary paint sets.

2. Paint containers must be sturdy and inexpensive. Following are some ideas for different types of paint containers:

   - Cupcake or muffin tins are excellent for painting with several colors at a time.

   - Egg cartons work well when children are painting with cotton swabs. Cut the cartons in thirds to make four-part containers, and pour small amounts of paint into each egg cup.

   - Store liquid tempera in recycled glue or dishwashing-liquid bottles. Paint can be squirted quickly and neatly into paint cups from these bottles.

   - Use baby-food jars as paint containers. Make a holder for them by cutting circles from an egg-carton lid. An empty six-pack soft-drink carton makes a great tote for baby-food jars of paint.

   - When using paint cups, make a nontipping cup holder from an empty half-gallon milk or juice carton. Cut holes along the length of the carton and pop in the cups.

   - Sponges can be good paint holders, too. Cut a hole the exact size of the paint jar or cup in the center of the sponge, then fit the jar/cup in the hole. Besides keeping paint containers upright, the sponges also catch drips.

   - Cotton-ball painting is more fun (and neater) when you clip spring-type clothespins to the cotton balls. Children use the clothespins like handles. The same clothespins can be used when printing with small sponge pieces.

(From Mayesky, Mary. *Creative Activites for Young Children*, 7th ed., Clifton Park, NY: Delmar Learning.)

- Cover unused tempera until its next use. Do not keep tempera too long, because it becomes sour smelling.

Enjoying the Painting Process

Young children naturally enjoy painting, but eager young painters may require some help learning how to:

- *Prepare paint trays for use.* With watercolor paint sets, put a drop or two of water in each paint color to moisten it. Remember to dip the brush in water to clean it before dipping it into another color.

PAINTING

- Use a variety of brush strokes.

- Paint directly on paper, using full, free strokes.

- Use the point, side, and flat surfaces of the brush. Try wide lines, thin lines, zigzag lines, and dots and dabs.

- Mix colors on paper.

- Dip one side of the brush in one color and the other side in a second color to blend paint in one stroke.

- Remove excess paint or water from a brush by using the side of the paint container.

- Clean paint trays with paper towels or sponges.

- Rinse brushes in water and dry them with the bristles up.

Exploring Finger Painting

Finger painting is an especially good activity for young children, because it can be done over and over again. This repetition stresses the process, not the product. This book has many finger-painting activities and recipes young children will enjoy.

For finger painting, you may purchase premixed finger paint, or you may mix powdered tempera paint with liquid starch to make your own finger paint. To make your own finger paint, pour a generous dollop of starch onto paper, then sprinkle it with dry tempera. Then, have the children mix the materials with their fingers. Some teachers like to stir the dry pigment into an entire container of liquid starch. No matter how you prepare the paint, be ready to add more ingredients as the children work. The results to strive for in mixing are rich, brilliant color and sufficient paint to fill the paper when the children wish. Children must also be allowed to experiment with the paint, using their fingers, the palms of their hands, their wrists, and their arms. The children may enjoy helping to mix a recipe from **Figure 4**, which tells how to make additional kinds of finger paint.

Remember that some children dislike the feel of finger paint. Never force these children to use finger paint. Instead, substitute painting with a brush.

Now enter the world of painting. Enjoy the trip!

FIGURE 4 · FINGER-PAINT RECIPES*

Starch and Soap Finger Paint

1 cup starch
1-1/2 cups boiling water
1/2 cup soap flakes (not soap powder)
1 tablespoon glycerine (optional, makes it smoother)

Method: Mix the starch with enough water to make a smooth paste. Add the boiling water, and cook until glossy. Stir in the soap flakes while the mixture is warm. When the mixture is cool, add glycerine and coloring (powder paint, poster paint, or vegetable coloring).

Flour and Salt Finger Paint, Cooked

2 cups flour
2 teaspoons salt
3 cups cold water
2 cups hot water

Method: Add the salt to the flour, then pour the mixture into the cold water gradually. Beat the mixture with an egg beater until the mixture is smooth. Add the hot water and boil until the mixture becomes glossy. Beat the mixture until smooth, then mix in the coloring.

Flour and Salt Finger Paint, Uncooked

1 cup flour
1-1/2 teaspoons salt
1 cup water

Method: Combine the flour and salt, then add the water. This mixture has a grainy quality, unlike other finger paints, providing a different sensory experience.

Argo™ Starch Finger Paint

1/2 cup boiling water
2 tablespoons Argo starch
6 tablespoons cold water

Method: Dissolve the starch in cold water in a cup. Add this mixture to the boiling water, stirring constantly. Heat the mixture until it becomes glossy. Add color.

Wheat Flour Finger Paint

3 parts water
1 part wheat flour

Method: Stir the flour into the water, and add food coloring. (Wheat flour can be bought at low cost in wallpaper or department stores.)

Tempera Finger Paint

Dry tempera paint
1/2 cup liquid starch or
1/2 cup liquid dishwashing detergent

Method: Mix the tempera paint with the starch or detergent, adding the starch gradually until the desired thickness is reached. Paint extender can also be added to dry tempera paint.

*Interesting smells can be obtained by adding different food flavorings (e.g., mint, cloves) or talcum powder to the finger paint, if desired.

(From Mayesky, Mary. *Creative Activites for Young Children*, 7th ed., Clifton Park, NY: Delmar Learning.)

PAINTING

Accordion Painting

5 Years Old and UP

MATERIALS

- ☐ construction paper
- ☐ tempera paint
- ☐ brushes

💡 HELPFUL HINTS

- This activity is appropriate for children with good, small motor development, because folding requires small motor skill in the fingers and hands.

- If you do this activity with younger children, you will need to fold the papers for them before they do the painting.

DEVELOPMENTAL GOALS

Develop creativity, small motor development, and hand-eye coordination and explore a new painting technique that practices paper folding.

PREPARATION

Practice with the children on how to accordion pleat the paper by folding it back and forth until the entire paper is folded.

PROCESS

1. Paint a picture or design on the construction paper.

2. Let the picture/design dry thoroughly.

3. Accordion pleat the painting.

4. This gives an interesting three-dimensional effect.

VARIATIONS

- Accordion pleat the paper before painting on it. This produces another interesting effect.
- Accordion pleat a finger painting or crayon or marker drawing.

NOTES FOR NEXT TIME: _____

_____

_____

_____

_____

4

Years Old and UP

MATERIALS

☐ any color bond (copy) paper

☐ cotton balls/ Q-Tips© or cotton swabs

☐ paintbrush

☐ baby oil

 **HELPFUL HINT**

- This activity works best on bond (copy) paper, because the baby oil quickly absorbs into it.

DEVELOPMENTAL GOALS

Develop creativity, small motor development, and hand-eye coordination and explore a new material for painting.

PREPARATION

Pour a small amount of baby oil into a shallow bowl for each child. Cover the work area with a newspaper.

PROCESS

1. Dip the cotton ball in the baby oil.

2. Draw on the paper with the cotton ball.

3. Dip the cotton swab or paintbrush in the baby oil and draw some more.

4. After it soaks in, lift the picture to the light to see the work of art.

VARIATION

- Use eyedroppers to draw with the baby oil.

NOTES FOR NEXT TIME: _____

_____

_____

_____

_____

PAINTING

A

All Ages

Bag Finger Painting

MATERIALS

☐ large sealable storage bags

☐ liquid starch

☐ tempera paint

 **HELPFUL HINT**

- Let the children who are able to help prepare the Ziploc© bags. It will save you time and they will love doing it!

DEVELOPMENTAL GOALS

Develop creativity, small motor development, and hand-eye coordination and explore a new way to mix colors.

PREPARATION

Put a small amount of liquid starch and a small amount of dry tempera paint inside the bag. Give each child one of the sealable storage bags.

PROCESS

1. Using the fingertips (no nails!), make a design on the bag.
2. Colors emerge as fingers move and mix the tempera into the liquid starch.

VARIATIONS

- Add two primary colors of dry tempera paint. Watch the colors mix!
- After mixing the paint, open the bag and squeeze it onto paper. Then, use a brush to make designs on the paper.

NOTES FOR NEXT TIME: _____

_____

_____

_____

_____

PAINTING

Batik Painting

MATERIALS

- ☐ paper
- ☐ crayons
- ☐ tempera paint
- ☐ brushes
- ☐ shallow container with water in it (a dishpan works well)
- ☐ paper towels

HELPFUL HINTS

- Dark paints make the most striking effects in batik activities.
- Bring in some batik cloth for the children to compare to their paintings. You will find batik cloth in a fabric store with the cotton fabrics.

DEVELOPMENTAL GOALS

Develop creativity, small motor development, and hand-eye coordination and explore a batik-painting technique.

PREPARATION

Dilute the tempera paint to a watery consistency.

PROCESS

1. Make a crayon drawing or design on paper.
2. Soak the paper in water.
3. Crumble the paper into a ball.
4. Uncrumble and flatten the paper.
5. Blot off the excess water with a paper towel.
6. Flow a diluted tempera paint over the surface with a brush.
7. Because the color will be more intense in the creased area, the finished drawing will have dramatic contrasts.

VARIATION

- Use different kinds of paper for the crayon drawings, such as brown paper bags, wrapping paper, and newspaper.

NOTES FOR NEXT TIME: _____

_____

_____

_____

PAINTING

Blow Painting

All Ages

MATERIALS

- ☐ typing or copy paper
- ☐ watery tempera in small containers
- ☐ plastic spoons
- ☐ straws

💡 HELPFUL HINT

- An adult will have to spoon the tempera paint onto the paper for very young children.

DEVELOPMENTAL GOALS

Develop creativity, small motor development, and hand-eye coordination and explore a new painting technique.

PREPARATION

Give each child a small amount of watery tempera paint in a container and a plastic spoon.

PROCESS

1. Spoon a very small puddle of tempera onto the paper.
2. Use the straw to blow the paint in various directions, creating a variety of patterns.
3. Blow gently, hard, and so forth.

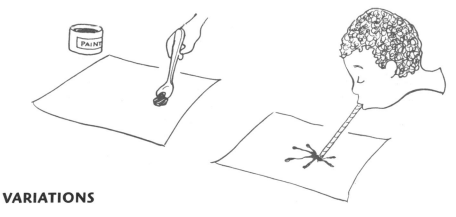

VARIATIONS

- Go outside and enjoy blow painting as the real wind blows!
- After the painting dries, add details with crayons and markers.
- Add a second color of tempera paint and blow paint on the same sheet of paper.

NOTES FOR NEXT TIME: _____

_____

_____

_____

Bubble Painting

MATERIALS

- ☐ 2/3 cup liquid detergent
- ☐ gallon container
- ☐ food coloring
- ☐ tempera paint
- ☐ paper towels
- ☐ straws or bubble pipes

 **HELPFUL HINT**

- Be sure to blow into the straws—You do not want children to drink "soap soup." Poke a small hole at the top of the straw to prevent accidental sipping.

DEVELOPMENTAL GOALS

Develop creativity, small motor development, and hand-eye coordination and explore a new painting technique that uses a familiar substance in a new way.

PREPARATION

Make a bubble solution by pouring 2/3 cup of liquid detergent into a gallon container. Add 1 tablespoon food coloring and enough water to fill the container. Let the solution sit for a few hours before using. Put the solution in clear plastic containers, and add liquid food coloring or tempera paint in primary colors.

PROCESS

1. Form secondary colors by mixing different food colors into primary colors. For example, place yellow food coloring in the red bubble solution to make orange.
2. Blow bubbles with straws.
3. Compare the bubbles made with these colored solutions to bubbles made with plain solution.
4. Blow colored bubbles over a paper towel.
5. Interesting spatter designs will result when the bubbles burst.

VARIATION

- Prepare a dark bubble solution. Place it in a cereal bowl. Blow bubbles with a straw until they fill the bowl, reaching barely above the edge of the bowl. Carefully place a light sheet of construction paper over the top of the bowl. Bubbles will pop on the paper and leave a circular design.

NOTES FOR NEXT TIME: _____

_____

_____

_____

_____

PAINTING

A

All Ages

Cardboard-Brush Painting

MATERIALS

- ☐ tempera paint in small shallow containers
- ☐ pieces of cardboard of varying lengths and widths
- ☐ paper

**HELPFUL HINT**

- Older children can help cut the cardboard into different widths and lengths.

DEVELOPMENTAL GOALS

Develop creativity, small motor development, and hand-eye coordination and explore a new use for cardboard.

PREPARATION

Give each child several pieces of cardboard of different lengths and widths.

PROCESS

1. Dip the piece of cardboard into the tempera paint.
2. Draw a picture or design using the cardboard as a brush.
3. Bend the top of the cardboard, dip it in paint, and dab it onto the picture.
4. Make wide lines, thin lines, zigzag lines, and dots and dabs.

VARIATIONS

- Mix colors on the page with the cardboard brush.
- Include white tempera paint with paint of primary colors. Watch how the colors change!

NOTES FOR NEXT TIME: _____

_____

_____

_____

_____

A

Chocolate-Pudding Finger Painting

MATERIALS

☐ package of instant chocolate pudding

☐ wax paper

 **HELPFUL HINTS**

- This is a good activity for very young children who put everything in their mouths.

  The only problem is that they might try to taste all the finger paint! Be watchful of this possibility.

- This is an excellent activity for creative expression, because it does not involve a permanent product. The process is the focus of this activity.

DEVELOPMENTAL GOALS

Develop creativity, small motor development, and hand-eye coordination and explore a new finger painting material.

PREPARATION

Mix the instant chocolate pudding according to the directions on the package.

PROCESS

1. Give each child a piece of wax paper.

2. Put a tablespoon or more of chocolate pudding on the wax paper.

3. Have the child finger paint with the chocolate pudding on the wax paper.

VARIATION

- Add mint flavoring to the pudding for an interesting smell and taste!

NOTES FOR NEXT TIME: _____

_____

_____

_____

PAINTING

A

Cold-Cream Finger Painting

MATERIALS

- ☐ any brand of cold cream
- ☐ dry tempera paint
- ☐ paper
- ☐ shallow dishes

 **HELPFUL HINTS**

- This is good for a first experience with a child reluctant to use colored paint with the fingers.

- Let the children mix the dry tempera into the cold cream. It is fun to see how the color mixes in and changes the cold cream's color. In addition, it is a good activity for the small muscles in the fingers and hands.

- Be aware of any allergies to the cream or ingredients in the cream.

DEVELOPMENTAL GOALS

Develop creativity, small motor development, and hand-eye coordination and explore a new material for finger painting.

PREPARATION

Divide the cold cream into separate shallow dishes.

PROCESS

1. Spoon dry tempera into the cold cream and mix.

2. Keep adding and mixing dry tempera until you get the desired color.

3. Finger paint on the paper with the colored cold cream.

DRY TEMPRA

cold cream

VARIATIONS

- Mix two colors of dry tempera into the cold cream and watch the colors mix.

- Finger paint directly on the tabletop with the colored cold cream. Make a print from the finger painting.

NOTES FOR NEXT TIME: _____

_____

_____

_____

_____

PAINTING

Comb Painting

MATERIALS

- ☐ plastic combs of different sizes
- ☐ tempera paint
- ☐ brushes
- ☐ paper

 **HELPFUL HINT**

- If you lack combs, a piece of notched cardboard will give similar results when drawn through the wet paint.

DEVELOPMENTAL GOALS

Develop creativity, small motor development, and hand-eye coordination and explore a new painting technique that uses recycled combs.

PREPARATION

Give each child several combs of different sizes.

PROCESS

1. The child makes a picture or design on paper with tempera paint.
2. Draw the comb(s) through the wet paint.
3. Make jabs, lines, and zigzags with the comb in the wet paint.

VARIATIONS

- Make a finger painting on paper. Draw combs through the wet finger paint.
- Use an old toothbrush or hairbrush and draw it through the wet paint.

NOTES FOR NEXT TIME: _____

_____

_____

_____

_____

3
Years Old and Up

Cotton-Ball Painting

MATERIALS

- ☐ cotton balls
- ☐ tempera paint in shallow containers
- ☐ paper

 HELPFUL HINTS

- For children who dislike getting paint on their fingers, use a clothespin to hold the cotton ball.

- This is an excellent activity for very young children just beginning to paint.

DEVELOPMENTAL GOALS

Develop creativity, small motor development, and hand-eye coordination and explore a new painting technique that uses cotton balls in a new way.

PREPARATION

Give each child several cotton balls.

PROCESS

1. Dip a cotton ball in a shallow dish of tempera paint.
2. Smear or squish the cotton ball on paper.
3. Dip another cotton ball in another color.
4. Repeat the process.

VARIATIONS

- Dip a cotton ball in dry powdered paint. Rub it across dry paper to create an interesting, soft effect.
- Use different kinds of papers, such as construction paper, wallpaper scraps, or cardboard.

NOTES FOR NEXT TIME: _____

_____

_____

_____

_____

Copyright © 2005, Thomson Delmar Learning

PAINTING

Crayon-Resist Painting

MATERIALS

- ☐ crayons
- ☐ paper
- ☐ tempera paint
- ☐ brushes

 HELPFUL HINTS

- Dark paints work best for crayon resist. The dark color fills all the areas the crayon has not covered.

- Crayon resist gives the feeling of a night picture. It thrills the child to see the changes that come when the paint crosses the paper.

DEVELOPMENTAL GOALS

Develop creativity, small motor development, and hand-eye coordination and explore a crayon-and-painting technique.

PREPARATION

Thin the tempera paint so it is watery.

PROCESS

1. Draw a picture or a design on the paper with crayons, pressing hard.

2. Paint over and around the crayon drawing with the thinned tempera.

3. In the areas covered with crayon, the crayon "resists," or is not covered by the paint.

VARIATIONS

- Use a piece of white cardboard from an old gift box instead of paper.
- Use a white paper plate for the crayon drawing.

NOTES FOR NEXT TIME: _____

_____

_____

_____

4

Crayons and Tempera Paint Washing

MATERIALS

- ☐ crayons
- ☐ construction paper
- ☐ tempera paint
- ☐ brushes

**HELPFUL HINTS**

- Children will need to press hard with their crayon for their drawings to show through the paint.

- This is a good activity to develop cooperation between children in art activities.

DEVELOPMENTAL GOALS

Develop creativity, small motor development, and hand-eye coordination and explore a new use for crayons and tempera paint.

PREPARATION

Mix water into dry tempera until it is a watery consistency. This watery paint is a "tempera wash."

PROCESS

1. Have the child draw a picture on a colored sheet of construction paper with the same color of crayon. The crayon drawing will be hard to see.

2. Exchange the drawing with a friend.

3. The friend paints over it with the thin tempera paint in the same color as the crayon.

4. This results in a translucent piece of artwork.

VARIATIONS

- Use two colors of crayons and one color of tempera paint.
- Let the same child who colors with the crayon do the tempera paint wash.

NOTES FOR NEXT TIME: _____

_____

_____

_____

_____

PAINTING

4 Years Old and Up

Dipping It!

MATERIALS

- [ ] two or three thin tempera paints in bright colors
- [ ] shallow containers
- [ ] white paper napkins or white paper towels

💡 HELPFUL HINTS

- Young children will need help folding the napkins or paper towels.
- These "tie-dyed" napkins can be used for various things, such as borders for bulletin boards or pictures, basket linings, and wrapping paper.

DEVELOPMENTAL GOALS

Develop creativity, small motor development, and hand-eye coordination and explore a new painting technique with paper.

PREPARATION

Put the paint in small containers, about 1 to 1-1/2" deep.

PROCESS

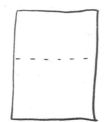

1. Give each child a white napkin or a sheet torn from a roll of white paper towels.
2. Fold the sheet in half twice.
3. Dip the corners of the napkin or towel into different colors of paint.
4. Open the napkins or towels and allow them to dry.
5. They dry into multicolored, bright designs.

VARIATIONS

- Dip the same corner into two different colors. Watch the colors blend.
- Refold the dried napkin and redip it into different colors.

NOTES FOR NEXT TIME: _____

_____

_____

_____

Copyright © 2005, Thomson Delmar Learning

Dragged Abstracts

MATERIALS

- ☐ three colors of tempera paint
- ☐ finger paint paper or white freezer paper

💡 HELPFUL HINTS

- These abstract paintings make great wrapping paper for child-made gifts.
- This is a good activity for mixing primary colors into secondary colors. Be sure to talk about how the colors mix as the children are doing the activity.

DEVELOPMENTAL GOALS

Develop creativity, small motor development, and hand-eye coordination and explore a new technique for mixing color.

PREPARATION

On a smooth surface, counter top, linoleum, or oilcloth, put small dabs of three colors of paint. About a half teaspoon is enough of each color.

PROCESS

1. Wet the paper over a sink.
2. Let it drip.
3. Lay the paper over the paint.
4. Wiggle and twist the paper back and forth until most of it is covered. See how the colors change!
5. Lay the paintings on newspapers to dry.

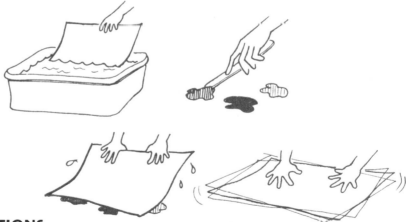

VARIATIONS

- Mix glitter with the tempera paint for an interesting effect.
- Move the paper back and forth with the feet. It is silly and fun!

NOTES FOR NEXT TIME: _____

_____

_____

_____

_____

PAINTING

Eye-Dropper Painting

MATERIALS

- ☐ eye droppers
- ☐ tempera paint
- ☐ paper

 **HELPFUL HINT**

- This activity is appropriate for children whose small motor development allows them to hold and manipulate an eyedropper.

DEVELOPMENTAL GOALS

Develop creativity, small motor development, and hand-eye coordination and explore using eye droppers for painting.

PREPARATION

Water down the tempera paint until it is very thin. Pour the paint into small containers. Put at least one eyedropper in each container.

PROCESS

1. Using the eyedropper, drop colors of paint onto the paper.

2. Drop colors over each other and watch them mix.

3. Pull the eyedropper across the paper, squeezing color onto the paper.

VARIATIONS

- Drop paint onto wet paper with the eyedropper for a different effect.
- Use food coloring instead of tempera paint.
- Drop paint onto a coffee filter for a tie-dyed effect.

NOTES FOR NEXT TIME: _____

_____

_____

_____

_____

PAINTING

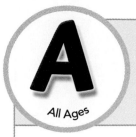

A

Finger Painting on Tabletops

MATERIALS

- [ ] finger paint
- [ ] Formica tabletop, an enamel-topped table, or linoleum
- [ ] newsprint paper

💡 HELPFUL HINT

- This is a good way to save on the cost of finger paint paper and to try something new and fun, too!

DEVELOPMENTAL GOALS

Develop creativity, small motor development, and hand-eye coordination and explore a new way of finger painting.

PREPARATION

Mix the finger paints to a thick consistency.

PROCESS

1. Put a dollop of finger paint directly onto the tabletop.
2. Have the child finger paint directly onto the chosen surface.
3. Lay a piece of newsprint paper on the finger painting.
4. Gently rub the paper with one hand.
5. Finger painting is transferred from the tabletop to the paper.

VARIATION

- Use several colors of finger paint and watch the colors mix!

NOTES FOR NEXT TIME: _____

_____

_____

_____

A

Finger Painting on Wax Paper

MATERIALS

- ☐ wax paper
- ☐ liquid dishwashing detergent
- ☐ dark-colored tempera paint

 **HELPFUL HINT**

- This is a good activity to emphasize process over product. Let the children enjoy the finger painting. When they are done, throw away the wax paper.

DEVELOPMENTAL GOALS

Develop creativity, small motor development, and hand-eye coordination and explore a new use for wax paper while learning a new finger-painting technique.

PREPARATION

Mix one part paint to one part soap. Give each child a generous supply of paint on individual pieces of wax paper.

PROCESS

1. Spread the dark-colored paint all over the wax paper to cover the sheet entirely.
2. Make finger-paint designs over and over on the wax paper.
3. The finger painting will have a translucent quality on the wax paper.

VARIATIONS

- Have the children help prepare the finger paint. It may be a bit messy for you, but it will be fun for the children!
- Use one long sheet of wax paper for a group finger-painting activity.

NOTES FOR NEXT TIME: _____

_____

_____

_____

_____

Years Old and Up

Finger Painting over Crayon

MATERIALS

- ☐ paper
- ☐ liquid starch
- ☐ powdered tempera
- ☐ crayons
- ☐ brushes

 **HELPFUL HINT**

- Press hard when making the crayon drawing. This way the drawing will show better under the finger painting.

DEVELOPMENTAL GOALS

Develop creativity, small motor development, and hand-eye coordination and explore the use of crayons and finger paint.

PREPARATION

Put liquid starch in shallow containers.

PROCESS

1. Cover the paper with brightly colored crayon designs or pictures.
2. Lay the crayoned paper on a smooth, flat surface.
3. Spread liquid starch over the crayoned picture.
4. Sprinkle a small amount of tempera paint in the liquid starch.
5. Be sure that its color contrasts with the crayon color(s).
6. Finger paint over the crayon drawing.
7. The color will mix as soon as the hand is drawn over the surface.

VARIATIONS

- Use two colors of dry tempera, such as red and yellow. Watch how it mixes to orange! Do the same with other primary colors.
- Add details by pasting bits of paper cut in shapes onto the artwork.
- Have one child do the crayon drawing and another do the finger painting.

NOTES FOR NEXT TIME: _____

_____

_____

PAINTING

A

Finger Painting with Shaving Cream

MATERIALS

- ☐ aerosol can of shaving cream
- ☐ washable tabletop or other washable surface
- ☐ dry tempera paint

 HELPFUL HINT

- Be watchful for children who put everything in their mouths. Shaving cream doesn't taste very good!! For this reason, this activity is most appropriate for children past that stage.

DEVELOPMENTAL GOALS

Develop creativity, small motor development, and hand-eye coordination and explore a new material for finger painting.

PREPARATION

Be sure the paint surface is washable.

PROCESS

1. Give each child a big glob of shaving cream.
2. Finger paint with the shaving cream directly on the tabletop surface.
3. Sprinkle dry tempera paint into the shaving cream.
4. Mix the paint into the shaving cream with the fingers.

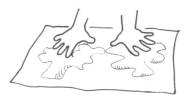

VARIATION

- Add spices for different smells, such as cinnamon or nutmeg.

NOTES FOR NEXT TIME: _____

_____

_____

_____

_____

Flour-and-Water Painting

MATERIALS

- [ ] flour
- [ ] water
- [ ] plastic squeeze bottles (the kind honey is sold in)
- [ ] Styrofoam or aluminum pans
- [ ] construction paper
- [ ] tempera paint or food coloring
- [ ] Popsicle sticks

💡 HELPFUL HINTS

- Be sure to test the plastic bottles for smooth flowing before beginning this activity. A stopped-up squeeze bottle can get in the way of a child's creative expression.
- Add more water to the flour mixture if the squeeze bottle gets "stuck" in the middle of the activity. Just add water and shake it to mix it in.

DEVELOPMENTAL GOALS

Develop creativity, small motor development, and hand-eye coordination and explore a new use for flour and water while learning a new painting technique.

PREPARATION

Mix one part flour with one part water. Add food coloring or tempera paint for coloring or leave the mixture white. Fill the plastic bottle halfway.

PROCESS

1. Have the child squeeze the flour mixture from the bottle, making designs on the construction paper.
2. Use a Popsicle stick to make more designs.
3. After the flour mixture dries, add more details with crayons and markers.

VARIATIONS

- Sprinkle wet designs with glitter for a sparkling effect.
- Bits of grass, leaves, or even feathers can be added before the flour mixture dries.

NOTES FOR NEXT TIME: _____

_____

_____

_____

_____

Fold-Over Painting

MATERIALS

- [ ] construction paper or any other heavy-duty paper
- [ ] tempera paint in several colors
- [ ] plastic spoons
- [ ] small shallow containers

 **HELPFUL HINT**

- This is a good activity for young children just beginning to use paints. Using the spoon with paint is easier than using a paint-brush for some children.

DEVELOPMENTAL GOALS

Develop creativity, small motor development, and hand-eye coordination and explore new painting technique that practices folding and making two images.

PREPARATION

Mix several colors of tempera paint and put them in shallow containers.

PROCESS

1. Give each child a plastic spoon and container(s) of tempera paint.
2. Fold the paper in half.
3. Drop small dots of paint onto one side.
4. Fold the paper.
5. Gently smooth hands over the paper.
6. Open the paper and the blotted halves will form a surprise picture.

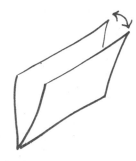 

VARIATIONS

- Use two or more colors for a color mixing experience.
- Use an eyedropper instead of a spoon to drop color onto the paper.

NOTES FOR NEXT TIME: _____

_____

_____

A

All Ages

Hide-and-Seek Painting

MATERIALS

- ☐ paper
- ☐ brushes
- ☐ paint
- ☐ blindfold

HELPFUL HINT

- Not all children like to be blindfolded. Never force a child to cover the eyes for this activity or any other.

DEVELOPMENTAL GOALS

Develop creativity, small motor development, and hand-eye coordination and explore a new painting technique.

PREPARATION

Tie a blindfold over the children's eyes.

PROCESS

1. Allow the child to feel the brushes, paper, and area before starting.
2. The child paints without seeing what the child is doing.
3. Take off the blindfold and view the artwork.

VARIATIONS:

- Play music while the children are painting blindfolded.
- Read a story or poem before or while they are painting.

NOTES FOR NEXT TIME: _____

_____

_____

_____

_____

PAINTING

A

All Ages

Ice-Cube Painting

MATERIALS

- ☐ ice-cube trays
- ☐ Popsicle sticks
- ☐ dry tempera paint
- ☐ finger paint paper

💡 HELPFUL HINTS

- This is a messy activity. Be sure to cover the work area and the children well!

- This activity provides a great opportunity to talk about freezing, melting, warm air, cold air, and many other science concepts.

DEVELOPMENTAL GOALS

Develop creativity, small motor development, and hand-eye coordination and explore a new painting technique that ties science to art activities.

PREPARATION

Fill the ice-cube trays with water. Insert a Popsicle stick into each hole. Make one for each child. Let the water freeze.

PROCESS

1. Give each child a sheet of finger-paint paper. (Any glossy paper will work.)

2. Sprinkle dry tempera onto the paper.

3. Have the child rub an ice cube over the paint.

4. Watch the ice melt into color!

VARIATIONS

- Use two primary colors of dry tempera. Watch the colors mix!

- If you live in a cold climate, let the ice cubes freeze outside. Children love checking on the progress of the freezing!

NOTES FOR NEXT TIME: _____

_____

_____

_____

_____

4

Years Old and Up

Leaf Painting

MATERIALS

- ☐ leaves of different shapes
- ☐ tempera paint
- ☐ crayons
- ☐ markers
- ☐ tag board or heavy construction paper
- ☐ small stones

💡 HELPFUL HINTS

- Gather the small stones on the same walk you take for gathering the leaves for this activity.

- This is a good activity to use the painted backpacks made in the "Making Painted Backpacks" activity of this book.

DEVELOPMENTAL GOALS

Develop creativity, small motor development, and hand-eye coordination and explore a new painting technique that ties science to art activities.

PREPARATION

Go outside and collect a supply of fallen leaves. If possible, collect bright fall-colored leaves. Fallen leaves that are not fall colored will work as well. Talk about the leaves—their shapes, their sizes, their colors, their lines.

PROCESS

1. Have the child choose a leaf for its color and/or shape.
2. Place the leaf on a piece of heavy construction or tag board.
3. Hold the leaf down with a small stone.
4. Paint around the outline of the leaf.
5. Choose another leaf and repeat the process until the paper is filled.
6. When the paint is dry, remove the stones to see the leaf's outline.

VARIATIONS

- Use crayons or markers to trace the leaf outline.
- Older children may want to label the leaf. Have the children look up the leaves they cannot identify.

NOTES FOR NEXT TIME: _____

_____

_____

_____

_____

Making Painted Backpacks

MATERIALS

- ☐ large, empty detergent boxes
- ☐ scissors
- ☐ construction paper
- ☐ paste
- ☐ tempera paint
- ☐ crayons
- ☐ markers
- ☐ heavy, soft yarn

HELPFUL HINTS

- Children can carry their favorite toys, dolls, and stuffed animals in their backpacks.

- These backpacks are great to take along on an outdoor walk for storing nature's treasures found along the way!

- Ask parents and friends to save detergent boxes for this activity.

DEVELOPMENTAL GOALS

Develop creativity, small motor development, and hand-eye coordination and create a useful object from recycled materials.

PREPARATION

Cut the top off the detergent box. Punch holes to string the heavy, soft yarn through the box.

PROCESS

1. Paste a piece of construction paper on the front of the box.

2. Paint a picture or design on the construction paper.

3. Add more details with crayons or markers after the paint has dried.

4. Loop the yarn through the holes in the box.

5. Try on the backpack and adjust the yarn so the backpack comfortably fits the child.

VARIATIONS

- Make detergent box totes with the yarn at both sides of the top of the box.

- Paint the child's name in large print on the backpack. Let it dry. Then, have the child decorate around his or her name. Wearing these on an outdoor walk is a good way to keep up with the children!

NOTES FOR NEXT TIME: _____

_____

_____

_____

PAINTING

Making Stand-Up Painted Faces

MATERIALS

- ☐ construction paper
- ☐ paste or tape
- ☐ tempera paint
- ☐ brushes
- ☐ bits of cloth or trim
- ☐ scraps of wrapping or wallpaper
- ☐ yarn

💡 HELPFUL HINTS

- Encourage the children to use as many facial details as possible. Some suggestions are eyes, nose, mouth, teeth, glasses, freckles, cheeks, ears, hair, and mustache.

- Remember to paint the back of the head, too!

DEVELOPMENTAL GOALS

Develop creativity, small motor development, and hand-eye coordination and create painted objects using paper.

PREPARATION

Roll a piece of paper to form a cylinder. Paper 12" × 12" works best. Paste or tape the edges. If using paste, press from the inside to make the paste hold securely. If using tape, tape on the inside of the cylinder.

PROCESS

1. Stand the cylinder on end.
2. Paint facial details on the cylinder.
3. Add clothing details with bits of construction paper, fabric or trim scraps, bits of wallpaper, or wrapping paper.

VARIATIONS

- Make stand-up animals.
- Older children enjoy making stand-up faces of favorite storybook characters.

NOTES FOR NEXT TIME: _____

_____

_____

_____

_____

PAINTING

Marble Painting

MATERIALS

- ☐ marbles
- ☐ paper
- ☐ scissors
- ☐ tempera paint in several colors
- ☐ round pan (a cake pan works well)

💡 HELPFUL HINTS

- Picking up the marbles and dipping them in paint will leave paint on the children's fingers. To make clean up a bit easier, mix a bit of liquid detergent into the tempera paint. Washing will be soapier and easier!
- Children can help cut out the round pieces of paper. Use the cake pan to trace around. Then, cut along the traced lines.
- Do not use marbles with children under age 3 as they may be a choking hazard!

DEVELOPMENTAL GOALS

Develop creativity, small motor development, and hand-eye coordination and explore a new painting technique.

PREPARATION

Cut the paper to fit into the bottom of the cake pan. Cut one for each child.

PROCESS

1. Dip the marble in the tempera paint.
2. Put the marble into the pan lined with paper.
3. Roll the marble around, making lines and squiggles of tempera paint.
4. Repeat with another color of paint.

VARIATIONS

- Use other round objects, such as ping-pong balls and beads.
- Use related colors of paint, such as red, yellow, and orange. Watch how the colors mix!
- Use different kinds of paper, such as construction paper, newsprint, newspapers, and wallpaper scraps.

NOTES FOR NEXT TIME: _____

_____

_____

_____

PAINTING

3
Years Old and Up

Newspaper Painting

MATERIALS

- ☐ sheets of newspaper
- ☐ tempera paint
- ☐ brushes

 **HELPFUL HINT**

- The paintings will have a transparent effect and the newspaper printing will show through the paint.

DEVELOPMENTAL GOALS

Develop creativity, small motor development, and hand-eye coordination and explore a new material for brush painting using recycled newspapers.

PREPARATION

Have several colors of tempera paint, including light colors, ready.

PROCESS

1. Paint background colors using light-colored paint over the paper.
2. The printing shows through the paint.
3. Paint designs or pictures over the background color.

VARIATIONS

- Mix sawdust or salt into the paint for an interesting, rough texture.
- Add details with crayons or markers.
- Use various objects to print designs onto the newspaper painting.

NOTES FOR NEXT TIME: _____

_____

_____

_____

PAINTING

Painting on Cardboard

MATERIALS

- ☐ tempera paint
- ☐ paintbrushes
- ☐ pieces of cardboard

 **HELPFUL HINT**

- This activity might frustrate children just beginning to paint with brushes, because the paint is not easy to control on cardboard.

DEVELOPMENTAL GOALS

Develop creativity, small motor development, and hand-eye coordination and explore painting on cardboard.

PREPARATION

Tear the top layer of paper from the cardboard so the lines (ridges) are visible.

PROCESS

1. Paint a picture or design directly onto the lined side of the cardboard.
2. Watch how the paint moves into the lines.
3. Paint along the lines.
4. Paint across the lines.

VARIATIONS

- While the painting is wet, place a piece of paper over it and press. This will make a print of the painting on the paper.
- While the paint is wet, sprinkle glitter on it. It will stick to the dried paint and give it a sparkly effect.

NOTES FOR NEXT TIME: _____

_____

_____

_____

_____

3 Years Old and Up

Painting on Damp Paper

DEVELOPMENTAL GOALS

Develop creativity, small motor development, and hand-eye coordination and explore a new technique for brush painting.

MATERIALS

- ☐ dry or liquid tempera paint
- ☐ paint brushes
- ☐ paper
- ☐ water container
- ☐ blotting material (e.g., rag, sponge, paper towel)

💡 **HELPFUL HINTS**

- Damp paper tempera painting must be done hurriedly to be lively.
- Do not expect complete success on the first try. Only experience will tell just how wet the paper must be and how much paint should be used.
- Clean the brush and the water in the container often during this activity.
- This activity is not suitable for beginning painters. It is better for children who are used to painting with brushes.

PREPARATION

Soak the paper thoroughly in water.

PROCESS

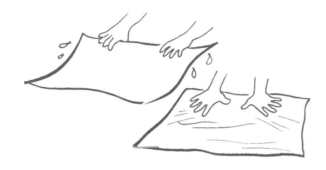

1. Lay the wet paper on the tabletop and smooth all the wrinkles.
2. Blot any pools of water with blotting material.
3. Paint directly on the damp paper.
4. Paint light colors at first, and second and third colors before the paper dries, so the colors will mingle and blend into soft shapes.
5. Details can be painted in when the painting is dry.

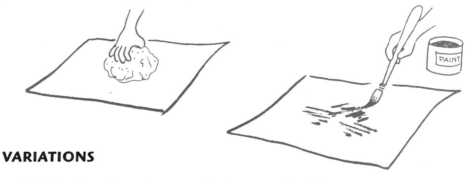

VARIATIONS

- Sprinkle glitter into the wet paint for a sparkly effect.
- Glue on bits of scrap fabric or trim for added texture.

NOTES FOR NEXT TIME: _____

_____

_____

PAINTING 175

PAINTING

Painting Snow Pictures with Cotton

MATERIALS

- ☐ colored construction paper
- ☐ tempera paint
- ☐ brushes
- ☐ cotton balls
- ☐ paste

💡 HELPFUL HINTS

- White paste works best with cotton balls.
- Remind the children to dip the cotton balls in paste and to not use their fingers to apply the paste. If the children have paste on their fingers, the cotton will stick to them!

DEVELOPMENTAL GOALS

Develop creativity, small motor development, and hand-eye coordination and explore a new tool for painting.

PREPARATION

Talk about the first day of snow or just after a big storm. For those in temperate climates, talk about pictures the children have seen of snow. Discuss how snow piles up on roofs, trees, cars, and so on.

PROCESS

1. Have the child paint a picture on colored construction paper.
2. Once the painting is finished, add cotton to represent snow.
3. Roll cotton into small balls to make it look like snow falling, snowballs, or even snowmen.
4. Glue the cotton bits to the painting.

VARIATIONS

- Glue glitter to the "snow" for an interesting effect.
- Draw pictures of houses and trees and add "snow" to them.

NOTES FOR NEXT TIME: _____

_____

_____

_____

_____

PAINTING

Painting through Tissue

MATERIALS

- ☐ white tissue paper
- ☐ tempera paint
- ☐ brushes
- ☐ heavyweight paper or pieces of cardboard or pieces of white gift boxes

 **HELPFUL HINT**

- This is an excellent activity for children who have a lot of experience painting with brushes.

DEVELOPMENTAL GOALS

Develop creativity, small motor development, and hand-eye coordination and explore painting on tissue paper.

PREPARATION

Soak the heavyweight paper, pieces of cardboard, or white gift boxes in water.

PROCESS

1. Lay a sheet of white tissue paper over the wet heavyweight paper.
2. Carefully apply more water to the tissue.
3. Paint the tissue.
4. Enjoy the wrinkles and "bubbled areas" that result on the tissue.

5. When the tissue painting dries, carefully remove and discard the tissue paper.
6. See how the tissue "painted" the heavyweight paper beneath the tissue.

VARIATIONS

- Brush or drop on tempera paint in related colors, such as red, yellow, and orange; yellow, blue, and green; or red, blue and purple.
- On the dried artwork, add details with colored pencils, markers, or tempera paint.

NOTES FOR NEXT TIME: _____

_____

_____

_____

_____

PAINTING

A

Painting to Music

MATERIALS

- ☐ tempera paint
- ☐ paper
- ☐ brushes
- ☐ tapes or CDs
- ☐ tape or CD player

 **HELPFUL HINT**

- Children will enjoy taking turns choosing the music for this activity.

DEVELOPMENTAL GOALS

Develop creativity, small motor development, and hand-eye coordination and explore a new way to paint that ties music to art activities.

PREPARATION

Choose music to play while the children paint. Begin with music that has a definite beat that is easy to hear.

PROCESS

1. Play the music for the children.
2. Discuss the beat and the way the music makes the children feel or want to move.
3. Have the children paint pictures or designs while the music is playing.
4. Encourage the children to make brush strokes to "go with the music."
5. After the children are finished, talk about the paintings and how the music made them feel while they were painting.

VARIATIONS

- Finger paint to music
- Make a collage to music.
- Work with clay or play dough to music.

NOTES FOR NEXT TIME: _____

_____

_____

_____

_____

3

Years Old and Up

Painting with Weeds

MATERIALS

- ☐ tempera paint in shallow containers (e.g., aluminum pie tins)
- ☐ paper
- ☐ weeds collected outdoors

 **HELPFUL HINTS**

- Queen Ann's lace makes an excellent paintbrush.
- In the fall, many weeds are at maximum heights and can be collected on class walks for later use in art activities.
- Wild oats and golden rod also work well for this activity. Be sure the children are not allergic to these weeds or any others used in this activity.

DEVELOPMENTAL GOALS

Develop creativity, small motor development, and hand-eye coordination and explore a new painting technique that ties nature to art activities.

PREPARATION

Mix the tempera paint and pour enough of it in the pie pan to cover the bottom. Give each child a piece of paper.

PROCESS

1. Have the child choose a weed to use as a brush.
2. Dip the weed in the paint.
3. Make a design or a picture on the paper.

VARIATIONS

- Choose another weed to use on the painting or on a new painting.
- Save the weeds used for painting to add to later collage activities.
- Let the weeds dry, and use them later in dough-sculpture designs.

NOTES FOR NEXT TIME: _____

_____

_____

_____

_____

PAINTING

Paper-Towel Painting

MATERIALS

- ☐ paper towels
- ☐ tempera paint
- ☐ shallow containers
- ☐ paper

 HELPFUL HINT

- Be sure to have the children wad the paper. It is fun for them and a good small motor activity, as well!

DEVELOPMENTAL GOALS

Develop creativity, small motor development, and hand-eye coordination and explore a new painting technique that uses paper towels in a new way.

PREPARATION

Wad the paper towel into a ball.

PROCESS

1. Dip the paper towel in paint.
2. Dab, press, or rub the paper towel on the paper.
3. Dip the paper towel in another color of paint.
4. Repeat the process.

VARIATIONS

- Use other kinds of paper, such as foil, wax paper, and wallpaper scraps.
- Wad two towels. Dip in paint and paint with both hands!

NOTES FOR NEXT TIME: _____

_____

_____

_____

_____

Plastic-Wrap Painting

MATERIALS

- ☐ heavy paper (e.g., cardboard, pieces of white gift boxes)
- ☐ tempera paint
- ☐ plastic wrap (the kind used in cooking)

💡 HELPFUL HINTS

- This activity is most appropriate for children who have a good amount of experience in painting with a brush.

- The wetter the paint, the better the plastic wrap will stick to and wrinkle on the paint.

DEVELOPMENTAL GOALS

Develop creativity, small motor development, and hand-eye coordination and explore a new use for plastic wrap that teaches a new painting technique.

PREPARATION

Be ready to cut the plastic wrap when the child needs it in this activity.

PROCESS

1. Quickly paint a piece of heavy paper with tempera paint.

2. Squeeze some more drops of liquid tempera over the surface.

3. Lay a sheet of plastic wrap over the wet surface.

4. Shapes and patterns will result from the wrinkled areas.

5. When the painting is dry, remove the plastic.

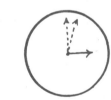

VARIATION

- Add more details to the artwork with crayons, markers, or more paint.

NOTES FOR NEXT TIME: _____

_____

_____

_____

PAINTING

Pulled-String Painting

MATERIALS

- ☐ string
- ☐ paper
- ☐ tempera paint
- ☐ heavy cardboard or piece of board
- ☐ brushes
- ☐ sponge

💡 HELPFUL HINT

- This activity is suitable for children who have fairly well developed small motor skills, usually ages 5 and up.

NOTES FOR NEXT TIME:

_____

_____

_____

_____

DEVELOPMENTAL GOALS

Develop creativity, small motor development, and hand-eye coordination and explore a new technique for painting.

PREPARATION

Mix the tempera paints so they are watery. Give each child several lengths of string, at least 12" long.

PROCESS

1. Place a sheet of paper on a flat surface.
2. Coat the string thoroughly with paint.
3. Arrange the paint-soaked string on the paper.
4. Twisted loops in the string make interesting effects.
5. Allow one or two ends to extend beyond the same edge of the paper.
6. Place another piece of paper over this string arrangement.
7. Cover the paper with a firm piece of cardboard or a piece of wood.
8. Hold the paper in place lightly with one hand.
9. With the other hand, grasp the ends of the string and pull it gently from between the papers.
10. Carefully peel the two papers apart. The design will be duplicated on the second sheet of paper.

VARIATIONS

- Coat the string with different colors of paint. Watch how the colors mix.
- Use different kinds of string, rope, and cording to make different sizes of lines.

Q-Tip© Painting

MATERIALS

☐ Q-tips© or cotton swabs

☐ tempera paint

☐ paper

💡 HELPFUL HINTS

- This activity requires good small motor development. It is suitable for children who are familiar with brush painting.

- Have a good supply of Q-tips© on hand, so children can use as many as they want in this activity.

DEVELOPMENTAL GOALS

Develop creativity, small motor development, and hand-eye coordination and explore painting with cotton swabs.

PREPARATION

Put the tempera paint in shallow containers. Give each child at least six Q-tips©.

PROCESS

1. Have the child dip a Q-tip© into the tempera paint.

2. Draw a picture or design with the Q-tip©.

3. Make dabs, dot, zigzags, and squiggles with the Q-tip©.

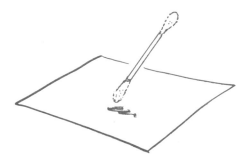

VARIATIONS

- Paint with cotton balls and Q-tips©.

- Add more details with a regular paintbrush.

NOTES FOR NEXT TIME: _____

_____

_____

_____

_____

PAINTING

Salty Painting

PAINTING

MATERIALS

- ☐ paper
- ☐ brushes
- ☐ tempera paint
- ☐ salt

 **HELPFUL HINTS**

- Have the children fill the various salt shakers. They will love doing this, and it is good hand-eye and small motor exercise for the children.

- Talk about the effects the salt makes on the paint. Encourage use of descriptive words like *splotchy, spotty, blobs,* and other such words.

DEVELOPMENTAL GOALS

Develop creativity, small motor development, and hand-eye coordination and explore a new painting technique that shows the effects of salt on paint.

PREPARATION

Put salt in shakers with various sizes of holes on top.

PROCESS

1. Paint a picture or design with tempera paint.
2. Sprinkle salt onto the wet tempera paint.
3. See the interesting splotches and runny spots appear.
4. Shake salt on with a shaker with a different size of holes on top.
5. See the difference in the splotches and spots.

VARIATION

- Shake salt on finger paintings.

NOTES FOR NEXT TIME: _____

_____

_____

_____

_____

3
Years Old and Up

Sand Painting

MATERIALS

- ☐ tempera paint
- ☐ brushes
- ☐ sand
- ☐ glue
- ☐ construction paper

 **HELPFUL HINT**

- Sand will, of course, fall here and there during this activity. Be prepared! Cover the work area with newspapers so the sand can be scooped up after the activity is over.

DEVELOPMENTAL GOALS

Develop creativity, small motor development, and hand-eye coordination and explore using sand with painting.

PREPARATION

Put sand in separate, small, shallow containers for each child's use.

PROCESS

1. Brush glue onto the construction paper.
2. Sprinkle sand onto the glue.
3. Paint a picture or design around the sand.

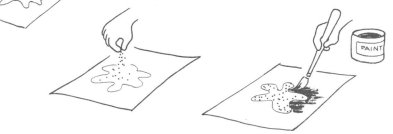

VARIATION

- Paint the sand. Watch what happens!

NOTES FOR NEXT TIME: _____

_____

_____

_____

_____

PAINTING

Spatter Painting

MATERIALS

☐ construction paper

☐ scissors (optional)

☐ toothbrushes

☐ piece of screen

☐ tempera paint

💡 HELPFUL HINTS

• This is a very messy activity, but it is worth the mess, because children are fascinated by seeing how the outline remains after the spattering is over.

• If you are using recycled toothbrushes for this activity, be sure to run them through the dishwasher or soak them in boiling water before using them with the children.

DEVELOPMENTAL GOALS

Develop creativity, small motor development, and hand-eye coordination and explore a spatter-painting technique.

PREPARATION

Cut a screen into pieces about 6 to 8" square. Put tempera paint in shallow containers (e.g., aluminum pie tins).

PROCESS

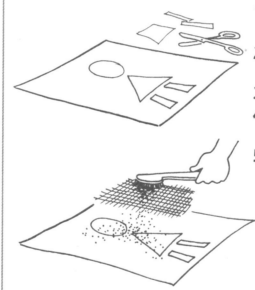

1. Have the child cut or tear a shape out of construction paper.

2. Place the shape on a background sheet of paper.

3. Dip a toothbrush in paint.

4. Rub the toothbrush over the screen.

5. When the shape is removed, its outline remains.

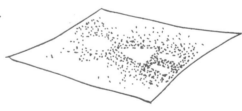

VARIATIONS

• Repeat the process using a different color of paint, placing the shape in a different place on the paper.

• Repeat the process using different shapes.

• Use natural forms, such as twigs, leaves, and grass.

NOTES FOR NEXT TIME: _____

_____

_____

_____

A

All Ages

Sponge Painting

MATERIALS

- ☐ sponge cut into a variety of sizes and shapes
- ☐ scissors
- ☐ liquid tempera paint
- ☐ paper
- ☐ brushes

HELPFUL HINTS

- An adult will need to assist very young children in soaking and smoothing the paper for this activity.
- Sometimes the process of soaking and smoothing the paper is as much fun as the sponge painting! Be prepared for this.

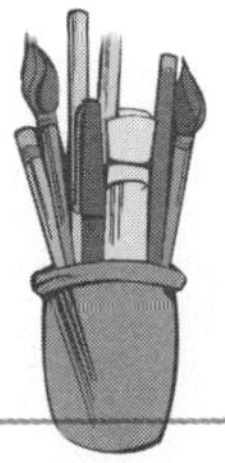

DEVELOPMENTAL GOALS

Develop creativity, small motor development, and hand-eye coordination and explore painting with sponges.

PREPARATION

Soak the paper thoroughly in water. Moisten the sponge pieces. Put tempera paint in shallow containers (e.g., aluminum pie tins).

PROCESS

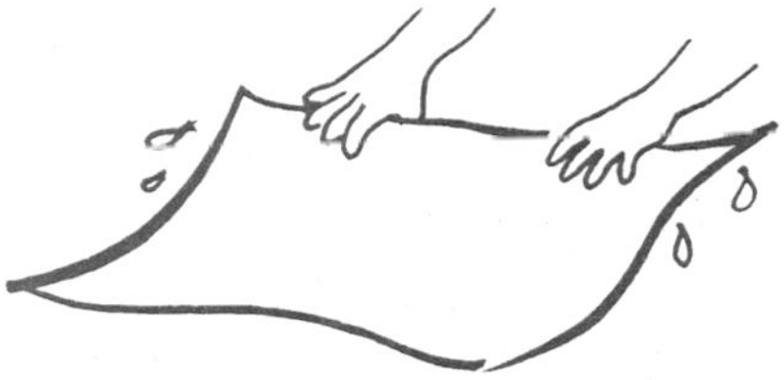

1. Lay the wet paper on a smooth surface and remove all the wrinkles and excess water.
2. Dip the sponge pieces in the tempera paint.
3. Apply the sponge to moist paper.
4. Make a picture or a design by using sponges of different shapes and sizes.
5. Allow the colors to mix and blend.

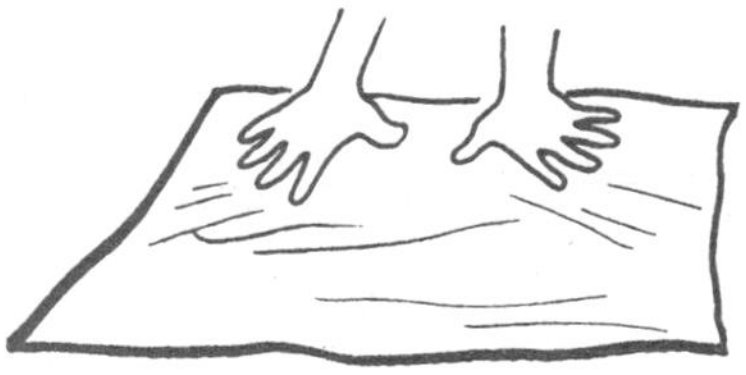

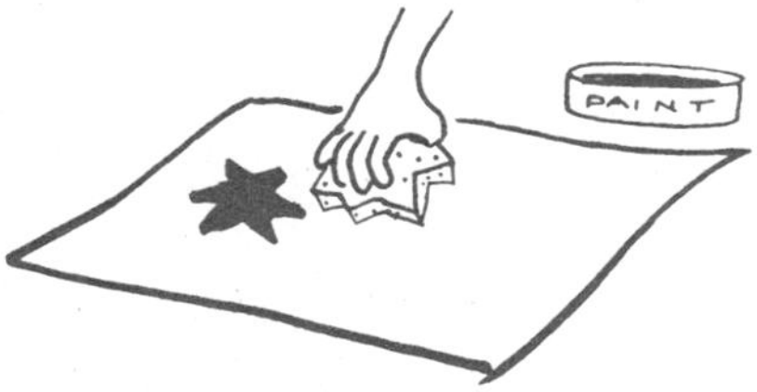

VARIATIONS

- Begin with two primary colors for younger children.
- Older children will enjoy several colors for this activity.
- Details and accents can be added with a brush when painting is dry.
- Experiment by trying this on both wet and dry paper.

NOTES FOR NEXT TIME: ______________________________

____

____

PAINTING

Spray Painting

PAINTING

MATERIALS

- ☐ construction paper shapes
- ☐ white construction paper
- ☐ spray bottles
- ☐ tempera paint
- ☐ small rocks to use as weights

💡 HELPFUL HINTS

- Plan an outdoor walk to gather the small stones to use as weights in this activity.

- Be sure you check that the spray bottle is not clogged before filling it with thinned tempera paint!

DEVELOPMENTAL GOALS

Develop creativity, small motor development, and hand-eye coordination and explore a new painting technique that shows how paint looks when sprayed.

PREPARATION

Mix a thin solution of tempera paint. Pour the paint into a plastic spray bottle. Set a small funnel on your spray bottle to make this easier to do.

PROCESS

1. Cut or tear shapes out of construction paper.
2. Arrange cut out shapes in some design over the sheet of white construction paper.
3. Weigh down the shapes with the small rocks.
4. Spray the tempera paint lightly over the shape design.
5. When the paint has dried, pick up the shapes to discover the designs left underneath.

VARIATIONS

- Use crayons or markers to complete the design after the paint has dried.
- Use heavy weight washers to hold down the shapes while spraying around them.
- Very young children enjoy just spraying paint without the shapes to spray around.

NOTES FOR NEXT TIME: _____

_____

_____

Tempera and White-Glue Resist Painting

MATERIALS

- ☐ tempera paint
- ☐ paper
- ☐ white glue
- ☐ brushes
- ☐ plastic knife

 **HELPFUL HINT**

- This activity involves waiting for the glue to dry. Very young children are not very good at waiting, so plan the first part of the activity before going outdoors. When it is time to come inside, the glue will probably be dry and the children can proceed with the rest of the activity.

DEVELOPMENTAL GOALS

Develop creativity, small motor development, and hand-eye coordination and explore a painting-resist technique.

PREPARATION

Have small brushes ready to use with the white glue. Be sure to caution the children not to use paintbrushes with the glue.

PROCESS

1. Paint a picture or design on the paper with the white glue by using the brush attached to the white glue jar or by applying with a finger.

2. Allow the glue to dry.

3. Paint over the glue picture/design with tempera paint.

4. Several colors can be mingled.

5. The glue will resist the paint.

6. Allow the paint to dry.

7. Clean away the glue with a plastic knife and expose the paper and original drawing.

VARIATION

- Glue can be painted over the areas previously painted with paint and repeated as often as desired. Make sure each is dry before applying the other.

NOTES FOR NEXT TIME: _____

_____

_____

PAINTING

Three-Dimensional Painting

PAINTING

MATERIALS

- ☐ paper
- ☐ tempera paint
- ☐ strips of construction paper
- ☐ tissue
- ☐ wrapping paper
- ☐ colored magazine paper
- ☐ glue
- ☐ scissors (optional)
- ☐ brushes

 **HELPFUL HINT**

- You may have to demonstrate how to glue down strips to make them "bump out," but avoid doing it for the children. They will learn by experimenting with the glue and paper in the process of this activity.

DEVELOPMENTAL GOALS

Develop creativity, small motor development, and hand-eye coordination and explore a new painting technique that reinforces design texture concepts and detail placement.

PREPARATION

Talk about how strips of paper can be added to make things "bump out" or be more "three-dimensional."

PROCESS

1. Paint a picture or design on the paper.
2. Glue pieces of different kinds of paper to the picture.
3. Glue them in alternating places, making them "bump out."
4. Glue strips so they look "wavy."

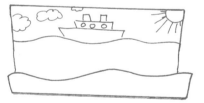

VARIATIONS

- Add other real-life objects, such as grasses, feathers, or shells.
- Glue on fabric and trim scraps for added effect.

NOTES FOR NEXT TIME: _____

_____

_____

_____

_____

5
Years Old and Up

Tie Dyeing

MATERIALS

☐ large pan of warm water
☐ marbles
☐ rubber bands
☐ pieces of old sheets
☐ undershirts, or cloth squares
☐ liquid tempera paint or liquid dye

💡 HELPFUL HINTS

• If possible, do this activity outdoors to avoid spilling the dye on the floor or furniture.

• Be very watchful of children around the warm water to avoid accidents.

DEVELOPMENTAL GOALS

Develop creativity, small motor development, and hand-eye coordination and explore a new technique that uses paint as a dye.

PREPARATION

Fill a large pot one-third full of warm water. Add the liquid dye or tempera paint and stir. The brightness of the color will depend on how much dye or tempera paint you add.

PROCESS

1. Place marbles inside the cloth pieces.

2. Fasten them with a rubber band. (Adults may need to tighten the rubber bands.)

3. Tie several marbles into the cloth at different places.

4. Dip the cloth in the dye.

5. Remove the rubber bands to see that the area under the rubber band is not dyed.

VARIATIONS

• Use old, white T-shirts from home to make tie dye designs.
• Use old pillowcases.

NOTES FOR NEXT TIME: _____

_____

_____

Tissue-Dab Painting

MATERIALS

- ☐ finger paint paper or freezer paper
- ☐ tempera paint
- ☐ brushes
- ☐ facial tissue

 **HELPFUL HINT**

- Do not let the children work at this activity so long that they start tearing the paper.

DEVELOPMENTAL GOALS

Develop creativity, small motor development, and hand-eye coordination and explore painting with tissues.

PREPARATION

Let each child wet a piece of finger paint paper or freezer paper.

PROCESS

1. Brush tempera paint over the paper quickly with a wide brush.
2. Put two colors of tempera together without stirring thoroughly.
3. Use a facial tissue to dab over the paper.
4. Take up paint randomly.
5. This provides a stippling effect, leaving light and shadowy areas.
6. Make short and curved strokes, quick dabs, or special designs.

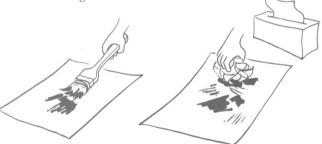

VARIATIONS

- Use bits of muslin to dab on the tempera paint. Then, let the muslin dry. The result is tie-dyed creations!
- Tissue-dab paintings make lovely wrapping paper for child-made gifts.
- They also make great bulletin-board backings.

NOTES FOR NEXT TIME: _____

_____

_____

_____

_____

Water Painting

MATERIALS

- ☐ plastic pails
- ☐ brushes of various sizes
- ☐ water

💡 HELPFUL HINT

- This is an excellent activity for beginning painters. You need not worry about messy cleanup, and the children get the same hand-eye and small muscle exercise as using real paint.

DEVELOPMENTAL GOALS

Develop creativity, small and large motor development, and hand-eye coordination and explore a new way to paint.

PREPARATION

Locate an outside area that has many easy-to-reach surfaces the children can reach to paint.

PROCESS

1. Give the child a bucket filled with water.

2. Using a paintbrush, have the child "paint" the fence, sidewalk, and so on with water.

3. Use different sizes of paintbrushes to continue painting surfaces.

VARIATIONS

- Fill plastic spray bottles with water and "spray paint" surfaces.
- Collect paper painter's hats for the "painters" to use in this activity.

NOTES FOR NEXT TIME: _____

_____

_____

_____

PAINTING

Wax-Paper Painting

MATERIALS

- ☐ wax paper
- ☐ heavy weight paper
- ☐ dry ballpoint pen
- ☐ Popsicle sticks
- ☐ water
- ☐ brushes
- ☐ tempera paint

💡 **HELPFUL HINT**

- This activity is suitable for children who have had experience painting with brushes.

DEVELOPMENTAL GOALS

Develop creativity, small motor development, and hand-eye coordination and explore painting on wax paper.

PREPARATION

Separate the wax paper into a piece for each child.

PROCESS

1. Lay a piece of wax paper over a heavyweight sheet of paper.
2. Make designs like squiggles and loops all over with a dry ballpoint pen or Popsicle stick.
3. Press on the tool while drawing, making heavy lines.
4. Remove the wax paper.
5. Brush water over the paper's surface.
6. Immediately drop or brush on liquid paint.
7. Note that the waxy lines resist the paint.

VARIATIONS

- Use more than one color paint.
- Use three related colors (e.g., red, yellow, and orange; yellow, blue, and green or red, blue and purple).
- Go back over the dried artwork with colored pencils or make designs with markers or ink in some of the small areas.

NOTES FOR NEXT TIME: _____

_____

_____

_____

 PAINTING

3

Years Old and Up

Window Gardening

MATERIALS

- ☐ markers
- ☐ black crayon
- ☐ thick tempera paint in various colors
- ☐ brushes
- ☐ paper

💡 HELPFUL HINTS

- Keep plenty of rags on hand for cleanup.
- This is a messy activity, so dress the children and cover the area accordingly, but it is worth the effort!

DEVELOPMENTAL GOALS

Develop creativity, small motor development, and hand-eye coordination and explore a new use for paint.

PREPARATION

Mix thick tempera paint in various colors with detergent so the paint sticks to the window.

PROCESS

1. Draw outlines of stems and leaves on the window(s). Make enough so each child has one flower each.
2. Work out flower pictures on paper first to get ideas for window painting.
3. Have the child use a black crayon to trace the outline on top of a stem on the window.
4. Fill the outlines with the thick tempera paint and a paintbrush.

VARIATION

- Paint bugs, birds, rainbows, and animals on the windows.

NOTES FOR NEXT TIME: _____

_____

_____

_____

Copyright © 2005, Thomson Delmar Learning

PAINTING

Windy-Day Painting

MATERIALS

- ☐ white construc-
tion paper
- ☐ red, yellow,
blue, and white
dry tempera
paint
- ☐ small strips of
cardboard

 **HELPFUL
HINT**

- With very young
children, begin
with only two
primary colors in
this activity. As
children's small
motor skills
improve, add
more colors.

DEVELOPMENTAL GOALS

Develop creativity, small motor development, and hand-eye coordination
and explore a new painting technique that ties science to art activities.

PREPARATION

Wet the white construction paper with water. Talk about the wind, how it
blows, how it makes things move, how it feels on the skin, and so on.

PROCESS

1. Give each child a small amount of red, yellow,
blue, and white dry tempera and several strips of
cardboard.

2. Have the child use the cardboard strips to paint a
windy day by quickly brushing the dry tempera onto
the wet surface.

3. Encourage the children to mix and blend the colors.

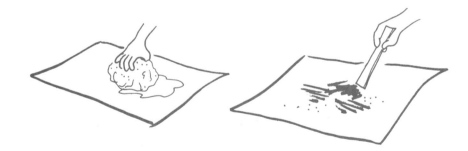

VARIATIONS

- Wind motion can be used to create unusual effects with the strips. Push,
pull, and twist the paint over the surface.
- Go outside and paint windy effects in the real wind!

NOTES FOR NEXT TIME: _____

_____

_____

_____

_____

PAINTING

Index by Ages

PAINTING

PART IV

Puppets

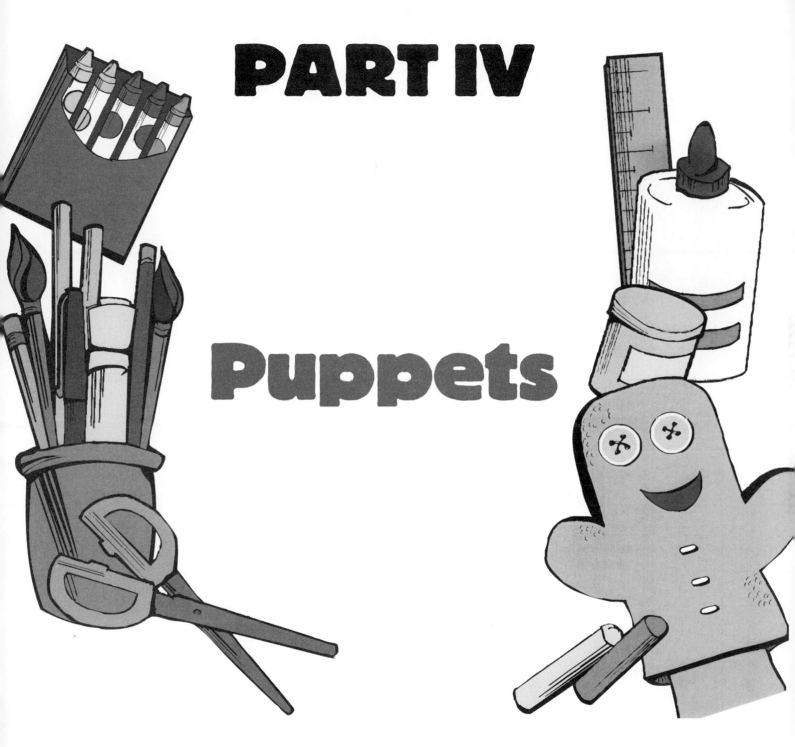

Fun with Puppets

Welcome to the world of puppets! You will see from the activities in this book that puppets are more than just familiar childhood toys. They are an art form.

Puppets fascinate and involve children in ways few other art forms can, because they allow children to enter the world of fantasy and drama easily. In this magic world, children are free to create whatever they need in their lives.

Traditional puppets, like stick and bag puppets, are found in this book, as are puppets made using such recyclables as paper-towel and toilet-tissue paper rolls, paper plates, paper bags, packaging materials, cardboard and cereal boxes. Once you start making and using these varied puppets, you will be encouraged to create many other unique kinds of puppets from your and the child's imaginations.

The activities in this book are designed for children aged 2 through 8. An icon representing a suggested age for the activity is listed at the top of each activity. However, use your knowledge of the child's abilities to guide you in choosing and using the activities in this book. Wherever appropriate, information is provided on how to adapt the activities for children over age 8.

The focus of this book is a creative approach to making and using puppets in art activities. The activities are meant to be starting points for exploring this art form. Both you and the children are encouraged to explore, experiment, and enjoy the world of puppets.

GETTING STARTED

Process vs. Product

The focus of this book and all early childhood art activities is the process, not the product. This means that the process of creating, not the product, is the main reason for the activity. The joys of creating, exploring materials, and discovering how things look and work are all part of the creative process. How the product looks, what it is "supposed to be," is unimportant to the child, and it should be unimportant to the adult.

Young children delight in the experience, the exploration, and the experimentation of art activities. The adult's role is to provide interesting materials and an environment that encourages children's creativity. Stand back when you are tempted to "help" children working with puppets. Instead, encourage all children to discover their own unique abilities.

Using Puppets

Puppets are usually first used in nursery or preschool, where they are invaluable. Puppets can teach finger plays; hand puppets can act out familiar nursery rhymes. The shy child who is reluctant to sing often will participate through a puppet. Puppetry is a sure means of stimulating creative storytelling in young children.

Puppets offer children two experiences: (1) the creative experience of making puppets and (2) the imaginative experience of making puppets come to life.

Considering the Child

Young children find it hard to wait patiently to use materials in an activity. Often, the excitement of creativity and patience do not mix. In addition, it is sometimes difficult for young children to share. With young children, plan to have enough materials for each child. For example, having enough fabric scraps for each child to dress a puppet makes the activity more fun and relaxed for young children.

Gathering Materials

Each activity in this book includes a list of required materials. It is important to gather all materials before starting an activity with children. Children's creative experiences are easily discouraged when children must sit and wait while the adult looks for the tape, extra scissors, or colored paper. Be sure to gather materials in a place the children can easily access.

Storing and Making Materials Available

Having the materials to make puppets is not enough. These materials must be stored and readily accessible to the children. For example, scraps of materials and trim bunched in a paper bag discourages children from using them. Storing such materials in a clear plastic box that is shallow enough for children to easily search works much better. Storing buttons in a recycled muffin tin or even in a fishing box with lots of compartments keeps these supplies orderly and encourages their use. Many teachers find clear-plastic shoeboxes invaluable for storing all the "fancy" materials children use to decorate their puppet creations. Such boxes, great for storing and stacking all kinds of art materials, are available at economy stores. **Figure 1** gives some added hints for storing materials for puppet making and other creative activities.

Be creative when thinking about storing and making materials available for your little puppet masters. Storing supplies in handy boxes and other containers makes creating puppets and cleaning up after puppet making more fun.

Using Food Products

Several activities involve the use of different kinds of foods. There are long-standing arguments for and against food use in art activities. For example, many teachers have long used potato printing as a traditional printing activity for young children. These teachers feel potatoes are an economical way to prepare printing objects for children. Using potatoes beyond their shelf life is an alternative to throwing them away. On the other hand, many teachers feel that food is for eating and should be used for nothing else.

This book has many activities that do not use food so that there will be options for teachers who oppose food use in art activities. Also, where possible, alternatives to food items are suggested. Whatever your opinion, creative puppet activities are provided for your and the children's exploration and enjoyment.

Employing Safe Materials

For all activities in this book and for any art activities for young children, be sure to use safe art supplies. Read labels on all art materials. Check materials for age appropriateness. The Art and Creative Materials Institute (ACMI) labels art materials AP (approved

FIGURE 1 · TIPS FOR STORING ART MATERIALS

The ways materials, supplies, and space are arranged can make or break children's and teachers' art experiences. Following are suggestions for arranging supplies for art experiences:

1. *Scissor holders.* Holders can be made from gallon milk or bleach containers. Simply punch holes in the containers and place scissors in the holes with the scissor points to the inside. Egg cartons turned upside down with slits in each mound also make excellent holders.

2. *Paint containers.* Containers can range from muffin tins and plastic egg cartons to plastic soft-drink cartons with baby food jars in them. These work especially well outdoors as well as indoors, because they are large and not easily tipped. Place one brush in each container. This prevents colors from mixing and makes cleanup easier.

3. *Crayon containers.* Juice and vegetable cans painted or covered with contact paper work very well.

4. Crayon pieces may be melted in muffin trays in a warm oven. These pieces, when cooled, are nice for rubbings or drawings. Crayola® makes a unit that is designed specifically for melting crayons safely.

5. Printing with tempera is easier if the tray is lined with a sponge or a paper towel.

6. A card file for art activities helps organize the program.

7. *Clay containers.* Airtight coffee cans and plastic food containers are excellent ways to keep clay moist and always ready for use.

8. *Paper scrap boxes.* By keeping two or more boxes of scrap paper of different sizes, children will be able to choose the size paper they want more easily.

9. Cover a wall area with pegboard and suspend heavy shopping bags or transparent plastic bags from hooks inserted in the pegboard to hold miscellaneous art supplies. Hang smocks in the same way on the pegboard (at child level, of course).

10. Use the back of a piano or bookcase to hang a shoe bag. Its pockets can hold many small items.

11. Use divided frozen food trays or a revolving lazy Susan to hold miscellaneous small items.

(From Mayesky, Mary. *Creative Activites for Young Children*, 7th ed., Clifton Park, NY: Delmar Learning.)

PUPPETS

product) and CL (certified label). Products with these labels are certified safe for use by young children.

The ACMI provides an extensive list of materials and manufacturers of safe materials for all young children. This information is available on the ACMI Web site at http://www.acminet.org or by writing to 715 Boylston Street, Boston, MA 02116.

Some basic safety hints for art activities are:

- Always use products that are appropriate for the child. Use nontoxic materials for children in Grades 6 and lower.

- Never use products for skin painting or food preparation unless the products are intended for those uses.

- Do not transfer art materials to other containers. You will lose the valuable safety information on the product packages.

- Do not eat or drink while using art and craft materials. Wash after use. Clean yourself and your supplies.

- Be sure that your work area is well ventilated.

Potentially unsafe art supplies for puppet making include:

- *Powdered clay.* Powdered clay is easily inhaled and contains silica, which harms the lungs. Instead, use wet clay, which cannot be inhaled.

- *Instant papier-mâché.* Instant Papier-mâché may contain lead or asbestos. Use only black-and-white newspaper and wheat paste or liquid starch.

- *Epoxy, instant glues, or other solvent-based glues.* Use only water-based, white glue.

- *Paints that require solvents like turpentine to clean.* Use only water-based paints.

- *Cold water or commercial dyes that contain chemical additives.* Use only natural vegetable dyes made from beets, onion skins, and so on.

- *Permanent markers.* Permanent markers may contain toxic solvents. Use only water-based markers.

Be aware of all children's allergies. Children with allergies to wheat, for example, may be irritated by the wheat paste used in papier-mâché . Other art materials that may cause allergic reactions include chalk or other dusty substances, water-based clay, and any material that contains petroleum products.

Also be aware of children's habits. Some young children put everything in their mouths. (This can be the case at any age.) Others may be shy and slow to accept new materials. Use your knowledge of children's tendencies to help you plan art activities that are safe for all children.

Creating a Child–Friendly Environment

It is difficult to be creative when you have to worry about keeping yourself and your work area clean. Remember to cover the children. Some good coverups are men's shirts (with the sleeves cut off), aprons, pillowcases with holes cut for the head and arms, and smocks. Some fun alternatives are sets of old clothes or shoes that can be worn as "art clothes." These old clothes could become "art journals" as they became covered with the traces of various art projects.

Creating a Child's Art Environment

Encourage young artists by displaying appropriate art prints and other works of art. Do not make the mistake of thinking young children do not enjoy "grownup art." Children are never too young to enjoy the colors, lines, patterns, and designs of artists' work. Art posters from a local museum, for example, can brighten an art area. Such posters also get children looking at and talking about art, which encourages the children's creative work.

Display pieces of pottery, shells and rocks, and other beautiful objects from nature to encourage children's appreciation of the lines, symmetries, and colors of nature. Even the youngest child can enjoy the look and feel of smooth, colored rocks or the colors of fall leaves. All these are natural parts of a child's world that can be talked about with young children as those children create artwork. Beautiful objects encourage creativity.

Starting to Collect

The more exciting "extras" you can collect, the more fun the puppet activities in this book will be for the children. You cannot start too soon collecting materials for these activities. You can probably add items to the following list, which suggests some puppet materials. Ask friends and parents to collect some of these materials, too.

Paper scraps
Fabric scraps
Wallpaper scraps
Rickrack and other sewing trims
Buttons
Pompoms
Sequins
Feathers
Popsicle/craft sticks
Paper bags
Paper plates
Styrofoam and paper cups
Boxes of varied sizes
Yarn and ribbon scraps
Straws

Enter the world of puppets in the pages that follow. Enjoy the trip!

Balloon Puppets

MATERIALS

- ☐ balloons
- ☐ markers
- ☐ glue
- ☐ pieces of yarn and trim
- ☐ masking tape

 **HELPFUL HINTS**

- These puppets are not made to last. Be prepared for a lot of popping fun as children create their balloon puppets.

- Have extra balloons on hand for children who work fast. They may want to make two or three.

DEVELOPMENTAL GOALS

Develop creativity, small muscles in hands and fingers, and hand-eye coordination and use familiar objects in new ways.

PREPARATION

You can blow up the balloons—one for each child—or, if the children are able, let them blow up the balloons. Some children will need some assistance. Tie the ends of the balloons. Talk about how to handle the balloons so they will not break. Have extras on hand in case they do break.

PROCESS

1. Tape the balloon to the table.
2. Use markers to make a face on the balloon.
3. Glue yarn on top for hair.
4. Add other pieces of fabric for clothing.
5. Untape the balloon when finished decorating it and enjoy!

VARIATIONS

- Never use balloons with children 3 and younger.
- Use balloons of different shapes to create fanciful animals.
- Make a balloon body with other balloons taped to the head.

NOTES FOR NEXT TIME: _____

_____

_____

_____

_____

PUPPETS

Basic Hand Puppets

MATERIALS

- ☐ scraps of fabric, felt pieces, yarn, and trim
- ☐ glue
- ☐ needle and thread (optional)
- ☐ scissors

💡 **HELPFUL HINTS**

- Older children enjoy sewing the puppets together themselves. Rug needles that have large eyes and somewhat blunt tips work well for this age group.

- You may have to help the child sew or staple the two puppet pieces together.

- Many fabric glues stick the two puppet pieces together very well.

DEVELOPMENTAL GOALS

Develop creativity and small muscles in hands and fingers; use familiar objects in new ways; and learn the design concepts of detail placement, color, and pattern.

PREPARATION

Use the child-sized hand pattern on the next page to cut out two hand-puppet pieces for each child.

PROCESS

1. Give each child two hand-puppet pattern pieces: one for the front of the puppet and one for the back.
2. Glue on bits of felt for facial features.
3. Glue on yarn for hair, in the front and back, if desired.
4. Sew or glue the two puppet pieces together.
5. When using glue, let the glue dry well before using the puppet.

VARIATIONS

- Staple the puppets together.
- Use buttons, odd bits of jewelry, and sequins for decorative details for children 4 and older.

NOTES FOR NEXT TIME: _____

_____

_____

_____

PUPPETS

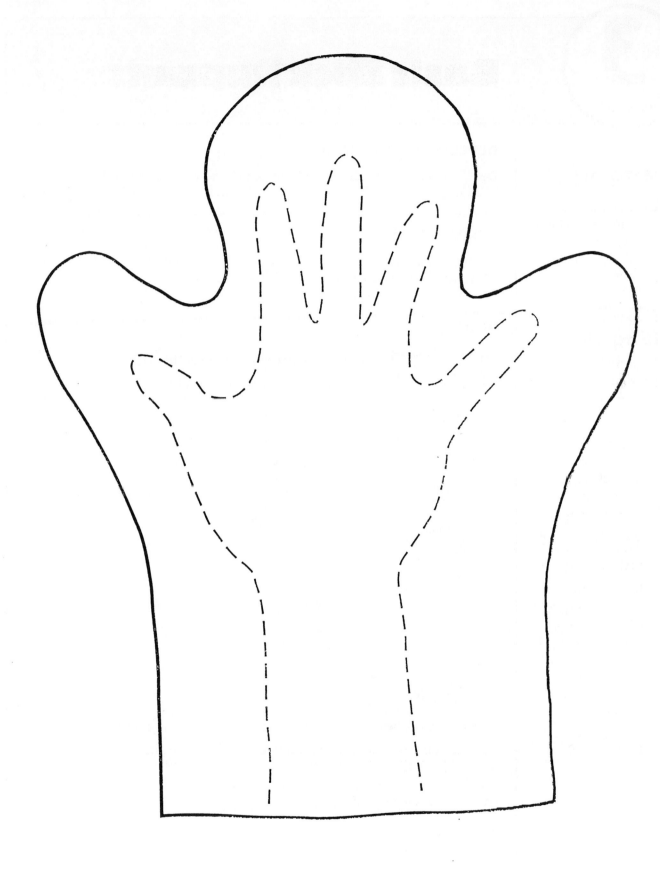

PUPPETS

Basic Stick Puppets

MATERIALS

- [ ] all types of sticks (e.g., large twigs, Popsicle sticks, small pieces of smooth lumber)
- [ ] pieces of cloth
- [ ] cotton balls
- [ ] newspaper
- [ ] rubber bands or strings

💡 HELPFUL HINTS

- Scrap yarn, wood shavings, and buttons are good materials for decorating the puppet's face.
- Using the stick, move the puppet side to side, up and down, or in any direction.

DEVELOPMENTAL GOALS

Develop creativity, small motor skills, and hand-eye coordination and encourage imagination.

PREPARATION

If using newspaper to stuff the puppet's head, wad the newspaper into small balls. Let the children help you do this—They love it!

PROCESS

1. Place a piece of cloth over the stick.
2. Stuff the cloth with wads of newspaper or cotton balls.
3. Attach the stuffed cloth to the stick with a piece of string or a rubber band, making a head.
4. Consider using a rubber band instead of string to form the head.

VARIATIONS

- Decorate the head with crayons or colored paper and paste.
- Use scrap pieces of fabric or wallpaper to dress the puppet.

NOTES FOR NEXT TIME: _____

_____

_____

_____

PUPPETS

Box Puppets

MATERIALS

- ☐ small boxes (from pudding or gelatin)
- ☐ construction paper
- ☐ paste
- ☐ scissors
- ☐ scrap pieces of fabric and trim
- ☐ masking tape
- ☐ markers
- ☐ crayons

💡 HELPFUL HINTS

- For some young artists, it may be better not to try to cover the box with construction paper. Instead, they may enjoy coloring directly onto the box.

- Covering boxes with construction paper to make box puppets is appropriate for children with well-developed small muscle skills.

DEVELOPMENTAL GOALS

Develop creativity, small muscles in hands and fingers, and hand-eye coordination; use familiar objects in new ways; and learn the design concepts of detail placement, color, and pattern.

PREPARATION

Give each child two small boxes.

PROCESS

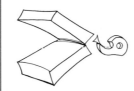

1. Tape the two boxes together, keeping the openings on both free.
2. Cover the boxes with construction paper.
3. The top box is the eye and top of the mouth.
4. The bottom box is the bottom part of the mouth
5. Add bits of colored paper for eyes, a mouth, and other details.
6. Add ears on the side of the boxes, if desired.
7. When all adhesives are dry, use and enjoy the puppet.
8. To use the puppet, place four fingers in the top box and the thumb in the bottom box to work the mouth.

VARIATIONS

- Use large boxes for big puppets. Be sure, however, that the boxes are small enough for little hands.
- Have fun making big tongues on the bottom box that will wag when the puppet talks.
- Add yarn hair that will be floppy and fun when the puppet moves.

NOTES FOR NEXT TIME: _____

_____

_____

PUPPETS

Bristle-Brush Puppets

MATERIALS

- ☐ wool sock or tube sock
- ☐ bristle brush
- ☐ buttons
- ☐ thumbtacks
- ☐ string
- ☐ glue

HELPFUL HINT

- This activity is appropriate for children 5 years and older.

DEVELOPMENTAL GOALS

Develop creativity, small muscles in hands and fingers, and hand-eye coordination; use familiar objects in new ways; and appreciate recycling.

PREPARATION

An adult should be available to help push thumbtacks through the sock and into the brush. The thumbtack is pushed from the inside of the sock into the base of the brush to attach the brush to the sock.

PROCESS

1. Try the sock on a hand to determine where the head will be.
2. Mark this spot.
3. Use thumbtacks to attach the brush to this spot. The brush becomes the puppet's hair.
4. Glue pieces of string to the sock for whiskers.
5. Glue buttons to the sock for eyes.
6. Tie a piece of string around the sock to make the puppet's neck.

VARIATIONS

- Use colored markers to add texture details to the sock.
- Make bristle puppets out of socks of varied sizes and colors.
- Glue on "wiggly" eyes.
- Use different sizes and shapes of brushes for the bristle tops.

NOTES FOR NEXT TIME: _____

_____

_____

_____

Coat-Hanger Puppets

MATERIALS

- ☐ wire coat hangers
- ☐ old nylon stockings or pantyhose
- ☐ cloth tape
- ☐ yarn
- ☐ felt scraps
- ☐ buttons
- ☐ scissors
- ☐ glue

💡 HELPFUL HINTS

- When using pantyhose, cut off the legs so they can be used separately.
- Some children may be able to stretch the hose over the hanger. Let them try.
- An adult must do the bending and taping of the hanger's hook.

DEVELOPMENTAL GOALS

Develop creativity, small muscles in hands and fingers, and hand-eye coordination and learn the design concepts of pattern, detail placement, and symmetry.

PREPARATION

Stretch the hanger into a diamond shape. Pull the stocking over it and tie at the bottom. Bend the hook into an oval and tape it in place so it will not poke the children.

PROCESS

1. Decorate the puppet by gluing on felt scraps for facial features.
2. Glue on yarn for hair, if desired.
3. Use buttons for eyes.
4. Work the puppet with the tape-covered oval as a handle.

VARIATIONS

- Make an original creation that does not have to be a person.
- Give the puppet a name and act out a story with it.
- Use different colors of hose for variety.

NOTES FOR NEXT TIME: _____

_____

_____

_____

PUPPETS

Cone Finger Puppets

MATERIALS

- ☐ thread cones
- ☐ glue
- ☐ scraps of fabric, felt, trim, and yarn
- ☐ buttons
- ☐ scissors
- ☐ construction paper
- ☐ crayons
- ☐ markers

HELPFUL HINT

- Tailor shops and dry-cleaning stores are good sources of thread cones.

DEVELOPMENTAL GOALS

Develop creativity, small muscles in fingers and hands, and hand-eye coordination and learn the design concepts of color, details, and pattern.

PREPARATION

Talk about the shape of the cone. Discuss what kind of puppet it would make. Talk about such details as face, body shape, and clothing type. Talk about what kind of animal it would make, too.

PROCESS

1. Cut a head from construction paper.
2. Add details with crayons and markers.
3. Glue head to the top of the cone.
4. Add fabric scraps to the cone for clothing.
5. Glue on construction paper arms, if desired.

VARIATIONS

- If thread cones are hard to find, make the cones out of paper or felt.
- Use a ping-pong ball for the head. Cut a hole in the bottom of the ping-pong ball and glue it to the top of the cone.
- Make cone finger puppets from another planet. Let the puppet talk about what it is like on his planet.
- Make cone finger puppets for story characters. Let the children guess which ones they are.

NOTES FOR NEXT TIME: _____

_____

_____

_____

PUPPETS

Cutout-Figure Stick Puppets

MATERIALS

- ☐ construction paper
- ☐ markers
- ☐ crayons
- ☐ paste
- ☐ Popsicle or craft sticks
- ☐ scraps of fabric and trim
- ☐ buttons
- ☐ sequins
- ☐ beads
- ☐ scissors

💡 HELPFUL HINTS

- Very young children will need help cutting out the figures.
- Let children who can cut well help other children cut out their figures.
- Do not use beads and sequins for children under 3 years old.

DEVELOPMENTAL GOALS

Develop creative thinking, small motor skills, and hand-eye coordination and reinforce the idea of recycling.

PREPARATION

Give each child a piece of construction paper. Talk about the kinds of puppet the children might like to make. Talk about favorite people in the children's lives, familiar story book or nursery rhyme characters, and so on.

PROCESS

1. Draw a figure on the construction paper.
2. Cut out the figure.
3. Paste the figure onto a Popsicle stick.
4. After the paste dries, decorate the figure.
5. Use pieces of fabric and trim to dress the stick figure.
6. Use beads and sequins as features and decorations.

VARIATIONS

- Cut pictures from magazines or old picture books. Glue the pictures to construction paper and cut them out, then glue them to sticks and decorate.
- Use old photographs for this activity. Cut out photos and glue them to sticks.

NOTES FOR NEXT TIME: _____

_____

_____

_____

PUPPETS

Cut-Up Puppets

MATERIALS

- ☐ damaged or outdated children's books
- ☐ Popsicle or craft sticks
- ☐ paste
- ☐ scissors

💡 HELPFUL HINTS

- Cut-up puppets make good use of damaged children's books.
- Let the children tell stories using the cut-out puppets.

DEVELOPMENTAL GOALS

Develop creativity and small muscles in hands and fingers and encourage recycling and dramatic play.

PREPARATION

Collect used and damaged children's books from garage or rummage sales.

PROCESS

1. Go through a book to choose pictures of people or animals.
2. Cut out the pictures.
3. Paste the pictures to a Popsicle stick.
4. Use the puppets to tell a story.

VARIATION

- Glue pictures of cartoon characters from advertisements to construction paper. Cut out and paste the pictures to Popsicle sticks to use as puppets.

NOTES FOR NEXT TIME: _____
_____
_____
_____

PUPPETS

Cylinder Puppets

4 Years Old and UP

MATERIALS

- ☐ pieces of 4-1/2" × 12" drawing or construction paper
- ☐ stapler and staples (or glue)
- ☐ yarn
- ☐ scraps of fabric and ribbon

💡 HELPFUL HINTS

- Be sure the cylinder fits over two of the child's fingers before stapling or gluing the cylinder closed.
- For very young children, make the cylinder fit over four of the child's fingers.

DEVELOPMENTAL GOALS

Develop creativity and small muscles in hands and fingers; understand design concepts of color, shape, and detail concepts; and encourage imagination.

PREPARATION

Give each child a piece of drawing or construction paper pre-cut to size indicated in list of materials.

PROCESS

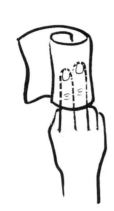

1. Roll the paper into a cylinder that fits over two of the child's fingers.
2. Staple or glue the cylinder together. This is the head of the puppet.
3. Using paper, scissors, and paste, make a face on the tube.
4. Use paper, yarn, and scrap bows to decorate the puppet.
5. Slip the puppet over two of the child's finger to use.

VARIATIONS

- Cut out a body, skirt, or suit and paste or staple it to the tube.
- Make real or imaginary animal cylinder puppets.

NOTES FOR NEXT TIME: _____

_____

_____

_____

PUPPETS

Detergent-Bottle Puppet Racks

MATERIALS

☐ small, plastic detergent bottles

☐ bolts

☐ scraps of lumber or drywall

 **HELPFUL HINT**

• Puppet racks are nice places for puppets to "rest." They are much nicer and more attractive than puppet piles!

DEVELOPMENTAL GOALS

Use familiar objects in new ways and develop sense of order.

PREPARATION

Wash and dry the plastic bottle. Keep the cap on the bottle.

PROCESS

1. Make a hole in the bottom of the plastic bottle.
2. Screw the bolt into the piece of lumber or drywall from the bottom up.
3. Keep screwing the bolt until it penetrates the top of the drywall or lumber.
4. Place the plastic bottle on top of the bolt.
5. Continue screwing the bolt until the plastic bottle is secured on the drywall or lumber.
6. Place a puppet over the detergent bottle for convenient storage.

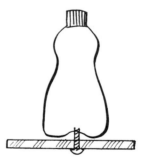

VARIATIONS

• When drywall and lumber pieces are unavailable, use heavy cardboard.
• Any plastic bottles the size of detergent bottles work well as puppet racks.

NOTES FOR NEXT TIME: _____

_____

_____

_____

PUPPETS

Envelope Puppets

MATERIALS

- [ ] white envelopes
- [ ] markers
- [ ] scissors
- [ ] crayons

💡 HELPFUL HINT

- Envelope puppets are appropriate for even very young children because they are easy to make and use. You may have to help young children cut off the bottom edges of the envelopes, however.

DEVELOPMENTAL GOALS

Develop creativity, small muscles in fingers and hands, and hand-eye coordination and use familiar objects in new ways.

PREPARATION

Give each child a white envelope.

PROCESS

1. Seal the envelope.
2. Draw a face on the envelope lengthwise.
3. Add facial details with markers and crayons.
4. Cut off the bottom edge of the envelope.
5. Slip the puppet on the hand and use as a puppet.

VARIATIONS

- Glue on yarn for hair, buttons for eyes, and any other decorative effect desired.
- Make envelope animals and act out "Farmer in the Dell."
- Make a family of envelope puppets for the housekeeping corner.

NOTES FOR NEXT TIME: _____

_____

_____

_____

Feeling Puppets

MATERIALS

- ☐ paper plates
- ☐ Popsicle or craft sticks
- ☐ glue
- ☐ stapler and staples
- ☐ crayons
- ☐ markers
- ☐ scraps of yarn, fabric, and trim

💡 HELPFUL HINT

- Shy children often find that puppets help them express their feelings.

DEVELOPMENTAL GOALS

Develop creativity, small muscles in fingers and hands, and hand-eye coordination and encourage feelings of expression.

PREPARATION

Talk about feelings. Ask the children to define words like *happy, sad, moody,* and *troubled.*

PROCESS

1. Give each child a paper plate.
2. Have the child choose an emotion to show on the paper-plate face.
3. Draw a face on the plate depicting the chosen emotion.
4. Add such details as yarn hair and button earrings.
5. Glue or staple a stick to the bottom of the plate.
6. Have the child use the puppet to explain what the puppet is feeling and why.

VARIATIONS

- From a group of feeling puppets, let the child choose a puppet and explain the puppet's feeling.
- Have each child make a happy and a sad puppet. Let the children express their feelings by choosing the corresponding puppet.

NOTES FOR NEXT TIME: _____

_____

_____

_____

PUPPETS

Finger-Leg Puppets

MATERIALS

- ☐ construction paper
- ☐ markers
- ☐ crayons
- ☐ buttons
- ☐ scraps of fabric and trim
- ☐ glue
- ☐ stapler and staples

HELPFUL HINT

- When making this type of puppet the first time, a sample may help the children, but try not to display the sample because doing so discourages creativity. Encourage the children to create their own finger-leg puppets.

DEVELOPMENTAL GOALS

Develop creativity, small muscles in hands and fingers, and hand-eye coordination and encourage imagination.

PREPARATION

Cut construction paper in strips 1-inch wide and wide enough to encircle the child's index and middle fingers.

PROCESS

1. Measure a construction paper strip around the child's index and middle fingers.
2. Glue or staple the strip so it forms a ring.
3. Draw and cut out the top part of a figure. Do not draw legs.
4. Glue or staple the figure to the paper ring.
5. Slip the puppet over the child's index and middle fingers. The child's fingers are the puppet's legs.

VARIATIONS

- Make animal finger-leg puppets.
- Do finger plays using finger-leg puppets.

NOTES FOR NEXT TIME: _____

_____

_____

_____

PUPPETS

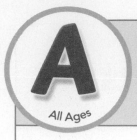
Finger-Cap Puppets

MATERIALS

- ☐ construction paper
- ☐ crayons
- ☐ markers
- ☐ scraps of fabric and trim
- ☐ glue
- ☐ buttons
- ☐ any other decorative items
- ☐ stapler and staples

HELPFUL HINTS

- Finger-cap puppets are great for all children, even toddlers, because they are easy to use. However, do not use buttons with toddlers and children under 3.
- Have older children measure each other for finger rings.

DEVELOPMENTAL GOALS

Develop creativity, small muscles in fingers and hands, and hand-eye coordination and encourage imagination.

PREPARATION

Cut 1-inch-wide strips of construction paper the length of the child's index finger.

PROCESS

1. Measure a 1-inch strip of construction paper around the child's index finger.
2. Glue or staple the strip so it forms a ring.
3. Draw a face on construction paper.
4. Decorate the face with yarn hair, buttons for eyes, and so on.
5. Glue the face to the construction-paper ring.
6. When the glue is dry, slip the ring over the child's index finger for play.

VARIATIONS

- Make a finger-cap puppet for each finger. Have a singalong using the finger-cap puppets as a chorus.
- Hold a performance with one child as the entire cast.
- Do fingerplays using the finger-cap puppets to act it out.

NOTES FOR NEXT TIME: _____

_____

_____

_____

PUPPETS

Finger-Face Puppets

3 Years Old and UP

MATERIALS

☐ felt-tip markers

HELPFUL HINTS

- Finger-face puppets are very easy to manipulate, even by toddlers.
- Finger puppets encourage small-muscle action, which is great for developing small motor control in the hands and fingers.
- Finger-face puppets are the least expensive, easiest puppets to make. Therefore, there is no excuse for excluding them from the young child's world.
- Ensure that parents approve of children drawing on their fingers.

DEVELOPMENTAL GOALS

Develop creativity, hand-eye coordination, and small muscles in hands and fingers and encourage imagination.

PREPARATION

Give each child a felt-tip pen.

PROCESS

1. Draw a face on the index finger with the felt-tip pen.
2. Draw faces on the three remaining fingers and the thumb, too.
3. The child's fingers become the puppets' faces.

VARIATIONS

- Let the children draw faces on each others' fingers.
- Do fingerplays with the finger-face puppets.
- Have one child perform a show as the entire cast.

NOTES FOR NEXT TIME. _____

_____

_____

PUPPETS

Foam-Tray Puppets

MATERIALS

- ☐ markers
- ☐ glue
- ☐ construction paper
- ☐ craft sticks
- ☐ recycled foam produce trays
- ☐ scraps of fabric and trim
- ☐ yarn and ribbon scraps
- ☐ buttons
- ☐ sequins
- ☐ scissors

💡 HELPFUL HINTS

- Ask parents to save foam trays for this and other art activities.
- Read or tell stories with memorable characters before this activity to stimulate children's creativity.

DEVELOPMENTAL GOALS

Develop creativity and small muscles in hands and fingers; use familiar objects in new ways; and learn the design concepts of detail placement, color, and line.

PREPARATION

Wash the foam trays. Give each child one tray.

PROCESS

1. Choose a favorite story character, or imagine one.
2. Draw the character on the foam tray with markers.
3. Add yarn for hair, buttons for eyes, and so on.
4. Glue a stick to the bottom of the tray to work the puppet.

VARIATIONS

- Spread areas of the tray with glue and sprinkle on glitter for added fun.
- Have older children work in groups to write their own stories, then create foam tray puppets to act those stories out.

NOTES FOR NEXT TIME: _____

_____

_____

_____

PUPPETS

Folded-Paper Puppets

MATERIALS

- ☐ rectangles of construction paper
- ☐ crayons
- ☐ markers
- ☐ wiggly eyes (optional)

💡 HELPFUL HINTS

- Have the children fold with you as you demonstrate.
- Children may need help folding the paper for this activity. Resist the temptation to fold the paper for the children. The children may need some help at the beginning, but let them do it themselves.

DEVELOPMENTAL GOALS

Develop creativity, small muscles in hands and fingers, and hand-eye coordination and use familiar objects in new ways.

PREPARATION

Give each child a rectangular piece of construction paper.

PROCESS

1. Fold the long rectangle into fourths, making a W.
2. The W is the puppet's body.
3. Draw eyes on the front of the W.
4. Or glue on wiggly eyes.
5. Cut a tongue from paper and glue the end of it in the puppet's mouth.
6. To use the puppet, put the thumb in the lower fold and put other fingers in the upper fold.

VARIATIONS

- Use green paper to make a frog with a big, red tongue.
- Use brown paper and make a forked tongue for a snake puppet.
- Glue on sequins and glitter for a sparkly snake or frog.

NOTES FOR NEXT TIME: _____

_____

_____

_____

PUPPETS

Food Puppets

MATERIALS

- ☐ apples, potatoes, or any other fruit or vegetable
- ☐ clothespins
- ☐ buttons
- ☐ old jewelry pieces
- ☐ yarn
- ☐ glue
- ☐ toothpicks
- ☐ scraps of fabric and trim

💡 HELPFUL HINTS

- Attach details with small pieces of toothpicks.
- Food puppets have limited shelf lives. Be sure to dispose of the puppets before they get moldy.

DEVELOPMENTAL GOALS

Develop creativity, see familiar things in new ways, gain small motor practice of hands and fingers, and encourage imagination.

PREPARATION

Give each child one piece of fruit or vegetable.

PROCESS

1. Use the piece of fruit or vegetable for the puppet's head.
2. Insert a clothespin into the piece of fruit or vegetable for a handle.
3. Glue buttons, pins, or old jewelry pieces to the fruit or vegetable to make a face.
4. Glue yarn to the fruit or vegetable for hair.

VARIATIONS

- Use bits of cloth or an old sock as a dress or suit.
- Use whole cloves as nice-smelling details on an apple-head puppet.
- Use raisins and seeds for details.

NOTES FOR NEXT TIME: _____

_____

_____

_____

PUPPETS

Glove Puppets

MATERIALS

- ☐ gloves
- ☐ large pom-poms
- ☐ scraps of felt
- ☐ glue
- ☐ scissors

💡 HELPFUL HINTS

- Glove puppets are a great way to recycle stray gloves.
- Heavy cotton garden gloves are inexpensive and work very well for this activity.

DEVELOPMENTAL GOALS

Develop creativity, small muscles in hands and fingers, and hand-eye coordination and use familiar objects in new ways.

PREPARATION

Give each child a glove. Discuss how each finger can be made into a finger puppet. Let the child try on the glove and move the fingers like five little puppets.

PROCESS

1. Glue pom-poms to each finger of the glove for the head.
2. Glue bits of felt or other fabric to the glove for facial or character details.
3. Let the glue dry, then enjoy!

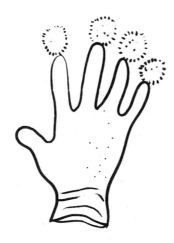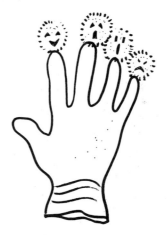

VARIATIONS

- Use old rubber gloves. Draw features on the rubber with felt-tip pens.
- Use garden gloves, and draw faces on the fabric.

NOTES FOR NEXT TIME: _____

_____

_____

_____

PUPPETS

Handkerchief Puppets

MATERIALS

- ☐ handkerchiefs
- ☐ markers
- ☐ cotton balls
- ☐ rubber band or string

💡 HELPFUL HINTS

- Because handkerchief puppets are so simple to make and use, they are excellent for very young children.

- Be prepared for children who finish their puppets quickly. Have enough materials for the children to make others.

DEVELOPMENTAL GOALS

Develop creativity and small muscles in fingers and hands, use familiar objects in new ways, and encourage dramatic play.

PREPARATION

Give each child a handkerchief.

PROCESS

1. Draw a face in the center of the handkerchief.
2. Stuff cotton or cloth inside the handkerchief, making the head.
3. Fasten the head with a piece of string or a rubber band.
4. Put the index finger in the head to work the puppet.

VARIATIONS

- Make a handkerchief puppet for each finger.
- Squares of muslin work as well as handkerchiefs.

NOTES FOR NEXT TIME: _____

_____

_____

_____

4

Years Old and UP

Humanettes

MATERIALS

- ☐ grocery bags
- ☐ crayons
- ☐ markers
- ☐ paint
- ☐ paintbrushes
- ☐ scraps of material, trim, yarn
- ☐ glue

💡 HELPFUL HINTS

- Turn the bag upward slightly above the shoulder or cut arm holes in the bag's sides.
- People puppets help children transition from puppetry to creative drama.
- A shy child may feel most protected behind a humanette.
- For children who do not like their heads covered, do not force them to use humanettes.

DEVELOPMENTAL GOALS

Develop creativity and small muscles in fingers and hands; encourage dramatic play; and learn the design concepts of color, detail placement, and line.

PREPARATION

Explain that humanettes are half-people and half-puppets.

PROCESS

1. Give each child a large grocery bag.
2. Identify locations for eye and mouth holes.
3. Cut eye and mouth holes.
4. Add facial features with markers, crayons, or paint.
5. Decorate with cut-out pieces of paper and scraps of fabric and yarn.
6. Place the bag over the head to become a puppet.

VARIATIONS

- Make imaginary animals using the grocery bags.
- Act out a story or a fingerplay wearing a humanette.

NOTES FOR NEXT TIME: _____

_____

_____

_____

PUPPETS

Juice-Box Puppets

MATERIALS

- ☐ juice boxes
- ☐ pipe cleaners
- ☐ scraps of felt
- ☐ tacky craft glue
- ☐ buttons
- ☐ Styrofoam ball (approximately 3 inches wide)
- ☐ yarn
- ☐ white pom-poms or small cotton balls
- ☐ scissors
- ☐ 3/8-inch dowel rod (8-inches long)

💡 HELPFUL HINT

- When wooden dowels are unavailable, pencils work just as well.

NOTES FOR NEXT TIME:

_____

_____

_____

_____

DEVELOPMENTAL GOALS

Develop creativity and small muscles in fingers and hands; use familiar objects in new ways; appreciate recycling; and learn the design concepts of detail placement, color, symmetry, and patterning.

PREPARATION

Wash and dry empty juice cartons. For each puppet, cut a dowel so that it extends about 3 1/2 inches at the bottom of the juice box and about 1 inch at the top.

PROCESS

1. Cut slits at the top and bottom of the juice box to put the dowel through.
2. Be sure the dowel extends about 3 1/2 inches at the bottom for a handle and 1 inch at the top for the head.
3. Press the Styrofoam ball onto the dowel for the puppet's head.
4. Cut small slits on sides of box and insert a pipe cleaner through.
5. Twist the ends to create a circle for hands.
6. Glue on bits of felt for facial details.
7. Glue on wiggly eyes or bits of felt for eyes.
8. Color on hair with markers or glue on yarn for hair.
9. Glue on scraps of fabric for clothes.

VARIATIONS

- Make juice-box animals.
- Have a puppet show with the juice-box puppets.
- Make juice-box puppets of favorite book characters. Then, act out the book.

PUPPETS

A

All Ages

Me Puppets

MATERIALS

- ☐ current pictures of children's faces
- ☐ poster board
- ☐ markers
- ☐ scissors
- ☐ glue
- ☐ glitter

💡 HELPFUL HINTS

- Do this activity at the beginning of the year and at the end of the year. Note the differences in the photos.

- Choose one or two children's me-puppets to focus on per week (or per day) as a way to get to know the children better. Let the puppets talk about themselves at group time or whenever appropriate in the day.

DEVELOPMENTAL GOALS

Develop creativity, small muscles in hands and fingers, and hand-eye coordination and encourage self-awareness and awareness of others.

PREPARATION

Collect current pictures of children's faces.

PROCESS

1. Measure two matching rectangles of poster board that are slightly larger than the child's picture.
2. Mark and cut out the rectangles with scissors.
3. On one rectangle, attach the child's picture with glue.
4. On the other rectangle, write the child's name with marker.
5. Make the name really fanciful with colored markers.
6. Make the area around the picture fancy, too.
7. Let the rectangle dry overnight.
8. Glue a wide craft stick between the two rectangles with the picture and name facing out.
9. Let the rectangle dry overnight.

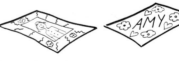

VARIATIONS

- Use pictures of the children when they were younger. See if the children can identify the children in the pictures.
- Spread glue and sprinkle glitter around the picture for a sparkly frame.
- If parents cannot provide pictures, buy a throw-away camera and take the children's pictures.

NOTES FOR NEXT TIME: _____

_____

_____

_____

PUPPETS

Milk-Carton Puppets

MATERIALS

- ☐ one pint milk or cream carton
- ☐ construction paper
- ☐ markers
- ☐ glue
- ☐ scissors
- ☐ crayons

💡 HELPFUL HINTS

- Older children may want to choose animals to make using the cartons. They can use a science book as a reference for details on their carton puppets.

- Older children may enjoy making imaginary creatures, then keeping journals of the creatures' adventures on earth and on other planets.

DEVELOPMENTAL GOALS

Develop creativity and small muscles in hands and fingers; use familiar objects in new ways; and learn the design concepts of detail placement, symmetry, and color.

PREPARATION

Wash the milk carton with hot, soapy water. Rinse and let dry. Cut a hole in the bottom of the carton large enough to put four fingers in to work the puppet. Talk about the kind of puppet the children can make from the milk carton. Discuss animals, people, objects, and imaginary things.

PROCESS

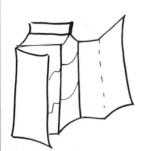

1. Cover the top and sides of the carton with construction paper.

2. For people or animals, glue feet near the bottom of the carton.

3. Cut out ears and glue them to the top of the carton.

4. Use markers or crayons on all sides of the carton to draw the animal's or person's hair.

5. For an animal, glue on a tail at the end of the carton.

VARIATIONS

- Make an imaginary visitor from the moon or another planet. Have the visitor tell its name. Tell about where it lives and what it is like to live there.

- For animals, use buttons for eyes, a scrap of felt for a tail, and a large pom-pom for a nose.

- Cover the carton with brown paper from a grocery bag. Draw on details with markers and crayons.

NOTES FOR NEXT TIME: _____

_____

PUPPETS

Mitten Puppets

MATERIALS

- ☐ old mittens
- ☐ glue
- ☐ buttons
- ☐ scrap pieces of felt, fabric, ribbon, trim, and yarn

💡 HELPFUL HINTS

- Mitten puppets are very easy to make and use. They are great for the youngest puppeteers.

- Mitten puppets make great use of single, worn-out, and outgrown mittens.

DEVELOPMENTAL GOALS

Develop creativity, small muscles in hands and fingers, and hand-eye coordination; use familiar objects in new ways; and encourage dramatic play.

PREPARATION

Collect lost-and-found mittens or mittens the children have outgrown.

PROCESS

1. Give each child a mitten.
2. Glue buttons to the mitten for eyes.
3. Glue a scrap piece of felt or another button to the mitten as a nose.
4. Glue another piece of felt to the mitten as the mouth.
5. Slip the hand into the mitten and make the puppet talk by moving the thumb upward and downward against the four fingers.

VARIATIONS

- Glue yarn to the mitten as hair.
- Dress the mitten puppet with scraps of fabric for a hat, a dress, a coat, and so on.
- Make a mitten puppet for each hand. Have a puppet conversation.

NOTES FOR NEXT TIME: _____

_____

_____

_____

PUPPETS

Nursery-Rhyme Finger Puppets

MATERIALS

- ☐ stiff paper, like construction paper or even thicker if available
- ☐ scissors
- ☐ markers
- ☐ crayons
- ☐ wiggly eyes (optional)
- ☐ glue
- ☐ cotton balls
- ☐ bits of yarn

💡 HELPFUL HINT

- This activity is most appropriate for children who can use scissors.

DEVELOPMENTAL GOALS

Develop creativity, small muscles in hands and fingers, and hand-eye coordination and practice language skills.

PREPARATION

Review nursery rhymes, such as Jack and Jill, Humpty Dumpty, and Peter, Peter, Pumpkin Eater.

PROCESS

1. Using stiff paper, draw out a puppet for a nursery rhyme.
2. Draw the puppet large enough so two fingers can be placed into the bottom of the figure.
3. Cut out the finger puppet and the finger hole(s).
4. Glue on wiggly eyes or draw on eyes.
5. Add cotton-ball or yarn hair.
6. Put fingers through the puppet to use it.

VARIATIONS

- Make finger puppets of storybook or comic book characters.
- Act out nursery rhymes with the finger puppets.
- Have the finger puppets talk about what it is like to be the characters.
- Let the children ask the puppet questions.
- Have older children make up nursery-rhyme puppets for younger children's use, or have the older children put on a puppet play for the younger children.

NOTES FOR NEXT TIME: _____

_____

_____

PUPPETS

5

Years Old and UP

Paper-Bag Zoo Creatures

MATERIALS

- ☐ small paper lunch bags
- ☐ scraps of construction paper
- ☐ glue
- ☐ scissors
- ☐ markers
- ☐ crayons
- ☐ wiggly eyes (optional)
- ☐ pipe cleaners (optional)

💡 HELPFUL HINTS

- This is a good activity for before or after a field trip to the zoo.
- Do not overlook imaginary animals. They count, too!

DEVELOPMENTAL GOALS

Develop creativity, small muscles in fingers and hands, and hand-eye coordination; use familiar objects in new ways; and learn the design concept of detail placement.

PREPARATION

Give each child a small paper lunch bag.

PROCESS

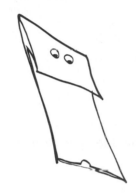

1. Cut out eyes from scraps of construction paper or use wiggly eyes.
2. Glue the eyes to the middle of the square on the bottom of the bag.
3. Glue a long tongue cut out of paper to the bottom of the square part of the bag.
4. Glue arms and legs to the sides of the bag.
5. Decorate the bag's front and back with crayons, markers, or glued-on pieces of construction paper.

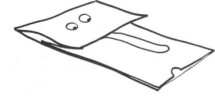

VARIATIONS

- Fold the two square edges of a paper bag under to form a different shaped head.
- Cut out different shaped ears to make different animals: long, pink ears for a rabbit; round, black ears for a panda; brown, floppy ears for a dog; round gray ears for a mouse.
- Thread pipe cleaners through the paper bag for whiskers for cats and mice.
- Use white lunch bags to make a panda, a polar bear, a pig, and a bunny.

NOTES FOR NEXT TIME: _____

_____

_____

PUPPETS

Paper-Chain Puppets

Years Old and UP

MATERIALS

- ☐ construction paper
- ☐ scissors
- ☐ glue
- ☐ markers or crayons
- ☐ string

💡 HELPFUL HINTS

- For young children with short attention spans, use fewer strips for shorter chains.

- Be sure to stand back and let the children glue their own strips together. They may take longer than you, but it is important that they do it themselves.

NOTES FOR NEXT TIME:

_____

_____

_____

DEVELOPMENTAL GOALS

Develop creativity, hand-eye coordination, and small muscles in fingers and hands and learn the design concepts of line, circles, color, and detail placement.

PREPARATION

Talk about insects and animals that are long and circular. Discuss such details as color, eyes, and if they have scales. Then, cut out 13 strips of paper that are 1 inch by 6 inches and one strip that is 4 inches square.

PROCESS

1. Form one of the strips into a circle and secure it with glue.
2. Form the paper strip into a circle connected to the first loop.
3. Continue until all 13 circles are connected, making a chain.
4. Each loop is a segment of the caterpillar.
5. Cut a circle from the paper square to make a head for the caterpillar.
6. Use markers or crayons to add eyes to the head.
7. Glue the head to one end of the chain.
8. Tie one piece of string to the head and another to the other end.
9. Use the string to move the chain as a puppet.

VARIATIONS

- Make paper-chain snakes, caterpillars, and even make-believe, snake-like creatures.
- Create an imaginary chain-thing from another planet. Name it. Let it tell the children all about itself.
- Make a nice, big paper-chain caterpillar. Make a nice, big leaf for the caterpillar to eat and rest on.
- Decorate each of the paper strips with crayons and markers for a very special puppet!
- Spread on glue and sprinkle on glitter for a sparkly chain puppet.

Paper-Plate Bugs and Stuff

4 Years Old and Up

MATERIALS

- ☐ paper plates
- ☐ scissors
- ☐ tape
- ☐ paint
- ☐ markers or crayons
- ☐ pipe cleaners
- ☐ hole punch
- ☐ buttons
- ☐ sequins

💡 HELPFUL HINTS

- This activity is appropriate for children ages 5 and up.
- Encourage the children to create bugs that are unique.

NOTES FOR NEXT TIME:
_____
_____
_____
_____

DEVELOPMENTAL GOALS

Develop creativity, small muscles in fingers and hands, and hand-eye coordination; use familiar objects in new ways; and learn the design concepts of detail placement, color, pattern, and symmetry.

PREPARATION

Talk about bugs. Discuss their sizes, shapes, colors, and such details as eyes, antennae, legs, and wings. Give each child two paper plates.

PROCESS

1. Fold a paper plate in half (fold it so that the back side of the plate is touching itself).
2. Using another paper plate, cut out a strip of the plate from the middle. Discard the middle strip.
3. Tape or staple each of the half-round pieces you just cut to the folded plate.
4. Position the plates so that the eating surfaces of the plates are facing each other.
5. Tape along the round edges only.
6. Step 5 forms two pockets in which to put fingers and control the puppet.
7. Draw a bug covering both sides of the plate.
8. Punch holes toward the top of the plate for antennae.
9. Loop a pipe cleaner through the holes for the antennae.
10. Slip the thumb and fingers into the pockets and bring the bug to life!

VARIATIONS

- Create an insect that has never been seen before. Name it. Have it tell everyone where it is from and what its life is like there.
- Make a paper-plate butterfly.
- Spread glue on part of the bug design and sprinkle glitter on the glue.
- Glue on buttons for eyes and sequins for shiny scales.

PUPPETS

Paper-Plate Puppets

3 Years Old and UP

MATERIALS

- ☐ paper plates
- ☐ Popsicle sticks
- ☐ stapler and staples
- ☐ crayons
- ☐ markers
- ☐ fabric scraps
- ☐ trim
- ☐ wallpaper
- ☐ yarn
- ☐ buttons
- ☐ paste
- ☐ construction paper

💡 HELPFUL HINTS

- Move the plate along a table edge as a puppet, or use it as a mask.
- Do not use sequins and beads for children under 3 years old.

DEVELOPMENTAL GOALS

Develop creative thinking, small motor skills in the hands and fingers, and hand-eye coordination; understand the concepts of color, contrast, and detail; and encourage imagination.

PREPARATION

Give each child a paper plate.

PROCESS

1. Make a face on the paper plate with crayons, paint, or glued-on colored-paper pieces.
2. Staple a Popsicle stick to the bottom of the plate for a handle.
3. Add such details as yarn for hair, buttons for eyes, and sequins for earrings.

VARIATIONS

- Make a hole for a mouth so the child can use one finger as a tongue to make the puppet talk.
- Make paper-plate animals for an imaginary zoo story.
- Have older children make paper-plate puppets of favorite storybook or fairy-tale characters.

NOTES FOR NEXT TIME: _____

_____

_____

_____

PUPPETS

All Ages

Paper-Tube Puppets

MATERIALS

- ☐ paper tubes from paper towels or toilet tissue
- ☐ paste
- ☐ scraps of fabric, yarn, ribbon, and trim
- ☐ small Styrofoam balls
- ☐ buttons
- ☐ pom-poms
- ☐ feathers
- ☐ glue

💡 HELPFUL HINTS

- Slip the puppet over one or two fingers to make it come alive.
- Cut paper tubes in varying lengths so the puppets can be all sizes.

DEVELOPMENTAL GOALS

Develop creativity and small muscles in hands and fingers; use familiar objects in new ways; and learn the design concepts of detail placement, color, and variety.

PREPARATION

Give each child a paper tube. Talk about what kinds of puppets the children could make. Discuss such features as eyes, noses, mouths, and hair.

PROCESS

1. The paper tube is the body.
2. Glue the Styrofoam ball to the tube to become the head.
3. Glue buttons to the ball for eyes.
4. Glue pom-poms to the ball for a nose or ears.
5. Decorate with pieces of trim for hair, hats, or other details.

VARIATIONS

- Make paper-tube animals. Sing "Farmer in the Dell" with the tube animals as the chorus.
- Make a family of tube puppets. Use the puppets to act out family stories.
- Have older children make their favorite fairy-tale or storybook characters.

NOTES FOR NEXT TIME: _____

_____

_____

_____

PUPPETS

PUPPETS

Paper/Styrofoam Cup Puppets

MATERIALS

- ☐ paper/Styrofoam cups
- ☐ markers
- ☐ pipe cleaners
- ☐ scraps of yarn, fabric, and trim
- ☐ construction paper
- ☐ glue

💡 HELPFUL HINTS

- Paper/Styrofoam cup puppets are great for all children, even toddlers, because they are very easy to make and use.

- Markers work best on Styrofoam. Crayons do not work well on Styrofoam.

DEVELOPMENTAL GOALS

Develop creativity, hand-eye coordination, and small muscles in fingers and hands; use familiar objects in new ways; and encourage imagination.

PREPARATION

Give each child a paper or Styrofoam cup.

PROCESS

1. Draw a face on the cup.
2. Or glue paper eyes, a nose, and a mouth on the cup.
3. Add yarn for hair.

VARIATIONS

- Make an animal by gluing ears to the top of the cup and a pipe-cleaner or paper-strip tail to the back.
- Create a family of cup puppets.
- Have older children create their favorite cartoon or storybook characters.

NOTES FOR NEXT TIME: _____

_____

_____

_____

PUPPETS

4 Years Old and Up

Pencil Puppets

MATERIALS

- ☐ pencils
- ☐ construction paper
- ☐ paste
- ☐ scraps of felt, fabric, and trim
- ☐ scissors

 **HELPFUL HINT**

- Cut figures from comics or magazines instead of drawing figures.

DEVELOPMENTAL GOALS

Develop creativity, small muscles in fingers and hands, hand-eye coordination and use familiar objects in new ways.

PREPARATION

Discuss the children's favorite characters and animals. Choose one favorite.

PROCESS

1. Draw the character on construction paper.
2. Cut the character out.
3. Glue on pieces of felt for facial details.
4. Glue on pieces of fabric for clothing.
5. Glue the character to a pencil.
6. Let the glue dry thoroughly before using the puppet.

VARIATIONS

- Make three little pigs as pencil puppets. Act out the story using these puppets.
- Make three bears as pencil puppets. Act out this story using the puppets.
- Older children may enjoy making pencil puppets for favorite stories. Have the children act out the story.

NOTES FOR NEXT TIME:

_____

_____

_____

PUPPETS

Ping-Pong Ball Puppets

MATERIALS

- [ ] ping-pong balls
- [ ] fabric scraps
- [ ] glue
- [ ] markers
- [ ] paste
- [ ] construction paper

💡 HELPFUL HINTS

- Use the ping-pong ball puppet as a finger puppet.
- Make sure the X shape is large enough to be comfortable but not too large as to make the puppet fall off.

DEVELOPMENTAL GOALS

Develop creativity, small muscles in hands and fingers, and hand-eye coordination; use familiar objects in new ways; and encourage imagination.

PREPARATION

Cut an "X" out of a ping-pong ball using sharp scissors.

PROCESS

1. Place a piece of lightweight fabric on a finger.
2. Cover the X area of the ball with sturdy glue.
3. Force the ball onto the fabric on your finger at the X.
4. Take the ball and fabric off your finger and let the glue dry.
5. While the glue is drying, draw or paste cut-out pieces of construction paper onto the puppet.

VARIATIONS

- Use old tennis balls instead of ping-pong balls.
- Have a pretend ping-pong game with these puppets. Have a ping-pong audience cheer the players on!

NOTES FOR NEXT TIME: _____

_____

_____

PUPPETS

Play Dough Puppets

MATERIALS

- ☐ play dough
- ☐ round cereal pieces
- ☐ raisins

 **HELPFUL HINTS**

- Be careful with very young children, because they may try to put inappropriate things in their mouths.

- Expect the young artists to "nibble" on the decorative elements before using them on the puppet. This is part of the fun!

DEVELOPMENTAL GOALS

Develop creativity, small muscles in fingers and hands, and hand-eye coordination; use play dough in new ways; and encourage imagination.

PREPARATION

Give each child a small amount of play dough.

PROCESS

1. Place a small amount of play dough on a finger.
2. Mold the play dough into a face shape covering the finger.
3. Add raisins, cereal, and so on for facial features.
4. The puppet is ready for play.

VARIATIONS

- Make a play dough puppet for each finger.
- Let the children make play dough puppets on each others' fingers.

NOTES FOR NEXT TIME: _____
_____
_____
_____

PUPPETS

Pom-Pom Puppets

MATERIALS

- ☐ pom-poms of varying sizes and colors
- ☐ Popsicle or craft sticks
- ☐ paste
- ☐ hole punch
- ☐ construction paper
- ☐ scraps of fabric, yarn, and trim

 **HELPFUL HINTS**

- This activity requires some degree of small motor control, because the pom-poms are small and difficult to handle.

- Have a good supply of pom-poms and sticks available for children who finish the puppet quickly. Fast children can make several.

PUPPETS

DEVELOPMENTAL GOALS

Develop creativity, small muscles in hands and fingers, and hand-eye coordination and learn the design concepts of pattern, symmetry, and details.

PREPARATION

Talk about the pom-poms. Discuss what kind of puppets could be made with them. Talk about colors, details, features, and so on.

PROCESS

1. Glue a large pom-pom to the stick.
2. Glue on pieces of construction paper for features and details.
3. Use smaller pom-poms for other details.
4. Use a hole punch on colored construction paper.
5. Glue on the colored circles from the hole punch, if desired.
6. Add fabric strips to the stick for clothing.
7. Glue on yarn for hair.

VARIATIONS

- Make a group of pom-pom puppets for a group singalong. Let the children choose the songs.
- Make animals for the song "Farmer in the Dell" and use them as you sing the song.
- Use cotton balls instead of pom-poms, but be aware that cotton balls are less stable decorations.

NOTES FOR NEXT TIME: _____

_____

_____

3
Years Old and UP

Popsicle-Stick Puppets

MATERIALS

- ☐ Popsicle sticks
- ☐ scraps of fabric, yarn, and trim
- ☐ scissors
- ☐ white glue
- ☐ fine-point colored markers
- ☐ wiggle eyes (optional)

💡 HELPFUL HINT

- You may have to show the children how to glue the fabric in place on the stick, but do not glue for them. Guide the children as they glue.

NOTES FOR NEXT TIME:

_____

_____

_____

_____

DEVELOPMENTAL GOALS

Develop creativity, small muscles in hands and fingers, and hand-eye coordination and use familiar objects in new ways.

PREPARATION

Talk about the kinds of puppets the children could make using Popsicle sticks. Discuss how the puppets could be mothers, fathers, kids, animals, and so on. Cut fabric into small scraps two to three times as wide as the Popsicle stick.

PROCESS

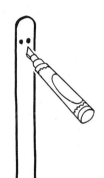

1. Give each child a Popsicle stick.
2. Draw eyes at the top of the stick or glue on wiggle eyes.
3. Be sure to leave enough room for hair or a hat.
4. Place a dot or two of glue on front of the stick, and place material on the glue.
5. Secure the material and wrap it around the stick, gluing it in place at the back of the stick.
6. Add such details as yarn hair to the top.
7. Glue a piece of ribbon as a belt in the middle of the stick.
8. Use markers to add facial details.

VARIATIONS

- Make a family of stick puppets. Act out a familiar family scene, such as mealtime or going to the store.
- Create the characters from a favorite story. Use the stick puppets to act out the story.
- Make a "mystery guest" stick puppet. Let the other children guess its identity.

PUPPETS

Pop-Up Puppets

MATERIALS

- ☐ paper or Styro-foam puppets
- ☐ craft or Popsicle sticks
- ☐ construction paper
- ☐ paste
- ☐ crayons
- ☐ markers
- ☐ pipe cleaners

💡 HELPFUL HINTS

- Some children may need help putting the stick into the cup. Let the children help each other do this.
- You can use pencils for this activity as well.

DEVELOPMENTAL GOALS

Develop creativity, small muscles in hands and fingers, and hand-eye coordination.

PREPARATION

Poke a large hole through the bottom of the cup so that a craft or Popsicle stick will fit through it.

PROCESS

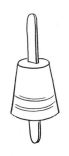

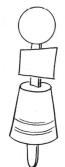

1. Give each child a cup and a craft or Popsicle stick.
2. Poke the stick through the hole in the cup and hold it so the top of the stick is a good deal above the top of the cup.
3. Tape a horizontal strip of construction paper to the stick for the puppet's body.
4. Use cut-out pieces of construction paper for the puppet's head.
5. Glue the head to the top of the stick.
6. Glue on pieces of pipe cleaners for arms.
7. Work the puppet by moving the stick up and down in the cup.

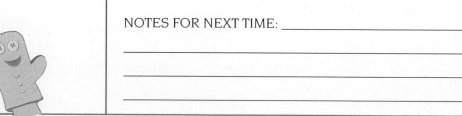

VARIATIONS

- Use cups of different sizes.
- Use fabric scraps for puppet's body.
- Make animal pop-up puppets.
- Act out fingerplays, rhymes, or poems with these puppets.

NOTES FOR NEXT TIME: _____

_____

_____

_____

Pringle™-Can Puppets

3 Years Old and Up

MATERIALS

- ☐ empty Pringle™ cans
- ☐ construction paper
- ☐ glue
- ☐ scissors
- ☐ scraps of fabric, yarn, trim
- ☐ beads (optional)
- ☐ feathers (optional)
- ☐ masking tape
- ☐ markers
- ☐ crayons
- ☐ paint
- ☐ paintbrushes

💡 **HELPFUL HINT**

- Have friends save Pringle™ cans for this activity, or have the children bring them from home.

DEVELOPMENTAL GOALS

Develop creativity, small muscles in hands and fingers, and hand-eye coordination; use familiar objects in new ways; and learn the design concepts of detail placement, color, line, and symmetry.

PREPARATION

Talk about the kinds of puppets Pringle™ cans can make. Discuss how they could be people, animals, objects, and imaginary or storybook characters. Wash out and dry the Pringle™ cans. Cover the metal on the open end with masking tape where the hand goes in to work the puppet.

PROCESS

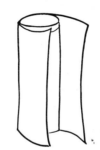

1. Give each child a Pringle™ can.
2. Glue construction paper on to cover the can.
3. Draw a face on the top (closed end) of the can.
4. Glue on yarn for hair.
5. Dress the puppet with fabric scraps and pieces of trim.
6. Glue on beads for eyes.

VARIATIONS

- Make favorite comic book, television, or storybook characters. Have the children act out a scene.
- Older children may want to make favorite historical characters. Have the other children guess who it is.
- Create a visitor from another planet. Have it tell you its name. Then, ask the creature questions about its home and how it is to live there.
- Make vegetable and fruit Pringle™ puppets. Put them together for a healthy meal. Have them talk about how they look, taste, and feel and why they are good for you.

NOTES FOR NEXT TIME: _____

_____

PUPPETS

247

PUPPETS

Shadow Puppets

MATERIALS

- ☐ heavy paper
- ☐ sticks
- ☐ glue or a stapler and staples
- ☐ a light source
- ☐ a blank wall area or screen

💡 HELPFUL HINTS

- Even very young children can make and enjoy hand shadow puppets.
- The stronger the light, the clearer the shadows.
- A flashlight works well for a small wall area. For a larger area, you may need a lamp.

DEVELOPMENTAL GOALS

Develop creativity and small muscles in fingers and hands and encourage creative movement and dramatics.

PREPARATION

Talk about shadows. Observe shadows during an outdoor walk. Show the children how to make and see hand shadows on the wall.

PROCESS

1. Draw and cut out a figure from heavy paper. (Recycled white gift boxes work well.)
2. Attach a stick to the figure.
3. Shine a light on an area of open wall space.
4. Move the puppet to see its shadow on the wall.
5. Watch the puppet's size and shape change as the puppet's or light's position changes.

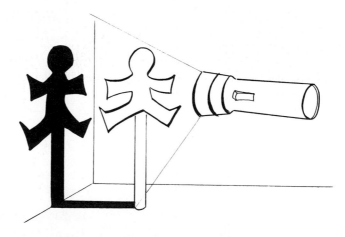

VARIATION

- Have some children use their hands for shadow puppets and stick puppets for shadow puppets. Compare how the puppets look. Let the puppets talk to each other as their shadows move on the wall.

NOTES FOR NEXT TIME: _____

_____

_____

PUPPETS

Shape Stick Puppets

MATERIALS

- ☐ construction paper
- ☐ cardboard or heavy-paper shapes
- ☐ scissors
- ☐ paste
- ☐ decorative items (e.g., beads, sequins, scraps of wallpaper, fabric, and trim)

💡 HELPFUL HINT

- This activity is appropriate for children who can cut with scissors.

NOTES FOR NEXT TIME:

_____

_____

_____

_____

DEVELOPMENTAL GOALS

Develop creative thinking, shape recognition, and small motor skills; understand design line and shape concepts; and encourage imagination.

PREPARATION

Talk about shapes. Review the circle, triangle, square, and rectangle.

PROCESS

1. Trace shapes on construction paper.
2. Cut out the shapes.
3. Arrange the shapes into a figure.
4. Use a circle for the head.
5. Make the body from a triangle, square, or rectangle.
6. Cut arms and legs from construction paper.
7. When satisfied with the arrangement, glue it to construction paper.
8. After the glue dries, cut the figure from the construction paper and decorate it with markers.
9. "Dress" the figure with scraps of fabric, wallpaper, and trim.
10. Glue the figure to a stick.

VARIATIONS

- Use pipe cleaners for arms and legs.
- Make shape animals.
- Make favorite cartoon or storybook characters.

PUPPETS (249)

PUPPETS

Single-Bag Puppets

MATERIALS

- ☐ small paper lunch bags
- ☐ crayons
- ☐ markers
- ☐ paint
- ☐ paintbrushes
- ☐ glue
- ☐ yarn
- ☐ colored construction paper
- ☐ pieces of fabric, wallpaper, and trim

 **HELPFUL HINT**

- This is a good first puppet for very young children. It is easy to make and easy to use.

DEVELOPMENTAL GOALS

Develop creativity and small motor skills, use familiar objects in new ways, and encourage imagination.

PREPARATION

Give each child a lunch bag.

PROCESS

1. On the bottom (square part) of the bag, draw facial features with crayons, markers, or paint to make the head.
2. Cut-out pieces of construction paper and glue them to the bag as other features.
3. Glue or staple on pieces of yarn for hair.
4. Decorate the rest of the bag as the puppet body.

VARIATIONS

- Make paper-bag animal puppets.
- Create a family of bag puppets.
- Make a paper-bag self-portrait.

NOTES FOR NEXT TIME: _____

_____

_____

_____

Sock Puppets

MATERIALS

- ☐ old socks
- ☐ buttons
- ☐ scraps of felt, fabric, and trim
- ☐ glue

💡 **HELPFUL HINTS**

- Sock puppets are traditional but great to use and fun to make.

- Exaggerate the puppets' features. For example, make a long, red tongue for a snake. Give the sock puppet character.

DEVELOPMENTAL GOALS

Develop creativity and small muscles in fingers and hands, use familiar objects in new ways, and encourage dramatic play.

PREPARATION

Give each child an old sock.

PROCESS

1. Pull the sock over the hand.
2. Glue facial features to the toe of the sock.
3. Add other decorative touches, such as yarn for hair and trim for clothes.
4. Let the glue dry, then put the puppet on and play!

VARIATIONS

- Make sock snakes, dogs, cats, and other animals.
- Use socks with prints and argyle designs as well as solid-colored socks.

NOTES FOR NEXT TIME. _____

_____

_____

Spool Puppets

MATERIALS

- ☐ spools
- ☐ pencils
- ☐ glue
- ☐ markers
- ☐ scraps of fabric, yarn, and trim

💡 HELPFUL HINTS

- The only reason to sharpen the pencils is to fit them in the bottom of the spool.
- Be watchful of young children with pencils.

NOTES FOR NEXT TIME:

_____

_____

_____

_____

DEVELOPMENTAL GOALS

Develop creativity, small muscles in hands and fingers, and hand-eye coordination and use familiar objects in new ways.

PREPARATION

Talk about what kind of puppet a spool would make. Discuss people, animals, objects, and imaginary creatures. Sharpen pencils to a point.

PROCESS

1. Give each child a spool and a pencil.
2. Draw a face on the spool.
3. Draw ears on the sides of the spool.
4. Glue on bits of yarn for hair on top and sides of the spool.
5. Add fabric scraps for clothing.
6. Put glue in the bottom hole of the spool.
7. Insert the sharpened end of the pencil into the bottom hole of the spool.
8. Let the glue dry thoroughly, then use and enjoy!

VARIATIONS

- Use old ballpoint pens instead of pencils.
- Create spool characters to act out fingerplays.
- Create a spool city full of imaginary creatures that have exciting stories to tell.
- Use cone spools instead of regular thread spools for an interesting variation. See what type of cone-headed characters you can create!

Stuffed-Animal Stick Puppets

MATERIALS

- ☐ Popsicle sticks
- ☐ twigs
- ☐ pencils
- ☐ small stuffed animals
- ☐ yarn or rubber bands

💡 HELPFUL HINTS

- Garage sales are good sources for stuffed animals.
- This is a good way to recycle old stuffed animals. Be sure to launder before using.

DEVELOPMENTAL GOALS

Develop creativity and small motor skills, see familiar things in new ways, and encourage imagination.

PREPARATION

Collect small stuffed animals.

PROCESS

1. Attach a small stuffed animal to a stick or a pencil with a piece of string or a rubber band.
2. Dress the puppet with scraps of fabric and trim.
3. Use this puppet like a stick puppet.

VARIATIONS

- Attach small dolls to sticks to make puppets.
- Act out a fairy tale or a favorite story with the stuffed-animal stick puppets.

NOTES FOR NEXT TIME: _____

_____

_____

_____

PUPPETS

Styrofoam-Ball Puppets

MATERIALS

- ☐ Styrofoam balls
- ☐ felt-tip pens
- ☐ scraps of colored paper
- ☐ fabric, trim
- ☐ buttons
- ☐ glue
- ☐ pencil

 **HELPFUL HINT**

- Felt-tip pens work best on Styrofoam. Crayons do not work well on Styrofoam.

DEVELOPMENTAL GOALS

Develop creativity, small muscles in fingers and hands, and hand-eye coordination; use familiar objects in new ways; and learn the design concepts of detail, color, and placement.

PREPARATION

Give each child a Styrofoam ball.

PROCESS

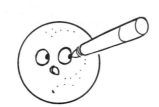

1. Make a face with felt-tip pens on the Styrofoam ball.
2. Or glue paper eyes, a nose, and a mouth to the ball.
3. Insert a pencil in the bottom of the ball for the puppet's handle.
4. Or make a hole in the Styrofoam ball in which to place a finger to work the puppet.

VARIATIONS

- Add such details as yarn for hair and buttons for eyes.
- Make real or imaginary animal Styrofoam-ball puppets.
- Create Styrofoam-ball puppets to use with fingerplays.

NOTES FOR NEXT TIME: _____

_____

_____

_____

PUPPETS

Tissue Puppets

MATERIALS

- ☐ facial tissue
- ☐ sticks (e.g., Popsicle sticks, large twigs, pencils)
- ☐ cotton
- ☐ string, or rubber bands

 **HELPFUL HINTS**

- Children may need some help securing the tissue to the stick.
- Make the string or the yarn used to fasten the head to the stick part of the tissue puppet's "costume" (e.g., a big bowtie made of yarn).
- Because tissue is a bit fragile, this material is most appropriate for children with the small motor development to handle this material.

DEVELOPMENTAL GOALS

Develop creativity, small motor skills, and hand-eye coordination and encourage imagination.

PREPARATION

Give each child two tissues (allow one for mistakes).

PROCESS

1. Place the tissue over the stick.
2. Stuff the tissue with cotton.
3. Attach the top of the tissue to the stick using string or a rubber band, making a head.
4. Draw a face on the head with markers.

VARIATIONS

- Make tissue "ghosts."
- Make a family of tissue puppets.
- Use the puppets to sing along with a favorite song.

NOTES FOR NEXT TIME: _____

_____

_____

_____

PUPPETS

Two-Bag Puppets

MATERIALS

- ☐ paper bags
- ☐ crayons
- ☐ markers
- ☐ paint
- ☐ paintbrushes
- ☐ yarn
- ☐ buttons
- ☐ paste
- ☐ colored construction paper
- ☐ scraps of fabric, yarn, trim
- ☐ newspaper
- ☐ glue

💡 HELPFUL HINT

- Encourage the children to search for the right materials for their puppets. The search is as much fun as the finished puppet!

DEVELOPMENTAL GOALS

Develop creativity, small motor skills in the fingers and hands, and hand-eye coordination and encourage imagination.

PREPARATION

Have the children crumple the newspaper into wads.

PROCESS

1. Give each child two paper bags: one for the head and one for the body.
2. Stuff one bag with wads of newspaper and staple or glue the bag shut. This is the head.
3. Make the body by stapling a second bag to the first. Leave room for the child's hand to slip in and work the puppet.
4. Make a face on the head with paint, crayons, or colored paper and paste.
5. "Dress" the body by gluing on scraps of fabric and trim.

VARIATIONS

- Use buttons to make eyes, crumpled tissue to make a nose, and yarn to make hair.
- Make paper-bag animals, cartoon characters, and family members.

NOTES FOR NEXT TIME: _____

_____

_____

Two-Faced Paper-Plate Puppets

MATERIALS

- ☐ white paper plates
- ☐ crayons
- ☐ markers
- ☐ Popsicle or craft sticks
- ☐ stapler and staples or glue
- ☐ buttons
- ☐ construction paper
- ☐ yarn

💡 HELPFUL HINT

- Two-faced puppets are good to use when talking about feelings. For example, ask a child to use the puppet's face to show how it feels about having vegetable soup for lunch.

DEVELOPMENTAL GOALS

Develop creativity, small muscles in hands and fingers, and hand-eye coordination; use familiar objects in new ways; and learn the design concepts of color, detail placement, and line.

PREPARATION

Give each child two paper plates.

PROCESS

1. Draw a face on the back of each paper plate.
2. Add details to the plates with buttons, pieces of yarn, and pieces of construction paper.
3. Insert a stick between the paper plates and staple or glue it in place.
4. Staple the edges of the plates together.

VARIATIONS

- Make an animal face on the back of each plate.
- Make a happy face on one plate and a sad face on the other.

NOTES FOR NEXT TIME: _____

_____

_____

_____

PUPPETS

Uncanny Puppets

MATERIALS

- ☐ clean cans of various sizes with open rims taped
- ☐ paint
- ☐ brushes
- ☐ construction paper
- ☐ paste
- ☐ markers
- ☐ scraps of fabric, trim, and yarn
- ☐ scissors
- ☐ masking tape
- ☐ markers
- ☐ crayons

HELPFUL HINTS

- Small cans can be worked by putting two or three fingers inside. Larger cans can be worked by putting the whole hand inside.

- Some children may have trouble waiting for the glue to dry on the paper. You might let them paint directly onto the can and skip the pasting step.

DEVELOPMENTAL GOALS

Develop creativity, small muscles in fingers and hands, and hand-eye coordination; use familiar objects in new ways; and encourage recycling.

PREPARATION

Be sure to wash all cans and let them dry thoroughly. Tape the open ends of the can with masking tape to completely cover the ends. Discuss what kind of people, animals, objects, and imaginary creatures could be made from these cans. Talk about the sizes, shapes, and feel of the cans.

PROCESS

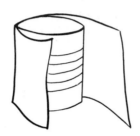

1. Give each child one can.
2. Spread glue on the can and cover it with construction paper.
3. Let the glue dry before decorating the can.
4. Draw on a face with crayons or markers.
5. Or make a face by gluing on pieces of construction paper.
6. Glue yarn hair to the top of the can.
7. Draw on clothing details or glue on fabric scraps for clothes.
8. Insert a hand into the bottom of the can to work the puppet.

VARIATIONS

- Use yogurt cups instead of tin cans for this activity.
- Make a family of can puppets with different sized cans. Act out a familiar family scene with these puppets.
- Make a "mystery" can puppet. Have the other children guess each other's puppets.
- Older children may enjoy making can puppets of favorite television, cartoon, or storybook characters.

NOTES FOR NEXT TIME: _____

_____

PUPPETS

Wooden-Spoon Puppets

3 Years Old and Up

MATERIALS

- ☐ wooden spoons
- ☐ yarn
- ☐ string
- ☐ scraps of fabric, trim, and yarn
- ☐ glue
- ☐ construction paper

💡 HELPFUL HINTS

- Wooden-spoon puppets are appropriate for very young children because they are very easy to use.
- Wooden-spoon puppets make great use of old kitchen spoons.

DEVELOPMENTAL GOALS

Develop creativity and small muscles in fingers and hands, use familiar objects in new ways, and encourage imagination.

PREPARATION

Give each child a wooden spoon.

PROCESS

1. Draw a face on the wooden spoon.
2. Glue yarn or string to the spoon for hair.
3. Glue scraps of fabric and trim to the spoon for clothing.
4. Use and enjoy.

VARIATIONS

- Make real or imaginary wooden-spoon animals.
- Create a family of spoon puppets. Use them in the housekeeping corner.
- Make yourself a spoon puppet.
- Make a new and unique creature that just happens to be a spoon puppet.

NOTES FOR NEXT TIME: _____

_____

_____

Index by Ages

PUPPETS

PART V

Print Making

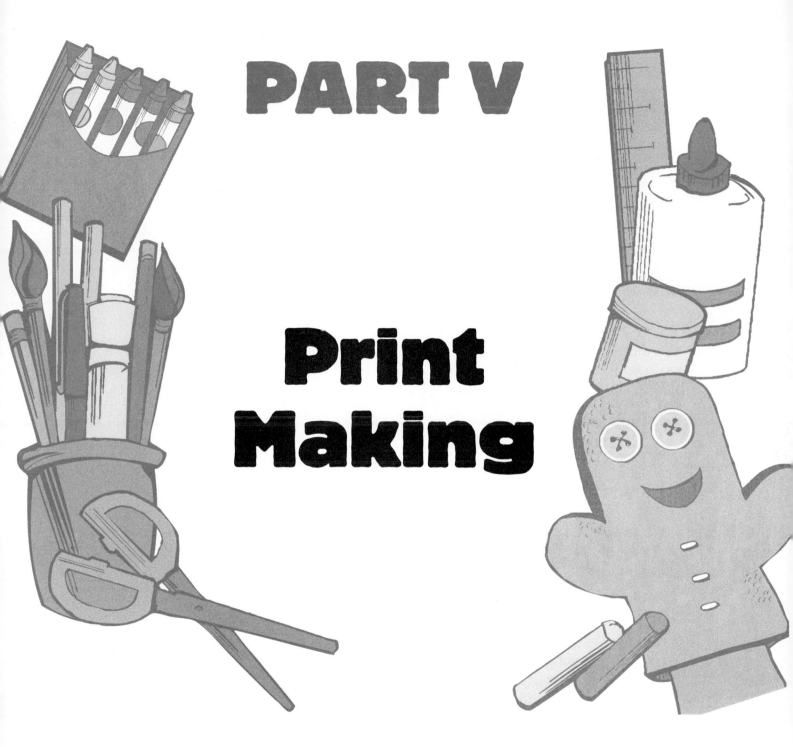

Fun with Print Making

Welcome to the world of print making! You will see from the activities in this book that print making is more than just a traditional art activity. Print making is an art form.

Long before they enter the classroom, most children have already discovered their footprints or handprints, made as they walk or play in snow, water, or wet sand. This is why printing with objects is an art activity that is appropriate for the age, ability, and interest level of young preschool children. In a basic printing activity, the child learns that an object dipped in or brushed with paint makes its own mark, or print, on paper. Children use small muscles in the hand, wrist, and fingers as they hold the object, dip it in paint, and print with it on paper. They learn that each object has its own unique quality, that each thing makes its own imprint.

While traditional forms of print making, like stick prints and vegetable prints, are found in this book, also included are such things as bottle caps, Styrofoam, tree bark, stones, and weeds. Once you start print making using these types of materials, you will be encouraged to find many other unique kinds of print making materials.

The activities in this book are designed for children ages 2 through 8. An icon representing a suggested age for the activity is listed at the top of each activity. However, use your own knowledge of the child's abilities to guide you in choosing and using the activities in this book. Wherever appropriate, information is provided on how to adapt the activity for children over age 8.

The focus of this book is creative print making. The activities are meant to be starting points for exploring this art form. Both you and the children are encouraged to explore, experiment, and enjoy the world of print making.

GETTING STARTED

Process vs. Product

The focus of this book and all early childhood art activities is the process, not the product. This means that the process of creating, not the product, is the main reason for the activity. The joys of creating, exploring materials, and discovering how things look and work are all part of the creative process. How the product looks, what it is "supposed to be," is unimportant to the child, and it should be unimportant to the adult.

Young children delight in the experience, the exploration, and the experimentation of art activities. The adult's role is to provide interesting materials and an environment that encourages children's creativity. Stand back when you are tempted to "help" children in their print making. Instead, encourage all children to discover their own unique abilities.

In their first attempts at print making, young children usually work randomly. This is the first step in print making: exploring the media. As children become more and more involved with printing, they develop better understandings of the process and possibilities for various designs.

Some ways to introduce print making activities to children are to:

- Have the children observe and discuss examples of repeat design in clothing, wrapping paper, and wallpaper in which objects appear again and again, up and down, across the material.
- When children are print making, talk about how the children can repeat designs across the material.
- Talk about how an object must be painted each time it is printed.
- Encourage children to experiment with various objects and techniques.

Gradually, through their printing experiences, children discover:

- The amount of paint needed to obtain clean edges
- The amount of pressure needed to get a print
- How the shape and texture of an object determines the shape and texture of the print
- How to repeat a print to create a design

Encourage children to search for objects from the home. Such household items as kitchen utensils, hardware, discarded materials, and many objects of nature are great printing materials. Gradually, children learn to look and discover textures, colors, and patterns all around.

Considering the Child

Young children often find it hard to wait patiently to use materials in an activity. Often, the excitement of creativity and patience do not mix. In addition, it is sometime difficult for young children to share. With young children, plan to have enough print-making materials for each child. For example, having enough sponge shapes so that each child can print without waiting encourages creative print making.

Gathering Materials

Each activity in this book includes a list of required materials. It is important that you gather all materials before starting the activity with children. Children's creative experiences are easily discouraged when they must sit and wait while the adult looks for the tape, extra scissors, or colored paper. Be sure to have the materials gathered in a place the children can easily access.

Storing and Making Materials Available

Having the materials for print making is not enough. These materials must be stored and readily available to the children. For example, scraps of printing materials bunched in a paper bag discourages children from using them. Storing those materials in a clear-plastic box that is shallow enough for children to easily search works much better. Storing small printing items in a recycled muffin tin or even in a fishing box with lots of compartments keeps these supplies orderly and encourages their use. Many teachers find clear-plastic shoe boxes invaluable for storing all the printing objects children use. Such boxes, great for storing and stacking all kinds of art materials, are available at economy stores. **Figure 1** gives more storage ideas.

FIGURE 1 · TIPS FOR STORING ART MATERIALS

The ways materials, supplies, and space are arranged can make or break children's and teachers' art experiences. Following are suggestions for arranging supplies for art experiences:

1. *Scissor holders.* Holders can be made from gallon milk or bleach containers. Simply punch holes in the containers and place scissors in the holes with the scissor points to the inside. Egg cartons turned upside down with slits in each mound also make excellent holders.

2. *Paint containers.* Containers can range from muffin tins and plastic egg cartons to plastic soft-drink cartons with baby food jars in them. These work especially well outdoors as well as indoors, because they are large and not easily tipped. Place one brush in each container. This prevents colors from mixing and makes cleanup easier.

3. *Crayon containers.* Juice and vegetable cans painted or covered with contact paper work very well.

4. Crayon pieces may be melted in muffin trays in a warm oven. These pieces, when cooled, are nice for rubbings or drawings. Crayola® makes a unit that is designed specifically for melting crayons safely.

5. Printing with tempera is easier if the tray is lined with a sponge or a paper towel.

6. A card file for art activities helps organize the program.

7. *Clay containers.* Airtight coffee cans and plastic food containers are excellent ways to keep clay moist and always ready for use.

8. *Paper scrap boxes.* By keeping two or more boxes of different sized scrap paper, children will be able to choose the paper size they want more easily.

9. Cover a wall area with pegboard and suspend heavy shopping bags or transparent plastic bags from hooks inserted in the pegboard to hold miscellaneous art supplies. Hang smocks in the same way on the pegboard (at child level, of course).

10. Use the back of a piano or bookcase to hang a shoe bag. Its pockets can hold many small items.

11. Use divided frozen food trays or a revolving lazy Susan to hold miscellaneous small items.

(From Mayesky, Mary. *Creative Activites for Young Children,* 7th ed., Clifton Park, NY: Delmar Learning.)

PRINT MAKING

Be creative when thinking about storing and making materials available for your little printing masters. Storing supplies in handy boxes and other containers makes creating art and cleaning up afterward more fun.

Identifying Print–Making Materials

Materials for print making may include the following:

- *Paint*—Tempera paint in sets of eight colors, powder paint in thin mixture, food coloring, and water-soluble printing ink are all suitable.

- *Stamp pad*—Place discarded pieces of felt or cotton inside a jar lid, a cut-down milk carton, a frozen-food tin, or similar waterproof container and saturate with color.

- *Paper*—Absorbent papers that are good for printing include newsprint, manila paper, tissue, construction paper, newspaper want-ad pages, and plain wrapping paper.

- *Cloth*—Absorbent pieces of discarded cloth, such as pillow cases, torn sheets, handkerchiefs, and old T-shirts, can be printed on.

- *Other items*—Other items you might need in print making include newspaper or plastic garbage bags for covering tables, brushes for applying paint when not using stamp pads, and cans for water.

Using Food Products

Several activities in this book involve the use of different kinds of foods. There are long-standing arguments for and against food use in art activities. For example, many teachers have long used potato printing as a traditional printing activity for young children. These teachers feel potatoes are an economical way to prepare printing objects for children. Using potatoes beyond their "shelf life" is an alternative to throwing them away. On the other hand, many teachers feel that food is for eating and should be used for nothing else.

This book has many activities that do not use food so that there will be options for teachers who oppose food use in art activities. Also, where possible, alternatives to food items are suggested. Whatever your opinion, creative activities in printing are provided for your and the children's exploration and enjoyment.

Employing Safe Materials

For all the activities in this book and for any art activities for young children, be sure to use safe art supplies. Read labels on all art materials. Check for age appropriateness. The Art and Creative Materials Institute (ACMI) labels art materials AP (approved product) and CL (certified label). Products with these labels are certified safe for use by young children. The ACMI provides an extensive list of materials and manufacturers of safe materials for all young children. This information is available on the ACMI Web site at http://www.acminet.org or by writing to 715 Boylston Street, Boston, MA 02116.

Some basic safety hints for art activities are:

- Always use products that are appropriate for the child. Use nontoxic materials for children in grade six and lower.

- Never use products for skin painting or food preparation unless the products are indicated for those uses.

- Do not transfer art materials to other containers. You will lose the valuable safety information on the product package.

- Do not eat or drink while using art and craft materials. Wash after use. Clean yourself and your supplies.
- Be sure that your work area is well ventilated.

Potentially unsafe art supplies for print making include:

- *Powdered clay.* Powered clay is easily inhaled and contains silica, which harms the lungs. Instead, use wet clay, which cannot be inhaled.

- *Instant papier-mâché.* Instant papier-mâché may contain lead or asbestos. Use only black-and-white newspaper and wheat paste or liquid starch.

- *Epoxy, instant glues, or other solvent-based glues.* Use only water-based, white glue, or glue sticks.

- *Paints that require solvents like turpentine to clean.* Use only water-based paints.

- *Cold water or commercial dyes that contain chemical additives.* Use only natural vegetable dyes made from beets, onion skins, and so on.

- *Permanent markers.* Permanent markers may contain toxic solvents. Use only water-based markers.

Be aware of all children's allergies. Children with allergies to wheat, for example, may be irritated by the wheat paste used in papier-mâché. Children who are allergic to peanuts must taste nothing containing peanut butter. In fact, some centers make it a rule to avoid all peanut butter use in food and art activities. Other art materials that may cause allergic reactions include chalk or other dusty substances, water-based clay, and any material containing petroleum products.

Also be aware of children's habits. Some young children put everything in their mouths. (This can be the case at any age.) Others may be shy and slow to accept new materials. Use your knowledge of children's tendencies to help you plan art activities that are safe for all children.

Finally, take the time to talk with the children about which things they may taste and which they may not. For example, when making anything mixed with glue, remind the children that glue is not to be tasted. You may find it helpful to use a large cut-out of a smiley face with a protruding tongue to indicate an activity that is an "edible" one—one with materials the children can taste. Use a smiley face with a large black "X" over the tongue to indicate a "no-taste" activity.

Creating a Child-Friendly Environment

It is difficult to be creative when you have to worry about keeping yourself and your work area clean. Cover all work areas with newspaper. It is best to tape the newspaper to the surface to prevent paint and other materials from seeping through the spaces. In addition, it is much easier to pick up and throw away paint-spattered newspaper than to clean a tabletop. Other coverups that work well are shower curtains and plastic tablecloths.

Also remember to cover the children. Some good child coverups are men's shirts (with the sleeves cut off), aprons, pillowcases with holes cut for heads and arms, and smocks. Some fun alternatives are sets of old clothes or shoes that can be worn as "art clothes." These old clothes could become "art journals" as they become covered with the traces of various art projects.

Other things to have on hand are paper towels or scrap paper for blotting printing items when changing colors during printing. A bucket of moist, child-sized sponges are also handy for cleanup.

Creating a Child's Art Environment

Encourage young artists by displaying art prints and other works of art. Do not make the mistake of thinking young children do not enjoy "grown-up art." Children are never too young to enjoy the colors, lines, patterns, and designs of artists' work. Art posters from a local museum, for example, can brighten an art area. Such posters also get children looking at and talking about art, which encourages the children's creative work.

Display pieces of pottery, shells and rocks, and other beautiful objects from nature to encourage children's appreciation of the lines, symmetries, and colors of nature, all part of the print-making experience. Even the youngest child can enjoy the look and feel of smooth, colored rocks or the colors of fall leaves. All these are natural parts of a child's world that can be talked about with young children as those children create artwork. Beautiful objects encourage creativity.

Starting to Collect

The more exciting "extras" you can collect, the more fun the print-making activities in this book will be for the children. You cannot start too soon collecting materials for these activities. You can probably add items to the following list, which suggests some print-making materials. Ask friends and parents to start collecting some of these materials.

Paper for printing (e.g., newsprint, manila paper, wallpaper, tissue, construction paper, newspaper want ads, plain wrapping paper)

Cloth (e.g., old pillowcases, torn sheets, handkerchiefs, old T-shirts)

Spools

Buttons

Rocks

Stamp pads with washable ink

Paint, paintbrushes

"Found" objects (e.g., forks, kitchen utensils, bottle tops, sticks, corks)

Natural objects (e.g., leaves, weeds, stones, grasses)

Vegetables (e.g., potatoes, carrots, other firm vegetables)

Styrofoam trays (but not those used for meat, as they may contain salmonella)

Styrofoam or paper cups (in states where Styrofoam cups are not prohibited in licensed child-care centers)

Paper plates

Boxes of varied sizes

Pieces of screen

Enter the world of print making in the pages that follow. Enjoy the trip!

A

All Ages

ABCs and 123s

MATERIALS

- ☐ collection of plastic alphabet letters and numbers
- ☐ paper
- ☐ tempera paint
- ☐ shallow container for paint or stamp pad (see the "Printing Stamps" activity for more information)
- ☐ paintbrushes (optional)

💡 HELPFUL HINT

- Very young artists will enjoy this activity. They need not identify letters or numbers by name; they just enjoy printing with them. You may give the name or the letter or number as the children print. Do not overdo this, because printing is the object of the activity.

DEVELOPMENTAL GOALS

Develop creativity, small motor development, and hand-eye coordination; recognize letters and numbers; and learn the design concept of pattern.

PREPARATION

For children learning about numbers and letters, discuss the letters and their sounds. Let children who can identify the letters do so. Talk about the plastic numbers. Let children who can identify the numbers do so. Talk about how the children could make designs with letters and numbers. With toddlers, simply identify the letters and numbers.

PROCESS

1. Dip plastic alphabet letters and numbers in paint.
2. Print them on paper.
3. Encourage the children to make patterns with single letters or numbers.
4. Make more patterns or lines with other letters or numbers.
5. Let children who can print their names and ages do so.

VARIATIONS

- Print initials on several sheets of paper to make personalized, original stationery.
- Print a letter. Then, using crayons or markers, draw pictures of words that start with that letter.
- Print letters or numbers on a page leaving large spaces between each. Trace around the drawings several times with crayons or markers to make another kind of design.

NOTES FOR NEXT TIME: _____

_____

Apple Prints

MATERIALS

- ☐ apples
- ☐ tempera paint
- ☐ paper plate
- ☐ shallow tray, or wide paint brushes
- ☐ paper
- ☐ knife

💡 HELPFUL HINTS

- To paint on a T-shirt, put a thick layer of paper inside the shirt to prevent the paint from bleeding through to the back of the fabric.

- An adult must cut the apples.

DEVELOPMENTAL GOALS

Develop creativity, small motor development, and hand-eye coordination and learn the design concept of pattern.

PREPARATION

An adult must cut the apple in half through the middle or cut it from top to bottom. Middle cuts make circle stamps with stars in the middle. Top-to-bottom cuts make apple shapes.

PROCESS

1. Dip the apple in paint.

2. Press the apple onto the paper to make a print.

3. Continue printing until desired design or pattern is created.

VARIATIONS

- Decorate a T-shirt with apple designs. Be sure to get fabric paints, and be sure the children are dressed in painting smocks or old clothes.

- Brush paint onto the children's hands, and decorate a T-shirt with these special handprints.

- Use several colors of paint for printing with apples.

NOTES FOR NEXT TIME: _____

_____

_____

_____

_____

PRINT MAKING

Background Paper Experiments

4 Years Old and UP

MATERIALS

- ☐ first, read the following "Process" section to gather the appropriate paper
- ☐ tempera paint, and objects to print

💡 HELPFUL HINTS

- Encourage the children to find new backgrounds for prints of their own.
- Ask parents and friends to save interesting kinds of paper and other objects for printing.

DEVELOPMENTAL GOALS

To develop creativity, small motor development, and hand-eye coordination and learn the design concept of contrast.

PREPARATION

Talk with children about contrast—how light colors look against dark colors. Discuss how large things look against smaller ones. Let the children give their own examples of contrast.

PROCESS

1. Paint the background paper and allow it to dry before printing on it with contrasting color paint.

2. Paste pieces of tissue or colored construction paper onto background paper. Allow them to dry. Then, print on this paper.

3. Print a design on background paper with pieces of sponge. Allow it to dry. Then, print on this paper.

4. Draw a design with crayons or markers on a piece of paper. Print over the design.

5. Try using a variety of shapes and sizes of paper to print on.

6. Place flat objects under the paper, then rub over with the side of the crayon to reveal the pattern. Print over this pattern with thin tempera paint.

VARIATIONS

- Print on various types of cloth, such as muslin, cotton, and denim.
- Print on wood scraps.
- Print with permanent ink on old T-shirts.
- Print on pieces cut from white gift boxes. Cover with clear contact paper and use as placemats.

NOTES FOR NEXT TIME: _____

_____

_____

PRINT MAKING

All Ages

Berry Nice Prints

MATERIALS

- ☐ plastic berry baskets
- ☐ construction paper
- ☐ tempera paint
- ☐ container for paint (large enough to dip berry basket in)
- ☐ paper

 **HELPFUL HINT**

- This is a good activity for beginning printers. The berry basket is easy to hold and to print on paper.

DEVELOPMENTAL GOALS

Develop creativity, small motor development, and hand-eye coordination and learn the design concept of line.

PREPARATION

Talk about the lines they see in the plastic berry basket. Discuss how the lines cross and how they make squares. Talk about which kind of prints the children think the baskets will make on paper.

PROCESS

1. Dip the berry basket in paint.
2. Press the basket onto the paper.
3. Repeat, overlapping shapes.
4. Continue until the pattern or design is completed.

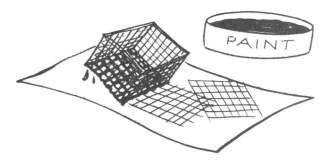

VARIATIONS

- Make contrasting designs by printing with white paint on black paper.
- Spread glue in spots and sprinkle glitter on them for a glittery effect.
- Print with different colors of primary colors. Watch the colors mix!

NOTES FOR NEXT TIME: _____

_____

_____

_____

A

All Ages

Bubble Prints

MATERIALS

- ☐ 1 cup water
- ☐ food coloring
- ☐ 1/4 cup liquid detergent
- ☐ 1/4 cup liquid starch
- ☐ straws
- ☐ printing paper
- ☐ measuring cups
- ☐ 6 to 8 inch bowl

HELPFUL HINTS

- Be sure children do not sip with the straws. To avoid this, poke a hole in the top of the straw.

- If the bubbles pop too quickly, add a few table-spoons of sugar to the water.

DEVELOPMENTAL GOALS

Develop creativity, small motor development, and hand-eye coordination and use familiar materials in new ways.

PREPARATION

In a 6 to 8 inch bowl, mix the water, drops of food coloring, liquid detergent, and liquid starch. Let the children do the measuring and mixing.

PROCESS

1. Blow bubbles using a straw.

2. Blow until the bubbles form a structure above the rim of the bowl.

3. Make a print by laying a sheet of white paper across the bowl rim and allowing the bubbles to pop against the paper.

4. Talk about the lines, shapes, and patterns the bubbles make on the paper.

VARIATIONS

- Use newspaper or brown wrapping paper.
- Use the printed paper for stationery or gift wrap.
- Have two or three bowls of differently colored bubble mixture. Make bubble prints with all the colors. Talk about how the colors mix.
- Make bubble prints outside on a sunny day.
- Blow bubbles with paper towel tubes.

NOTES FOR NEXT TIME: _____

_____

PRINT MAKING

All Ages

Can-Top Prints

MATERIALS

- ☐ all sizes of cans (e.g., juice, spray-can tops, bottle caps, soup cans)
- ☐ paper
- ☐ paint in shallow containers

💡 HELPFUL HINTS

- This is a good beginning printing activity because it concentrates on one shape and allows the children to concentrate on the process.
- Young printers are easily distracted by too many materials.
- Give children large sheets of paper for this activity, particularly if it is the children's first time. Let them experiment with making designs of their choosing.
- Later, give a group of children a large piece of butcher paper that covers part of a bulletin board and let the little printers print to their hearts' content.
- Give other groups the paper that will complete a bulletin-board cover. Cover your bulletin board with this paper as a background for your displays.

DEVELOPMENTAL GOALS

Develop creativity, small motor development, and hand-eye coordination; use familiar objects in new ways; learn the design concept of pattern and use a circle and its variations to make a pattern.

PREPARATION

Talk about the circular shape and the sizes of the cans. Discuss the idea of pattern—repeating a design on the paper. Wash the cans thoroughly and let them dry.

PROCESS

1. Give each child a piece of paper.
2. Dip the can lightly in paint.
3. Make a print on the paper with the can top.
4. Make can top prints in vertical lines, circular lines, zigzags, and so on.
5. See how many different kinds of designs the children can make with the can top.

VARIATIONS

- Add other circular objects, like paper-towel and tissue rolls, to the print.
- Provide small boxes of rectangular or square shapes to use for printing another shape.
- Use different kinds of paper, like newsprint, classified ads, brown wrapping paper.

NOTES FOR NEXT TIME: _____

_____

_____

PRINT MAKING

Cardboard or Rubber Block Prints

MATERIALS

- ☐ a piece of innertube or cardboard
- ☐ scissors
- ☐ paste or glue
- ☐ heavy cardboard
- ☐ floor tile or a piece of wood
- ☐ thick mixture of tempera paint
- ☐ spoon
- ☐ brayer (or small trim paint roller)
- ☐ ink slab (9" × 9" floor tile or piece of Plexiglas®/clear plastic with edges taped)
- ☐ paper
- ☐ newspaper

💡 HELPFUL HINTS

- This is an excellent activity for experienced print makers, children generally 5 years and older.

- Use scrap paper for practice prints to get the children used to using a brayer or roller.

- Use a smooth bottom of a small jar to rub the entire design before printing.

- Peel back a corner of the paper to see whether further rubbing is necessary for a strong print.

DEVELOPMENTAL GOALS

Develop creativity, small motor development, and hand-eye coordination; practice using a brayer; and learn the design concepts of shape, line, and pattern.

PREPARATION

Discuss which designs the children would like to make and print. Talk about how to make a pattern by repeating designs or objects. Give the children time to practice using a brayer (roller) if the children have never used a brayer before.

PROCESS

 **1.** Cut shapes from pieces of cardboard or inner tubes and glue them to a cardboard background for printing.

 **2.** Spoon a small amount of paint onto the piece of Plexiglas® or floor tile.

 **3.** Roll the ink with a brayer (or small trim paint roller) until it is spread smoothly on the inking slab.

 **4.** Roll the ink brayer over the mounted design from side and top to bottom to ensure an even distribution over the entire surface.

 **5.** Place a piece of paper over the inked design and rub gently and evenly with the fingers until the entire design is reproduced.

 **6.** Re-ink the design for more prints.

VARIATIONS

- Use water-soluble or oil base printer's ink. This produces a very clear print. If you use oil-base printer's ink, you will need to use turpentine to clean the brayer.

- Try different shapes, sizes, and colors of paper for printing.

- Print on fabric squares. Join all the different prints for a group "print quilt."

NOTES FOR NEXT TIME: _____

_____

Cardboard Relief Prints

MATERIALS

- ☐ pieces of cardboard
- ☐ carpenter's nails
- ☐ thick tempera paint
- ☐ paper
- ☐ paintbrushes

💡 HELPFUL HINTS

- Use small paint rollers to roll out the paint onto the cardboard.

- Use nails long and big enough for children to handle like pencils. A ten-penny nail works well.

NOTES FOR NEXT TIME:

_____

_____

_____

_____

_____

DEVELOPMENTAL GOALS

Develop creativity, small motor development, and hand-eye coordination; learn the design concepts of pattern and line; and understand relief printing.

PREPARATION

Discuss what relief printing is—printing from a raised surface. A simple example of relief printing is a rubber stamp pressed into a stamp pad and pressed onto a piece of paper. Relief printing plates are made from flat sheets of material (in this activity—cardboard). After drawing a picture on the surface, the artist uses tools to cut away the areas that will not be printed.

PROCESS

1. Scratch out a design on the cardboard with a carpenter's nail.

2. Remember that the printed image will appear in reverse!

3. Use a paintbrush to cover the cardboard with tempera paint.

4. Lay the paper on top.

5. Press lightly with the palm of the hand.

6. Peel away the paper and see the print!

VARIATIONS

- Instead of drawing into the Styrofoam, press areas you do not want printed.

- You could also cut out sections of the Styrofoam, ink them up separately, pop the pieces back together, and print.

- Repeat the process so you have an edition of prints.

- Use different colors, shapes and kinds of paper to make relief prints.

PRINT MAKING

A

All Ages

Circle Challenge

MATERIALS

- ☐ paper cups of various sizes
- ☐ large, round pasta, and any other circular shapes to print
- ☐ tempera paint
- ☐ shallow container for paint
- ☐ brushes
- ☐ paper

 **HELPFUL HINT**

- This is a good beginning printing activity for very young artists. Only one or two circular objects are required for very young artists. This is because they are learning the process, and too many choices for printing objects distracts them. As children grow more adept in the process, add more objects for printing.

DEVELOPMENTAL GOALS

Develop creativity, small motor development, and hand-eye coordination and recognize shapes.

PREPARATION

Talk about circles. Have the children identify as many circles as they can in the room. Discuss which circular things the children can think of to use in print making. Challenge the children to bring from home as many of these items as they can. Include these items with those listed previously.

PROCESS

1. Begin by printing with one circular printing object.
2. Print this on the page, making a pattern or a random design.
3. Use another circular object and print with it on the page.
4. Try printing one line with one size circle.
5. Do another with a differently sized circle.
6. Alternate large and small circular shapes in one line.
7. Print zigzag, horizontal, and vertical lines with circle shapes.

VARIATIONS

- Repeat the activity with another shape—square, rectangle, even triangles!
- Have several containers of different colors of paint. Print each shape with a different color.
- Let the print dry. Then, print more circular shapes over the existing print using black or white tempera paint for a contrasting effect.

NOTES FOR NEXT TIME: _____

_____

PRINT MAKING

5

Years Old and Up

Cloth Prints

MATERIALS

- ☐ soft cloth
- ☐ felt markers (permanent markers if cloth is going to be washed and water-soluble markers if cloth is not going to be washed)
- ☐ heavy paper (recycled gift boxes work well)
- ☐ practice paper

💡 HELPFUL HINTS

- When using permanent markers for this activity, be sure the children are well covered so they get no marker on their clothing.

- Embroidery hoops help hold the fabric taut when the printing is done.

DEVELOPMENTAL GOALS

Develop creativity, small motor development, hand-eye coordination; learn the design concepts of pattern and line; and use familiar materials in new ways.

PREPARATION

Discuss pattern—how it is made of a repeating figure or design. Talk about how shapes can be used to make a pattern.

PROCESS

1. Cut shapes from heavy paper. Recycled gift boxes work well.
2. Trace around the shapes on the practice paper.
3. Repeat the shapes until a pattern emerges.
4. Encourage the children to do such things as overlap, turn, and reverse shapes.
5. Once the practice design on paper is made, repeat it on cloth.
6. Each child helps another by holding the paper shape in place as the other traces around it.
7. Complete the practice design on the cloth.

VARIATIONS

- Cut seasonal shapes, such as leaves in the fall, and make a design on cloth with them.
- Use "found" objects to print on the cloth, such as bottle caps, and buttons.

NOTES FOR NEXT TIME: _____

_____

_____

_____

Cork Prints

MATERIALS

- ☐ corks
- ☐ knife
- ☐ paper
- ☐ paint
- ☐ paintbrushes
- ☐ newspapers
- ☐ scrap paper or paper towels (for practicing)

HELPFUL HINT

- Cut the corks before introducing the activity.

NOTES FOR
NEXT TIME:

_____

_____

_____

_____

DEVELOPMENTAL GOALS

Develop creativity, small motor development, and hand-eye coordination; use familiar objects in new ways; learn the design concepts of pattern and circle.

PREPARATION

Cut a design around the edge and/or in the middle of the corks.

PROCESS

1. Place a pad of newspapers under the paper to be printed.
2. Have a scrap paper or paper towel available to practice the design.
3. Cover the surface of the cork with paint.
4. Print on a scrap of paper to eliminate any excess paint.
5. Press the cork onto the paper to make a print.
6. Continue making prints to make a design or a pattern.

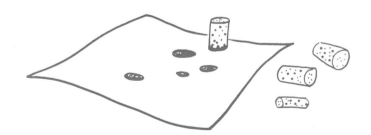

VARIATIONS

- Use several different colors of paint.
- Try different paper, such as brown wrapping paper, classified ads, or tissue paper.
- Apply different colors to different areas of the cork for interesting print results.

PRINT MAKING

Crayon Prints

MATERIALS

- ☐ wax crayon
- ☐ copy paper
- ☐ turpentine or mineral spirits
- ☐ shallow container
- ☐ brush
- ☐ cloth or paper towel

HELPFUL HINTS

- Mineral spirits is a solvent similar to turpentine. It is available in hardware or art-supply stores.

- Be careful that children do not get mineral spirits in their eyes. If they do, rinse the eyes thoroughly with water.

- This activity is inappropriate for beginning printers, because it involves waiting until the wax softens and the use of mineral spirits. It is appropriate for children ages 5 and up.

DEVELOPMENTAL GOALS

Develop creativity, small motor development, and hand-eye coordination and use familiar tools (crayons) in new ways.

PREPARATION

Discuss which type of picture or design the children will want to make.

PROCESS

1. Give each child a piece of copy paper.

2. Draw heavily with the crayon on the piece of paper.

3. The adult dips the brush in the mineral spirits and spreads a thin coat of mineral spirits on the back to soften the crayon wax.

4. When the wax is soft, lay a piece of paper over the picture and rub it with fingers or a flat tool until the picture transfers.

5. It may be possible to make several prints from one drawing.

VARIATIONS

- Make the crayon drawing over a piece of window screen for an interesting effect.
- Use different sizes, shapes, and kinds of paper for printing.

NOTES FOR NEXT TIME: _____

_____

PRINT MAKING

Crayon Shavings Prints

MATERIALS

- ☐ scrap pieces of crayon
- ☐ scraping tool (e.g., nail file, scissors, grater)
- ☐ aluminum foil
- ☐ paper
- ☐ salt shaker
- ☐ iron
- ☐ newspapers

💡 HELPFUL HINTS

- Exercise extreme caution around the children during the ironing processes in this activity. Only an adult should handle the iron and well away from the children's reach.

- This activity is appropriate for children who have printing experience.

- Give the children several chances to create a crayon-shavings print. As the children work with crayon shavings, they will learn how many to shake onto the paper to get a vibrant print.

DEVELOPMENTAL GOALS

Develop creativity, small motor development, and hand-eye coordination and use familiar tools (old crayons) in new ways.

PREPARATION

Have the children help shave scrap crayon into small pieces onto a piece of newspaper. Place the pieces in a clean, dry salt shaker or use any type of shaker with fairly large holes.

PROCESS

1. Sprinkle a few of the crayon shavings onto a piece of white paper.
2. Place this paper on a piece of newspaper.
3. Place a piece of foil over the crayon pieces.
4. An adult presses the foil with a moderately hot iron.
5. Remove the foil and place it on a second sheet of paper.
6. Press once again.
7. Separate the foil from the white paper, which has received the printed impression.

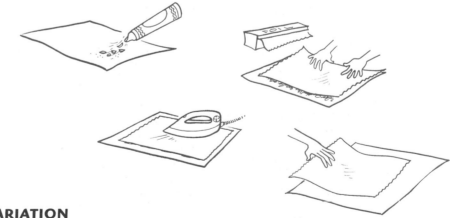

VARIATION

- To control color areas, fill several shakers with different colors of crayon shavings.

NOTES FOR NEXT TIME: _____

_____

All Ages

Creative Shoe Prints

MATERIALS

- ☐ white canvas tennis shoes
- ☐ tempera paint
- ☐ printing objects such as vegetables
- ☐ plastic letters and numbers
- ☐ cotton swabs
- ☐ paintbrushes
- ☐ stamp pad (see the "Printing Stamps" activity on page 33)
- ☐ fabric crayons and pens (optional)

💡 HELPFUL HINTS

- Even very young artists ages 2 and up can decorate their own shoes.
- There may be some running of colors if the shoes get too wet. This is not a problem if you use printer's ink or fabric crayons.

DEVELOPMENTAL GOALS

Develop creativity, small motor development, and hand-eye coordination and use art to decorate everyday objects.

PREPARATION

Each child needs a pair of white tennis shoes to decorate. Talk with the children about how they would like to decorate their shoes. Talk about shapes, patterns, and designs. Discuss types of lines, too.

PROCESS

1. Dip a printing object into tempera paint.
2. Press the object onto the shoe.
3. Repeat printing with the object and others.
4. Use paintbrushes and cotton swabs to make more designs on the shoes.
5. Dip plastic letters and numbers in paint.
6. Press them onto the shoes to print.
7. Let the shoes dry thoroughly before wearing.

VARIATIONS

- Paint the shoelaces, too. Take them out and lay them on some paper and start painting!
- Use school colors and have a pair of shoes that show school spirit. Alternately, use the colors of a favorite team.
- Fabric pens and crayons work great for drawing designs on the shoes.

NOTES FOR NEXT TIME: _____

_____

PRINT MAKING

Dip It!

3 Years Old and Up

MATERIALS

☐ two or three colors of thin tempera paint of bright colors

☐ shallow containers

☐ white paper napkins or white paper towels

💡 **HELPFUL HINTS**

- Young children may need help folding the napkins or paper towels.

- These "tie-dyed" napkins can be used for various things, such as borders for bulletin boards or pictures, basket linings, and wrapping paper.

DEVELOPMENTAL GOALS

Develop creativity, small motor development, and hand-eye coordination; use familiar objects in new ways; and learn the design concept of pattern.

PREPARATION

Put the paint in small containers, about 1 to 1-1/2 inches deep.

PROCESS

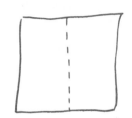

1. Give each child a white napkin or a sheet torn from a roll of white paper towels.

2. Fold the sheet in half twice.

3. Dip the corners of the napkin or towel into different colors of paint.

4. Open the napkins or towels and allow them to dry.

5. The sheets dry into multicolored, bright designs.

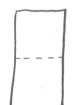

VARIATIONS

- Dip the same corner into two different colors. Watch the colors blend.

- Refold the dried napkin and redip it into different colors.

- Use square pieces of muslin instead of paper napkins.

NOTES FOR NEXT TIME: _____

_____

_____

_____

PRINT MAKING

All Ages

Finger Paint Prints

MATERIALS

- ☐ finger paint
- ☐ formica tabletop, enamel-topped table, or linoleum
- ☐ newsprint paper

HELPFUL HINTS

- This is a good way to save on the cost of finger paint paper and to try something new and fun.

- Some children may finish this activity quickly. Have enough newsprint paper available so they can make several finger paint prints.

- Be careful so that you do not rub too hard when transferring the finger painting to the newsprint. It may smear the painting. If this happens, just finger paint again and lay another piece of newsprint over it. The children get to finger paint again, which is just more fun!

DEVELOPMENTAL GOALS

Develop creativity, small motor development, and hand-eye coordination and gain initial experience with printing.

PREPARATION

Mix finger paints to a thick consistency.

PROCESS

1. Put a blob of finger paint directly on the tabletop.
2. Have the child finger paint directly on the tabletop.
3. When the child is finished painting, lay a piece of newsprint paper on the finger painting.
4. Gently rub the paper with one hand.
5. The finger paint transfers from the tabletop to the paper.

VARIATIONS

- Use several colors of finger paint and watch the colors mix.
- For children who do not like to use their fingers, let them brush the finger paint around on the tabletop.

NOTES FOR NEXT TIME: _____

_____

_____

_____

Finger Prints

MATERIALS

- ☐ stamp pad filled with washable ink or shallow container of paint
- ☐ paper
- ☐ markers
- ☐ crayons

 **HELPFUL HINTS**

- Some children may not want to put their fingers in the paint. Do not force them to do so. Have other items these children can use to print.

- After this activity has been introduced, you will probably see these prints every time the children get around paint!

- This is a good printing activity for young children because the prints are easily done, are relatively error proof, and unique.

DEVELOPMENTAL GOALS

Develop creativity, small motor development, and hand-eye coordination and learn the design concepts of pattern, line, and swirl.

PREPARATION

Have the children practice making their finger prints. Talk about how each child's finger prints are unique. Talk about the lines the children see: swirls, curvy, round. Discuss which designs or objects the children could make with their finger prints.

PROCESS

1. Give each child a piece of paper and a stamp pad. (See the "Printing Stamps" activity on page 33 to learn how to make simple stamp pads.)

2. Show the children how to place the ball of the finger in the paint and then make a print on paper.

3. Let the children practice to learn just how much paint is necessary and the best technique for making clear prints.

4. On a clean sheet of paper, make about six prints.

5. Put each child's name on the paper and let the paper dry.

6. Make characters or objects using the finger prints as the body.

VARIATIONS

- Make a picture using finger prints.
- Make a finger-print family. Draw the family members in their house or outside in the sun.
- Use different colors of paint, different kinds of paper.

NOTES FOR NEXT TIME: _____

_____

_____

_____

PRINT MAKING

First Experiments with Monoprints

MATERIALS

- ☐ thick mixture of tempera paint
- ☐ paintbrushes
- ☐ sheets of Plexiglas® (approximately 12" × 12")
- ☐ paper
- ☐ small paint roller (optional)
- ☐ Popsicle stick or pencil with eraser

💡 HELPFUL HINTS

- You can find Plexiglas® at a local lumberyard or hardware store. Ask for offcuts, which are normally thrown away.

- You can also use old political-yard signs, garage-sale signs, or any waxy-surface signs for the printing plate.

- Add flour to tempera paint to make it thicker and stickier like printer's ink.

DEVELOPMENTAL GOALS

Develop creativity, small motor development, and hand-eye coordination and learn the concept of monoprinting.

PREPARATION

Explain that monoprinting is the process of making only one print from the printing plate (the part on which the picture is first drawn).

PROCESS

1. Brush the paint onto the Plexiglas®, covering it completely, or use a small paint roller to roll it out to cover the Plexiglas®.

2. Using the end of a pencil or a Popsicle stick, draw an image on the Plexiglas®.

3. Place the paper on the Plexiglas® and rub lightly.

4. Peel away the paper and see the print.

VARIATIONS

- Repeat the process using a different color of paint and a different kind of paper.

- Use found objects to make a design on the paint. Make a monoprint of this design.

NOTES FOR NEXT TIME: _____

_____

_____

Glue and Leaf Prints

MATERIALS

- ☐ white glue
- ☐ leaves
- ☐ pieces of cardboard
- ☐ paint
- ☐ paintbrushes
- ☐ paper to print on

💡 HELPFUL HINTS

- Beginning printers often enjoy printing without creating patterns or designs. Expect random printing when children learn new art techniques.

- Both fallen leaves and green leaves work for this activity.

DEVELOPMENTAL GOALS

Develop creativity, small motor development, and hand-eye coordination and learn the design concepts of pattern and line.

PREPARATION

Collect leaves of different sizes and shapes. Talk about the leaves and their shapes and sizes. Discuss how the children can use the leaves to make patterns. Cut cardboard into pieces that are slightly bigger than the leaves.

PROCESS

1. Squeeze white glue around edges of the top side of a leaf.
2. Stick the leaf to a piece of cardboard.
3. Use a paintbrush to cover the leaf with paint.
4. Press the painted side of the leaf onto a piece of paper.
5. Repeat to make a design.

VARIATIONS

- Include sticks, pine cones, and other natural objects. Dip them into paint and add them to the leaf design.
- Use different colors of paint.
- Use different kinds of paper, such as tissue, classified ads, brown wrapping paper.

NOTES FOR NEXT TIME: _____

_____

_____

_____

Great Balls of Fun!

MATERIALS

- [ ] paper
- [ ] thin mixture of tempera paint
- [ ] containers for paint
- [ ] tennis balls
- [ ] smocks or old clothes for covering the children

HELPFUL HINTS

- This is a great outdoor activity because the mess is not a worry.
- Some dripping may occur, which adds interest to the finished print.

DEVELOPMENTAL GOALS

Develop creativity, small motor development, and hand-eye coordination and use familiar objects in new ways.

PREPARATION

Be sure children and the area are well covered. This is a very messy, but fun activity!

PROCESS

1. Dip the tennis ball in paint.
2. Dab or drop the balls onto the paper to make a print.
3. Repeat until satisfied with the print.
4. Let the prints dry thoroughly.

VARIATIONS

- Use balls of different sizes and weights. Golf balls leave interesting prints.
- Dip balls in different colors.
- Print on a piece of cloth or an old T-shirt using printer's ink for a permanent print.

NOTES FOR NEXT TIME: _____

_____

_____

_____

A

All Ages

Hair's the Thing

MATERIALS

- ☐ old combs
- ☐ brushes (e.g., hairbrushes, scrub brushes, toothbrushes)
- ☐ paper
- ☐ tempera paint
- ☐ shallow container for paint or stamp pad (see the "Printing Stamps" activity for directions.)

💡 HELPFUL HINTS

- With very young artists, use only one or two combs or brushes. Because these children are learning the process, too many items may confuse them.

- Run the combs and brushes through the dishwasher or soak them in soapy water before using them for this activity.

DEVELOPMENTAL GOALS

Develop creativity, small motor development, and hand-eye coordination and use familiar objects in new ways.

PREPARATION

Have children bring in brushes and combs that they can use for printing. Be sure the children know the brushes and combs must be old, because paint will not come out of them after printing.

PROCESS

1. Dip the comb into tempera paint.
2. Run the comb along the paper to make wavy printed lines.
3. Dip the comb in paint again and find another way to make marks with it.
4. Dip a brush into the paint.
5. Press the brush, dab it, and rub it along the paper to make more prints.
6. Use another brush and repeat the process.

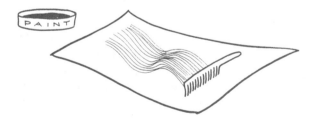

VARIATIONS

- Have several colors of paint. Use a different one with each brush or comb.
- Paint the items with a paintbrush, then press them onto the paper.
- Print using as many sides of the combs/brushes as possible.

NOTES FOR NEXT TIME: _____

_____

_____

_____

PRINT MAKING

Hand and Foot Prints

MATERIALS

- ☐ long piece of paper
- ☐ tempera paint in a shallow pan large enough to put feet and hands in
- ☐ pail of water with a bit of liquid detergent mixed in
- ☐ paper towels
- ☐ tape

💡 HELPFUL HINTS

- This is a great outdoor activity! Children will enjoy being outside and playing barefoot.
- Some children may not want to put their feet or hands in paint. Trace around their feet and hands with a marker or crayon.

DEVELOPMENTAL GOALS

To develop creativity, small motor development, and hand-eye coordination and develop an initial understanding of how prints are made.

PREPARATION

This is a fun but messy activity. Spread newspapers and tape them to the floor. Spread out the long piece of paper and tape it to the newspaper.

PROCESS

1. Have the children dip their feet in the paint.
2. Print the right foot and left foot.
3. Print the hands.
4. Write the child's name by the prints.
5. Continue until all children have made their prints.
6. Step into the pail of water to clean off the feet. Dip in the hands to clean them, too. Dry with paper towels.

VARIATIONS

- After making the first set of prints, let the child walk to the end of the paper, making a trail of footprints until the paint is "walked off."
- Use the foot and hand print sheet as a bulletin board for an "All About Us" theme.
- Print foot and hand prints on separate pieces of paper. Write down what the children want to tell about themselves near the prints. This could be the cover of a book "All About Me."

NOTES FOR NEXT TIME: _____

_____

_____

_____

PRINT MAKING

 292 PRINT MAKING

Kitchen Prints

MATERIALS

- ☐ kitchen utensils and equipment to be used for printing
- ☐ tempera paint
- ☐ shallow container for paint
- ☐ paper

 **HELPFUL HINT**

- This is a good activity to help develop children's thinking skills. It helps the children see things in the environment for their potential as art materials.

NOTES FOR NEXT TIME:

_____

_____

_____

_____

_____

DEVELOPMENTAL GOALS

Develop creativity, small motor development, and hand-eye coordination and use familiar objects in new ways.

PREPARATION

Challenge the children to come up with as many things in the kitchen that they can print (e.g., potato masher, forks, spoons, bowls, paper cups, spatula, funnels, wire strainers).

PROCESS

1. Choose one object with which to print.
2. Dip the object in tempera paint.
3. Press the object onto the paper.
4. Try printing on a different side of the same utensil.
5. Print with other utensils using various sides.
6. Try making a line with one kind of utensil.
7. Make another line using another utensil.
8. Alternate printing with different utensils for another type of pattern.

VARIATIONS

- Use several colors of paint. Use a different color for different utensils.
- Print on different shapes, colors, and kinds of paper.
- Use another room in the house for objects. For example, challenge the children to find as many objects as they can from their own bedrooms, bathrooms, or garages.

PRINT MAKING

Monoprints One More Time!

MATERIALS

- ☐ thick mixture of tempera paint
- ☐ paintbrushes
- ☐ sheets of Plexiglas® (12" × 12")
- ☐ paper
- ☐ small paint roller (optional)
- ☐ paper
- ☐ pencil

💡 HELPFUL HINTS

- Add flour to tempera to make it thicker and stickier like printer's ink.
- You can find Plexiglas® at hardware stores or lumber yards. Ask for off-cuts they often throw away.
- Old yard signs or political signs also work well. Any sturdy paper with a waxy surface works, too.

DEVELOPMENTAL GOALS

Develop creativity, small motor development, and hand-eye coordination and understand monoprinting.

PREPARATION

Discuss monoprinting—a process in which only one print is made from the printing plate (the part on which the picture/design is made).

PROCESS

1. Cover the Plexiglas® completely by brushing on the tempera paint. Or you can use a small paint roller to roll it on the Plexiglas®.

2. Place paper over the Plexiglas®.
3. Using a pencil, draw an image on the paper.
4. When you peel away the paper, the image will have transferred itself.
5. This is similar to carbon paper.

VARIATIONS

- Make a design using different thicknesses of pencils.
- Use sticks and twigs to make the design.
- Print with different kinds of paper and different colors of paint.

NOTES FOR NEXT TIME: _____

_____

_____

_____

_____

PRINT MAKING

4 Years Old and Up

Monoprints—Even One More Way!

MATERIALS

- ☐ tempera paint
- ☐ paintbrushes
- ☐ sheets of Plexiglas® (approximately 12" × 12")
- ☐ paper

 **HELPFUL HINTS**

- Thicken the tempera paint with a little bit of flour to make it sticky like printer's ink.
- You can find Plexiglas® at lumber yards or hardware stores. Ask for offcuts that are normally thrown away.
- Old yard signs or political signs work well, too.

DEVELOPMENTAL GOALS

Develop creativity, small motor development, and hand-eye coordination and understand monoprinting.

PREPARATION

Discuss monoprinting. Explain that it is a process of making only one print from the printing plate (the part that holds the picture/design).

PROCESS

1. Using a paintbrush, paint a design or picture on the Plexiglas®.
2. Use many or a few colors.
3. Do not let the paint dry!
4. Place paper over the Plexiglas®.
5. Rub lightly with the palm of the hand.
6. Peel the paper away.

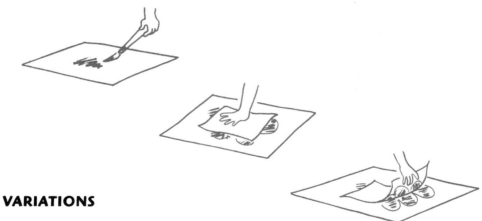

VARIATIONS

- Use small and large paintbrushes in the design. Even try a house paint type of paintbrush!
- Try different sizes and colors of paper.

NOTES FOR NEXT TIME: _____

_____

_____

_____

PRINT MAKING

Nature Spatter Prints

MATERIALS

- ☐ toothbrushes
- ☐ paint
- ☐ leaves
- ☐ weeds
- ☐ grasses
- ☐ paper
- ☐ pieces of screen

 **HELPFUL HINTS**

- Spatter painting is messy but fun. Be sure to prepare the area and the children.

- Encourage the children to take time to arrange and rearrange their items until they create designs they like. Some children will do this quickly; others will need more time.

- Spatter prints are more interesting in contrasting colors or paint.

DEVELOPMENTAL GOALS

Develop creativity, small motor development, and hand-eye coordination and see design and pattern in nature.

PREPARATION

Put paint in small, shallow containers. Talk about the natural objects collected for this project. Discuss how the children could arrange the objects on the paper. Demonstrate how to rub the toothbrush across the screen and over the paper to get paint spatters on the paper.

PROCESS

1. Arrange the natural objects on the paper in a design.
2. Dip the toothbrush in the paint.
3. Rub the paint-filled toothbrush across a piece of screen over a part of the arrangement on the paper.
4. Paint will spatter on the paper around the arrangement.

5. Continue spatter painting until the whole area around the arrangement is covered with paint spatters.
6. Remove the arrangement to see the print.

VARIATIONS

- Use different colors of paint.
- Use different kinds of paper, such as brown wrapping paper, white tissue paper, and construction paper.

NOTES FOR NEXT TIME: _____

_____

_____

PRINT MAKING

Paint Monoprints

5 Years Old and UP

MATERIALS

- ☐ smooth, nonabsorbent hard surface (e.g., glass, plastic, tabletop)
- ☐ drawing paper
- ☐ tempera paint
- ☐ brush
- ☐ water container

💡 HELPFUL HINT

- This is an excellent printing activity for older children, because the children are more able to wait for the painting to dry. They can also dampen the drawing paper themselves.

NOTES FOR NEXT TIME:

_____

_____

_____

DEVELOPMENTAL GOALS

Develop creativity, small motor development, and hand-eye coordination and learn the design concept of mirror image.

PREPARATION

Discuss which kind of pattern, design, or picture the children may want to do. Remind the children that rubbing on a painting with another piece of paper will result in a mirror image. Talk about what a mirror image is—the reverse image.

PROCESS

1. Paint a picture or design on a nonabsorbent surface.
2. Allow the surface to dry.
3. Thoroughly dampen a sheet of drawing paper.
4. Press the dampened paper firmly and evenly over the painted design with the palm of the hand.
5. Carefully peel the paper from the design.
6. One impression printing will appear on the paper as a mirror image.

VARIATION

- Older children may enjoy including names or numbers on their designs. They will have to draw them backward for them to print correctly. This is a definite challenge!

PRINT MAKING

Pasta Prints

MATERIALS

- [ ] all shapes of pasta (e.g., elbows, shells, wheels, spaghetti)
- [ ] paste
- [ ] construction paper
- [ ] tempera paint
- [ ] shallow containers for paint
- [ ] paper for printing

💡 HELPFUL HINT

- Because the pasta is bumpy, the whole piece will not print on the paper. It will still make an interesting print.

- Do not use buttons or beads with children three years and younger.

DEVELOPMENTAL GOALS

Develop creativity, small motor development, and hand-eye coordination and learn the design concepts of shapes and pattern.

PREPARATION

Discuss the various shapes of pasta. Talk about how the shapes could make designs or patterns.

PROCESS

1. Paste pasta pieces onto construction paper.

2. Make a design, picture, or pattern.

3. Brush tempera paint over the pasta design.

4. Press a piece of paper over the pasta.

5. Tap lightly over the pasta with the palm of the hand.

6. Remove the paper and see the print.

VARIATIONS

- For those who are opposed to using food in art activities, use such non-food items as buttons and beads.

- Include other items in the design, such as buttons, rice, and twigs.

- Brush again over the pasta with a different color of paint. Make another pasta print.

- Encourage the children to make patterns with the pasta. Try alternating shapes in a line. Make one line of one type of pasta, another line with a different kind.

NOTES FOR NEXT TIME: _____

_____

_____

PRINT MAKING

Pine Cone Prints

MATERIALS

- ☐ pine cones
- ☐ thin mixture of tempera paint
- ☐ container for paint
- ☐ paper

 **HELPFUL HINT**

- If pine trees are not in your area, buy bags of pine cones at craft stores.

DEVELOPMENTAL GOALS

Develop creativity, small motor development, and hand-eye coordination and appreciate pattern and beauty in nature.

PREPARATION

Go outdoors and collect pine cones. Talk about their shapes, how they feel, and how they smell.

PROCESS

1. Give each child a piece of paper.
2. Dip a pine cone in tempera paint.
3. Press the pine cone onto the paper.
4. Use all sides of the pine cone to make prints.

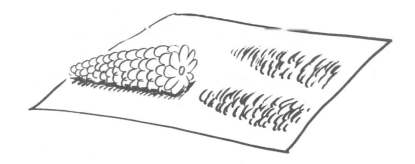

VARIATIONS

- Include twigs, acorns, and small stones for printing.
- Save painted pine cones to use as part of natural arrangements.

NOTES FOR NEXT TIME: _____

_____

_____

_____

PRINT MAKING

Play Dough Prints

Years Old and Up

MATERIALS

- ☐ play dough
- ☐ Popsicle or craft sticks
- ☐ paper
- ☐ tempera paint
- ☐ shallow containers for paint

💡 HELPFUL HINTS

- Young children may enjoy simply printing with the play dough without carving designs. This is to be expected with beginning printers.

- Encourage speedy finishers to make several different carvings to print.

DEVELOPMENTAL GOALS

Develop creativity, small motor development, and hand-eye coordination and learn the design concept of pattern.

PREPARATION

Discuss stamps and how to print with them. Talk about which kind of stamps the children would like to make from play dough.

PROCESS

1. Give the child a lump of play dough the size of an apple or a small grapefruit.
2. Pound the play dough into small, flat cakes about 1 inch thick.
3. Carve a design on the flat surface with a Popsicle or craft stick.
4. Brush the design with paint or dip it in paint.
5. Press the design onto paper to print.

VARIATIONS

- Carve several different designs on the play dough. Print each in a different color.
- Carve letters or numbers. Print on sheets of paper to make original stationery.
- Make one line of one design, then another of a second design. Try alternating two designs in one line.
- Print horizontal, vertical, and zigzag lines.
- Printed sheets make great wrapping paper, backing for photos, and covers for jars.

NOTES FOR NEXT TIME: _____

_____

PRINT MAKING

300 **PRINT MAKING**

A

All Ages

Plunge into It!

MATERIALS

- ☐ new plungers of various sizes
- ☐ large sheets of butcher paper
- ☐ various colors of tempera paint
- ☐ foam trays or plates

💡 HELPFUL HINTS

- This is a great outdoor activity!
- Foot and hand prints are a logical next step from this activity. They can be added to the print after the plunger prints are done.

DEVELOPMENTAL GOALS

Develop creativity, large and small motor development, and hand-eye coordination and learn the design concepts of pattern and circular shapes.

PREPARATION

Cover the art area with newspaper. Tape the newspaper to the floor. Lay out butcher paper, and tape it to the floor, as well. Prepare paints in trays. Set plungers in paint trays.

PROCESS

1. Dip the plunger in paint.
2. Press the plunger onto the butcher paper to make a print.
3. Continue printing to create a design or pattern.

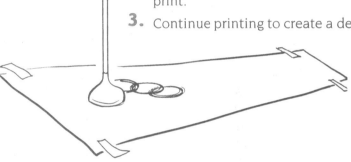

VARIATIONS

- Add other round objects to print, such as paper cups or towel rolls.
- Use two plungers at a time—each with a different color of paint.
- Use the paper as a giant class mural.
- Use the print as wrapping paper or book covers.

NOTES FOR NEXT TIME: _____

_____

_____

_____

PRINT MAKING

Print All Over—Body Part Prints

MATERIALS

- ☐ tempera paint
- ☐ large sheets of paper
- ☐ shallow pans
- ☐ old hand towels

💡 HELPFUL HINTS

- This is a great activity for outdoors! Outside, the children can rinse themselves in soapy water, hose off, and dry with old towels.

- Be prepared for prints that are a bit unusual—such as bottom prints. If you have prepared the children in old painting clothes, the unusual will not be a problem.

- This activity is appropriate for even very young artists, because it is simple and easy to do and understand.

DEVELOPMENTAL GOALS

Develop creativity, small motor development, and hand-eye coordination and explore a new print technique.

PREPARATION

If the children have done hand and foot prints, talk about the process. Discuss which other parts of the body the children can print with (e.g., nose, chin, knee, forearm).

Make a stamp pad by folding old hand towels into thirds. The towels should be about 7" × 14" with three layers. Soak each towel with tempera paint and place it in a cookie sheet or another shallow pan.

PROCESS

1. Press a body part on the pad and then on the paper.
2. Let the child make as many prints of as many body parts as desired.
3. Give child enough paper to make more if they are interested.

VARIATIONS

- Have several color stamp pads for multicolor body prints.
- Tape a long sheet of paper to the wall and print on it.
- Print on pieces of muslin.
- Use printed sheets for wrapping paper or for background on bulletin boards.

NOTES FOR NEXT TIME: _____

_____

_____

PRINT MAKING

Printing Stamps

 Years Old and Up

MATERIALS

- ☐ string
- ☐ glue
- ☐ block of wood
- ☐ paper
- ☐ thin mixture of tempera paint
- ☐ brush
- ☐ shallow container for paint

💡 HELPFUL HINTS

- String may be soaked in glue rather than drawn through it.
- Be sure the mixture of tempera is thin for this printing activity. You might want to start with a thicker mixture and test it with commercial stamps to ensure the proper consistency.
- Do not use string longer than 12 inches.

DEVELOPMENTAL GOALS

Develop creativity, small motor development, and hand-eye coordination; use familiar materials in new ways; learn the design concept of pattern.

PREPARATION

Discuss various kinds of stamps (e.g., stamps used to send letters, stamps for entry to a show). Discuss which kinds of designs and/or patterns the children could make as stamps.

PROCESS

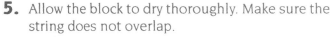

1. Cover one side of the wood block with a thin coat of glue.
2. Deposit a small amount of glue on a piece of cardboard and pull the string through the glue.
3. Give the string an even coat of glue.
4. Place the string in the glue on the block so it forms a design.
5. Allow the block to dry thoroughly. Make sure the string does not overlap.
6. Paint the string on the block.
7. Lay the printing paper over several thicknesses of newspaper.
8. Press the block on a scrap of paper to eliminate any excess paint.
9. Several prints can be made from the printing paper before applying more paint.

VARIATIONS

- Instead of painting the design, make a print by stamping on an ink pad.
- Make original stationery by stamping several sheets of paper with the stamp.
- Vary the colors of paint between printings. When one color runs dry after several prints, dip the stamp in another color for new prints.
- Make initialed stationery by stamping letters onto pieces of paper. Remember that the letters must be backward on the stamp to appear correctly on the print.

NOTES FOR NEXT TIME: _____

_____

PRINT MAKING

Recycled Puzzle Prints

3 Years Old and Up

MATERIALS

- ☐ old puzzle pieces
- ☐ white glue
- ☐ cereal box cardboard
- ☐ scissors
- ☐ tempera paint
- ☐ paintbrush
- ☐ paper
- ☐ construction paper

💡 HELPFUL HINTS

- Garage or yard sales are good sources of inexpensive puzzles. Also, ask friends to save puzzles with missing pieces.

- You may use a small trim paint roller and printer's ink instead of tempera paint. Water-based printing ink can be purchased from any art-supply store or educational-supply store. It can be used for any of the print-making activities in this book.

- If the tempera paint is too thin, thicken it with some regular household flour or even white glue.

DEVELOPMENTAL GOALS

Develop creativity, small motor development, and hand-eye coordination; use familiar objects in new ways; recycle puzzle pieces and learn the design concept of pattern.

PREPARATION

Talk about print making and how you can make several of the same image. Discuss what a pattern is—a repeat design. Talk about how patterns can be made of repeated lines of the same object (e.g., lines with alternating objects). Cut cereal boxes into pieces about 6" × 8".

PROCESS

1. Take several puzzle pieces and arrange them on the nonprinted side of the cereal box cardboard.
2. The pieces can be arranged to create a picture, a random design, or a pattern.
3. Once happy with the way the pieces look, glue them down and let the glue dry for an hour or so.
4. Use a paintbrush to cover the puzzle pieces with paint.
5. Lay a sheet of paper on top of the painted puzzle pieces.
6. Rub gently with the palm of the hand.
7. Peel off the paper to see the print.

VARIATIONS

- Repeat the process with a different color of ink. There may be some color mixing!
- Glue other objects to the puzzle print pattern, such as small twigs, beads, and cut-out pieces of Styrofoam. Repaint the design and print again.

NOTES FOR NEXT TIME: _____

_____

PRINT MAKING

Sandpaper Rubbings

MATERIALS

- ☐ different grades of sand paper
- ☐ scissors
- ☐ crayons
- ☐ paper
- ☐ tempera paint
- ☐ paintbrushes

💡 HELPFUL HINT

- Shapes can be torn from sandpaper if children do not yet use scissors.

DEVELOPMENTAL GOALS

Develop creativity, small motor development, and hand-eye coordination; use familiar materials in new ways; and learn the design concepts of line and pattern.

PREPARATION

Talk about the different textures of the sandpaper. Let the children feel each kind of sandpaper.

PROCESS

1. Cut the sandpaper into different shapes.

2. Put the paper over the sandpaper shape.

3. Color over the sandpaper with crayons.

4. Each grade of sandpaper will make a different texture.

VARIATIONS

- Paint over the sandpaper shape. Press it onto a piece of paper to make a print.

- Cut the sandpaper into letters.

- Make a sandpaper A. Do a crayon rubbing of it. Draw pictures of things that start with the letter A around the printed letter A. Repeat with other letters.

NOTES FOR NEXT TIME: _____

_____

_____

_____

PRINT MAKING

Spatter Prints on Fabric

MATERIALS

- ☐ washable fabric (e.g., old sheet, piece of burlap, or unbleached muslin)
- ☐ 1/4 cup liquid dye or 1/2 package of powdered dye in 1 pint of hot water
- ☐ bowls
- ☐ mixing spoon
- ☐ paintbrushes (or toothbrushes)
- ☐ craft sticks (or old combs)
- ☐ small, shallow containers (cut-down 1/2 pint milk containers work well)

💡 HELPFUL HINTS

- If the fabric is to be used as a covering, brush or spray on a protective coat of clear shellac.
- Do this in a well-ventilated area, preferably outdoors.
- Do not use spatter-dyed fabric for articles that directly contact other articles (e.g., pillow covers), because the dye may rub off.
- An adult should mix the dye.
- Mix a bit of liquid soap into the dye mixture to make clean up easier on the hands.

DEVELOPMENTAL GOALS

Develop creativity, small motor development, and hand-eye coordination and learn the design concept of pattern.

PREPARATION

Mix liquid or powdered dye. Put the dye mixture in the small, shallow containers.

PROCESS

1. Place the material on a flat surface with newspapers around the work area.
2. Dip a toothbrush or paintbrush in dye.
3. Run a comb or craft stick across the brush, making dye spatters.
4. Continue spattering a design onto the fabric.
5. Use two or three colors for interesting patterns.
6. Allow the fabric to dry.

VARIATIONS

- Use liquid tempera paint instead of dye if the fabric will not be washed.
- Spatter paint around cut-out construction paper designs.

NOTES FOR NEXT TIME: _____

_____

_____

PRINT MAKING

A

All Ages

Sponge Prints

MATERIALS

- ☐ sponges
- ☐ scissors
- ☐ liquid tempera paint in shallow container (aluminum pie tins work well)
- ☐ paper

 **HELPFUL HINTS**

- Some children may not want to get their fingers in the paint. Let them hold the sponge with a spring-type clothespin, then print.

- The younger the printer, the fewer the shapes required for printing. These children are at the stage where they are just learning the process. With fewer choices with which to print, they can better concentrate on the process.

DEVELOPMENTAL GOALS

Develop creativity, small motor development, and hand-eye coordination; use familiar objects in new ways; and learn the design concept of pattern.

PREPARATION

Cut sponges into a variety of sizes and shapes.

PROCESS

1. Dip the sponge pieces in tempera paint.
2. Apply the sponge to paper to print.
3. Continue printing to make an overall pattern.
4. Print one line of one shape, another line with a different shape.
5. Print in zigzag lines and vertical or horizontal lines.

VARIATIONS

- Soak the paper in water. Lay the wet paper on a smooth surface and remove all the wrinkles and excess water. Print on the moist paper for a softer, blurry-type print.
- Print with several different colors of paint.
- Print on different kinds of paper, such as tissue, construction paper, cardboard, and pieces of white gift boxes.

NOTES FOR NEXT TIME: _____

_____

_____

_____

PRINT MAKING

All Ages

Spray Prints

MATERIALS

☐ construction paper

☐ scissors

☐ large sheets of white construction paper

☐ spray bottles

☐ tempera paint

☐ small rocks to use as weights

 **HELPFUL HINTS**

• Plan an outdoor walk to gather the small stones to use as weights in this activity.

• Be sure you check that the spray bottle is not clogged before filling it with paint.

• Because the spray covers a wide area, the larger the sheet of paper the better for this activity.

DEVELOPMENTAL GOALS

Develop creativity, small motor development, and hand-eye coordination and learn the design concepts of pattern, shape, and placement.

PREPARATION

Mix a thin solution of tempera paint. Pour the paint into a plastic spray bottle. Set a small funnel over the spray bottle to make this easier to do.

PROCESS

1. Cut or tear shapes out of construction paper.

2. Arrange the cut-out shapes in some design or pattern over the sheet of white construction paper.

3. Weigh down the shapes with the small rocks.

4. Spray the tempera paint lightly over the shape design.

5. When the paint has dried, pick up the shapes to discover the designs underneath.

VARIATIONS

• Use crayons or markers to complete the design after the paint is dried.

• Use heavy-weight washers to hold down the shapes while spraying around them.

• Use different colors of construction paper for the background.

• Very young children enjoy just spraying paint without the shapes

• Use several colors of paint for spraying.

NOTES FOR NEXT TIME: _____

_____

All Ages

Stick Prints

MATERIALS

☐ small sticks, 2 to 3 inches long, of various sizes and shapes

☐ tempera paint

☐ brush

☐ paper

☐ pad of newspaper

💡 HELPFUL HINTS

- Beginning printers do not need to make drawings first. They can simply print with the stick in any fashion they choose.

- Go outdoors and have the children collect the sticks for this activity. It is much more fun than collecting them yourself!

- Older children may enjoy making mosaic effects with stick printing. This is done by leaving a narrow space of background paper between each print.

DEVELOPMENTAL GOALS

Develop creativity, small motor development, and hand-eye coordination and learn the design concepts of pattern and placement.

PREPARATION

Cut a number of sticks of different sizes and shapes, 2 or 3 inches long, making sure the ends are cut straight.

PROCESS

1. Make a light pencil drawing or design on paper.

2. Mix a small amount of paint on a piece of nonabsorbent scrap paper and smooth it with a brush to an even consistency.

3. Dip the stick in the paint.

4. Press the stick to a scrap of paper and print one or two images to remove any excess paint.

5. Press the stick to the drawing/design that has been placed on a pad of newspaper and repeat printing with the stick until the image becomes too light.

6. Repeat the process until the picture/design is complete.

VARIATIONS

- Things like jar lids and matchbox folders are also possible printing tools for this activity.

- Unusual patterns may be created by dipping the edges of any of the objects in paint.

- Interesting effects can be created by overlapping individual prints and colors.

- Try twisting the stick when printing for a different effect.

- Vary colors when printing with the stick.

- Use different shapes, colors, and kinds of paper.

- Use printing designs for wrapping paper, placemats, and box covers.

NOTES FOR NEXT TIME: _____

_____

PRINT MAKING

3 Years Old and Up

Styrofoam Tray Prints

MATERIALS

- ☐ Styrofoam tray
- ☐ tempera paint
- ☐ small paint rollers (the kind used for painting trim)
- ☐ rolling pin
- ☐ paper or fabric
- ☐ pen or pencil
- ☐ shallow container for paint

💡 HELPFUL HINTS

- This activity is appropriate for children whose small motor skills are developed enough to handle the print roller.

- Allow the children using the roller for the first time to practice using the roller on scrap paper. Some children may enjoy just using the roller itself!

- When using recycled Styrofoam trays, be sure to wash the trays in bleach before using them. Do not use Styrofoam trays that were used to hold meat.

DEVELOPMENTAL GOALS

Develop creativity, small motor development, hand-eye coordination and learn the design concepts of pattern, line, and size.

PREPARATION

Talk about how repeating a design makes a pattern. Discuss the types of designs the children might like to make. Explain that the idea of this activity is to create a design on the tray by indenting a pen or a pencil into the tray.

PROCESS

1. Give each child a Styrofoam tray.
2. Use a pen or a pencil to make a design in the Styrofoam. Press hard enough to dent the Styrofoam.
3. Remember that letters print reversed, so if the children want letters they must draw them backward.
4. After the design is complete, roll ink evenly onto the tray.
5. Place a piece of paper on the ink.
6. Use a rolling pin to help transfer the design onto the paper.
7. Carefully, lift the paper evenly. There is the print.

VARIATIONS

- Use different kinds of paper, such as brown wrapping paper, newsprint, construction paper, and classified ads.
- Use different colors of ink.

NOTES FOR NEXT TIME: _____

_____

_____

PRINT MAKING

Texture Prints

MATERIALS

- ☐ materials with interesting textures such as cardboard
- ☐ sandpaper
- ☐ bristle brushes
- ☐ wadded cloth
- ☐ burlap
- ☐ paper
- ☐ paint in small, shallow containers

HELPFUL HINTS

- With very young children, demonstrate the printing process initially (dip the object in paint, press the object onto the paper). Do this once and only once.

- Let the children experiment on their own from there.

- With beginning printers, it is generally best to use one color of paint. This allows the printers to concentrate on the process and avoid distraction by the number of colors.

DEVELOPMENTAL GOALS

Develop creativity, small motor development, hand-eye coordination and learn the design concept of pattern.

PREPARATION

Talk with the children about how things look and feel. Use the word *texture* in your discussion. Discuss the items collected for this activity and how each looks and feels.

PROCESS

1. Give each child a piece of paper and a shallow container filled with paint.

2. Challenge each child to print with as many differently textured items as they can.

3. Encourage the children to repeat prints to create patterns.

VARIATIONS

- Use different colors of paint with the same object.
- Use different objects with the same color of paint.
- Print in a zigzag pattern, a vertical line, and in a horizontal line. Alternate colors in any of these patterns.

NOTES FOR NEXT TIME: _____

_____

_____

Try These—Experiments with Color

MATERIALS

- ☐ paint
- ☐ printing objects
- ☐ paper (see following for specifics)

 **HELPFUL HINT**

- Recycled muffin tins work well using different consistencies of paint. Each muffin tin compartment can hold a different thickness or type of paint.

NOTES FOR
NEXT TIME:

_____

_____

_____

_____

_____

_____

DEVELOPMENTAL GOALS

To develop creativity, small motor development, and hand-eye coordination and learn the design concepts of pattern, tone, and contrast.

PREPARATION

First, read the following "Process" section. Then, prepare the paint and gather the kind of paper needed for the printing variation.

PROCESS

1. Alternate thin transparent watercolor with thick tempera paint when printing with objects.

2. Use a light color to print on dark paper or vice versa.

3. Use thin, transparent paint on colored paper or cloth so that the color of the background shows through.

4. Combine two objects of the same shape and size and use a different color for each.

5. Combine objects of different sizes and shapes, using a different color for each.

6. Vary the amount of paint used—heavier amounts make deeper colors, lesser amounts make lighter colors.

VARIATIONS

- Dip the object in two colors of paint and see how the colors mix.
- Use one of the preceding color variations on newspaper classified ads.
- Use printed paper for book covers for stories, poems, pictures, and notes.
- Use printed paper for place cards, gift wrapping, and gift-container covers.

Try These—Experiments with Pattern

3 Years Old and Up

MATERIALS

- [ ] paper
- [ ] printing objects of your choice
- [ ] paint in shallow containers

💡 HELPFUL HINTS

- Beginning printers will probably be able to do overall-pattern prints.
- Encourage experienced printers to create their own patterns.

NOTES FOR NEXT TIME:

_____

_____

_____

_____

_____

_____

_____

DEVELOPMENTAL GOALS

Develop creativity, small motor development, and hand-eye coordination and learn the design concept of pattern.

PREPARATION

Talk about pattern—how it is made by repeating a design. Give each child a large piece of paper, access to shallow containers of paint, and objects to print.

PROCESS

1. Suggest printing a design in the following ways.
2. Print a shape in straight rows or zigzags. Repeat the design to create an all-over pattern.
3. Use a different shape for each row and add a second color in alternate rows.
4. Group shapes in units of two or three and print a rhythmic design. Move shapes to alternate positions and print in a second color.
5. Print in a border design with one shape or group of shapes in a regular, repeated manner.

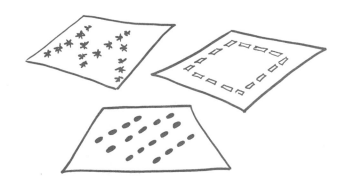

VARIATIONS

- Use different kinds of paper, such as cardboard, tissue and brown wrapping paper.
- Dip objects in one, then another color. See how the colors mix.
- Use the border prints for things like writing paper and place mats.

PRINT MAKING

Vegetable Prints

MATERIALS

- ☐ firm vegetables such as potatoes and carrots
- ☐ plastic knife
- ☐ shallow containers of paint
- ☐ paper for printing

💡 HELPFUL HINTS

- This is a good activity for vegetables that are getting old. Even limp vegetables are still good for printing. In fact, vegetables are easier to carve when they are not fresh.
- Encourage children to identify different vegetables for print making. How about rutabaga or turnips?

DEVELOPMENTAL GOALS

Develop creativity, small motor development, and hand-eye coordination and learn the design concepts of pattern and line.

PREPARATION

Carve a simple design into the vegetable by notching the edges or carving holes with a small, plastic knife. Talk about pattern with the children. Discuss how a pattern has the same object repeated in different lines.

PROCESS

1. Give each child a potato for printing.
2. Let older children carve the potato for printing.
3. For younger children, carve a simple design in the potato.
4. Dip the potato in the paint.
5. Press the potato onto paper to make a print.
6. Encourage the children to make patterns by printing lines, swirls, zigzags, and so on.

VARIATIONS

- Instead of food, carve out pieces of packaging Styrofoam for this activity.
- Have several colors of paint with which to print.
- Use different kinds of paper to print on, such as newspaper want ads, cardboard pieces, and brown wrapping paper.
- Use the print to wrap gifts for parents and friends.

NOTES FOR NEXT TIME: _____

_____

_____

_____

Weed Prints

MATERIALS

- ☐ a variety of weeds
- ☐ paper
- ☐ tempera paint in shallow containers.

HELPFUL HINTS

- If the weeds get too dry, they will not print as well.
- Be sure children do not have allergies to any of the weeds used in this activity.

DEVELOPMENTAL GOALS

Develop creativity, small motor development, and hand-eye coordination and appreciate pattern and beauty in nature.

PREPARATION

Go on a walk and collect weeds for printing. Weeds in flower (e.g., golden-rod, Queen Anne's lace) generally work best.

PROCESS

1. Give each child a piece of paper.
2. Dip the top (flowering part) into paint.
3. Press the weed onto the paper.
4. Continue dipping and printing with the weeds until a design and/or pattern emerges.

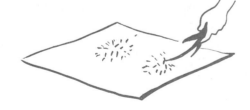

VARIATION

- Print with other natural objects, such as small stones and twigs added to the printed weed design.

NOTES FOR NEXT TIME: _____

_____

_____

PRINT MAKING

What Can It Be?

MATERIALS

- ☐ long pieces of newsprint paper (18" × 24") (or classified ads from the newspaper)
- ☐ tempera paint in shallow pan (cookie sheets work well)
- ☐ crayons
- ☐ markers
- ☐ pail of soapy water
- ☐ paper towels

💡 HELPFUL HINTS

- Toddlers will enjoy the simple process of printing without making prints.
- The more foot and hand prints, the more chances for creating.
- This is a fun activity to do outdoors where there are fewer worries about mess and cleanup.

DEVELOPMENTAL GOALS

Develop creativity, small motor development, and hand-eye coordination and create designs from foot and hand prints.

PREPARATION

Cover the floor by taping down newspapers. Tape long sheets of paper onto newspapers.

PROCESS

1. Have the child step into a pan of paint and put the hands in the paint.
2. Step out of the paint onto the paper to make foot and hand prints.
3. Let the prints dry completely.
4. Using crayons and markers, use the foot and hand prints to make a design or any kind of original creation.
5. Give the children some ideas to get them started (e.g., foot "people," hand "trees," foot "animals").

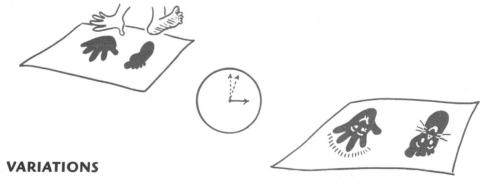

VARIATIONS

- Use other body parts to make prints, like elbows, forearms, and knees. Make designs and pictures with these prints.
- For children who do not want to get messy, trace around the children's shoes onto pieces of paper. Then, let the children use crayons or markers to make anything they choose.

NOTES FOR NEXT TIME: _____

_____

PRINT MAKING

A

All Ages

Wheelies!

MATERIALS

- ☐ liquid tempera paint
- ☐ liquid starch
- ☐ cookie sheet or tray with sides
- ☐ paintbrush for mixing
- ☐ small wheel toys (cars, trucks, etc.)
- ☐ large sheets of paper

 **HELPFUL HINT**

- This activity inspires even the most reluctant artists. It is fun, messy, and uses toys that are familiar to most children.

DEVELOPMENTAL GOALS

Develop creativity, small motor development, and hand-eye coordination and use familiar materials in new ways.

PREPARATION

Pour a big glob of liquid starch onto the cookie sheet or tray. Put a big spoonful of paint in the starch glob. Mix the paint and starch with a paintbrush.

PROCESS

1. Have the child choose a small wheel toy.
2. Roll the toy through the paint.
3. Drive the car over a piece of paper, making designs and tracks.
4. Use other wheel toys to roll through the paint and over the paper.
5. Let the painting dry completely.

VARIATIONS

- Use different colors of paint in the tray. This way colors will mix both in the tray and on the paper.
- Have the children bring small wheel toys from home for this activity.
- Use a stamp pad to wheel over. Then, roll the wheel onto the paper.
- Tape paper to the wall near the floor and paint source. Wheel the paint-dipped toy up and down on the paper.

NOTES FOR NEXT TIME: _____

_____

_____

_____

PRINT MAKING

Wood-Block and String Prints

MATERIALS

- ☐ wooden block
- ☐ string
- ☐ paste or glue
- ☐ paper
- ☐ tempera paint
- ☐ brush

 **HELPFUL HINT**

- Make the first print on scrap paper to eliminate any excess paint.

NOTES FOR
NEXT TIME:

_____

_____

_____

_____

DEVELOPMENTAL GOALS

Develop creativity, small motor development, and hand-eye coordination and learn the design concepts of pattern and repeated images.

PREPARATION

Discuss which designs children would like to make. Explain that these designs will be made with string.

PROCESS

1. Coat the entire length of the string with paste or glue.

2. While the string is still wet, wrap it around the wooden block to form a design.

3. Place a small amount of tempera paint on a piece of scrap paper, and smooth it with a brush to an even consistency.

4. Choose the side of the string-wrapped block that has the most pleasing design.

5. Dip that side into the paint, or apply the paint to the string with a brush.

6. Lift the block from the paint, and press it against the paper with some pressure.

7. Several prints can be made before applying more paint.

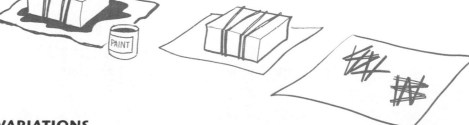

VARIATIONS

- Make all-over patterns by alternating the sides of the block in printing.
- Make wrapping paper using wood-block and string printing.
- Use different colors of paint.

Yarn Prints

MATERIALS

- ☐ yarn
- ☐ glue
- ☐ scissors
- ☐ cardboard or oaktag
- ☐ paper
- ☐ tempera paint
- ☐ crayons

💡 HELPFUL HINTS

- The thicker the yarn, the better the print.
- Thin the glue with a little water so it runs easily from the container.

NOTES FOR NEXT TIME:

_____

_____

_____

_____

DEVELOPMENTAL GOALS

Develop creativity, small motor development, and hand-eye coordination; use familiar materials in new ways and learn the design concepts of pattern and line.

PREPARATION

Talk about how designs can be repeated to make patterns. Discuss how lines can be zigzag, horizontal, vertical, and so on.

PROCESS

1. Use crayons to draw a pattern, design, or picture on the cardboard.
2. Outline parts or all of the picture with glue.
3. Apply glue to the yarn.
4. Let the yarn and glue dry thoroughly.
5. Brush tempera paint over the picture.
6. Place another piece of paper over the picture.
7. Press lightly with the palm of the hand.
8. Peel off the paper to see the string print!

VARIATIONS

- Use thinner yarn, string, or even rope to outline the design.
- Draw a simple object with crayons onto a square piece of cardboard about 4" × 4". Glue yarn around the object. Let it dry. Print with it on paper to make original stationery.

PRINT MAKING

Index by Ages

PART VI

Paper Art

Fun with Paper Art

Welcome to the world of paper art! You will see from the activities in this book that paper is more than just an art material. It is an art form.

Traditional forms of paper, like construction paper and tissue paper, are used in many of the activities in this book, but included are activities using such recyclables as paper-towel and toilet-tissue paper rolls, paper plates, paper bags, packaging materials, cardboard, and cereal boxes. Once you start using the activities, you will be encouraged to find many other unique uses for paper in other activities.

The activities in this book are designed for children aged 2 through 8. An icon representing a suggested age for the activity is listed at the top of each activity. However, use your knowledge of the child's abilities to guide you in choosing and using the activities in this book. Wherever appropriate, information is provided on how to adapt the activity for children over age 8.

The focus of this book is a creative approach to using paper in art activities. The activities are meant to be a starting point for exploring this art form. Both you and the children are encouraged to explore, experiment, and enjoy the world of paper art!

GETTING STARTED

Process vs. Product

The focus of this book and all early childhood art activities is the process, not the product. This means that the process of creating, not the product, is the main reason for the activity. The joys of creating, exploring materials, and discovering how things look and work are all part of the creative process. How the product looks, what it is "supposed to be," is unimportant to the child, and it should be unimportant to the adult.

Young children delight in the experience, the exploration, and the experimentation of art activities. The adult's role is to provide interesting materials and an environment that encourages children's creativity. Stand back when you are tempted to "help" children with their artwork. Instead, encourage all children to discover their own unique abilities.

Considering the Child

Young children find it hard to wait patiently to use materials in an activity. Often, the excitement of creativity and patience do not mix. In addition, it is sometimes difficult for young children to share. With young children, plan to have enough materials for each child. For example, having a dab of paste on a small piece of wax paper for each child to use makes the process of pasting more fun and relaxed for young children.

Gathering Materials

Each activity in this book includes a list of required materials. It is important to gather all the materials before starting the activity with children. Children's creative experiences are easily discouraged when they must sit and wait while the adult looks for tape, extra scissors, or colored paper. Be sure to gather the materials in a place the children can easily access.

Storing and Making Materials Available

Having the appropriate materials for paper art is not enough. These materials must be stored and readily accessible to the children. For example, a basket jumbling together such paper-art materials as crayons, markers, and chalk is not ideal storage. Instead, use boxes to assemble these materials so that each child has an individual, complete set. In addition to enhancing creativity and organization, this system cuts down on arguments and means that all materials are available to each child when those materials are needed. A recycled muffin tin works well for storing the small pieces used in paper-art activities, such as buttons and pom-poms. A fishing box with multiple compartments also works well for this purpose.

Another approach is to store paper-art materials in a clear-plastic box that is shallow enough to be easily searched. Some teachers find clear-plastic shoeboxes invaluable for storing children's paper-art materials. For example, use one box for fabric scraps, another for trim scraps, and another for colorful yarn pieces. These clear-plastic boxes, available at economy stores, are great for storing and stacking all kinds of art materials.

Be creative when thinking about storing and making available art materials for your little artists. Storing supplies in handy boxes and other containers makes creating art, and cleaning up after, more fun. See Figure 1 for more storage ideas.

Employing Safe Materials

For all activities in this book and for any art activities for young children, be sure to use safe art supplies. Read labels on all art materials. Check materials for age appropriateness. The Art and Creative Materials Institute (ACMI) labels art materials AP (approved product) and CL (certified label). Products with these labels are certified safe for use by young children.

The ACMI provides an extensive list of materials and manufacturers of safe materials for all young children. This information is available on the ACMI Web site at http://www.acminet.org or by writing to 715 Boylston Street, Boston, MA 02116.

Some basic safety hints for art activities are:

- Always use products that are appropriate for the child. Use nontoxic materials for children in Grades 6 and lower.
- Never use products for skin painting or food preparation unless the products are intended for those uses.
- Do not transfer art materials to other containers. You will lose the valuable safety information on the product packages.
- Do not eat or drink while using art and craft materials. Wash after use. Clean yourself and your supplies.
- Be sure that your work area is well ventilated.

FIGURE 1 · TIPS FOR STORING ART MATERIALS

The ways materials, supplies, and space are arranged can make or break children's and teachers' art experiences. Following are suggestions for arranging supplies for art experiences:

1. *Scissor holders*. Holders can be made from gallon milk or bleach containers. Simply punch holes in the containers and place scissors in the holes with the scissor points to the inside. Egg cartons turned upside down with slits in each mound also make excellent holders.

2. *Paint containers*. Containers can range from muffin tins and plastic egg cartons to plastic soft-drink cartons with baby food jars in them. These work especially well outdoors as well as indoors, because they are large and not easily tipped. Place one brush in each container. This prevents colors from mixing and makes cleanup easier.

3. *Crayon containers*. Juice and vegetable cans painted or covered with contact paper work very well.

4. Crayon pieces may be melted in muffin trays in a warm oven. These pieces, when cooled, are nice for rubbings or drawings. Crayola® makes a unit that is designed specifically for melting crayons safely.

5. Printing with tempera is easier if the tray is lined with a sponge or a paper towel.

6. A card file for art activities helps organize the program.

7. *Clay containers*. Airtight coffee cans and plastic food containers are excellent ways to keep clay moist and always ready for use.

8. *Paper scrap boxes*. By keeping two or more boxes of scrap paper of different sizes, children will be able to choose the size paper they want more easily.

9. Cover a wall area with pegboard and suspend heavy shopping bags or transparent plastic bags from hooks inserted in the pegboard to hold miscellaneous art supplies. Hang smocks in the same way on the pegboard (at child level, of course).

10. Use the back of a piano or bookcase to hang a shoe bag. Its pockets can hold many small items.

11. Use divided frozen food trays or a revolving lazy Susan to hold miscellaneous small items.

(From Mayesky, Mary. *Creative Activities for Young Children*, 7th ed., Clifton Park, NY: Delmar Learning)

Potentially unsafe paper-art supplies include:

- *Epoxy, instant glues, or other solvent-based glues.* Use only water-based white glue.

- *Paints that require solvents like turpentine to clean.* Use only water-based paints.

- *Cold water or commercial dyes that contain chemical additives.* Use only natural vegetable dyes made from beets, onion skins, and so on.

- *Permanent markers.* Permanent markers may contain toxic solvents. Use only water-based markers.

Be aware of all children's allergies. Children with allergies to wheat, for example, may be irritated by the wheat paste used in papier-mâché. Other art materials that may cause allergic reactions include chalk or other dusty substances, water-based clay, and any material that contains petroleum products.

Also be aware of children's habits. Some young children put everything in their mouths. (This can be the case at any age.) Others may be shy and slow to accept new materials. Use your knowledge of children's tendencies to help you plan art activities that are safe for all children.

Creating a Child-Friendly Environment

It is difficult to be creative when you have to worry about keeping yourself and your work area clean. Cover all work areas with newspaper. It is best to tape the newspaper to the work surface to prevent paint or other materials from seeping through the spaces. In addition, it is much easier to pick up and throw away paint-spattered newspaper than it is to clean a stained tabletop! Other coverups that work well are shower curtains and plastic tablecloths.

Remember to cover the children, too! Some good child coverups are men's shirts (with the sleeves cut off), aprons, pillowcases with holes cut for the head and arms, and smocks. Some fun alternatives are sets of old clothes or shoes that can be worn as "art clothes." These old clothes could become "art journals" as they became covered with the traces of various art projects.

Creating a Child's Art Environment

Encourage young artists by displaying appropriate art prints and other works of art. Do not make the mistake of thinking young children do not enjoy "grownup art." Children are never too young to enjoy the colors, lines, patterns, and designs of artists' work. Art posters from a local museum, for example, can brighten the art area. Such posters also get children looking at and talking about art, which encourages the children's creative work.

Display pieces of pottery, shells and rocks, and other beautiful objects from nature to encourage children's appreciation of the lines, symmetries, and colors of nature. Even the youngest child can enjoy the look and feel of smooth, colored rocks or the colors of fall leaves. All these are natural parts of a child's world that can be talked about with young children as those children create artwork. Beautiful objects encourage creativity.

Starting to Collect

The more exciting "extras" you can collect, the more fun the paper-art activities in this book will be for the children. Ask parents and other community members for help in gathering art materials. Send a list of needed materials home with the children, or post the list on the classroom door. Following are some of the materials you can start collecting for paper artwork. You will probably think of more items as you progress.

Paper scraps
Fabric scraps
Wallpaper scraps
Rickrack and other sewing trims
Buttons
Pom-poms
Styrofoam "worms"
Junk mail
Sequins
Feathers
Straws
Popsicle sticks
Tissue paper
Wrapping paper
Ribbon
Corrugated cardboard
Recycled gift boxes

A Group Collage Made for Touching

MATERIALS

- ☐ sandpaper
- ☐ flannel
- ☐ velvet
- ☐ burlap
- ☐ cardboard
- ☐ glue
- ☐ plastic wrap
- ☐ large piece of cardboard for backing

 **HELPFUL HINT**

- Use this activity to encourage the use of vocabulary-expanding words (e.g., *coarse, smooth*).

DEVELOPMENTAL GOALS

Develop creativity, small motor development, and hand-eye coordination and explore group collage techniques.

PREPARATION

Discuss the textures of the materials gathered for this activity. Talk about how they look and feel. Use words such as *bumpy, smooth*, and *prickly* to develop the child's vocabulary of texture words.

PROCESS

1. Each child in the group chooses pieces of textured paper and cloth.
2. Have the children place pieces on the cardboard base.
3. Allow the children time to arrange and rearrange pieces until they are satisfied.
4. Have the children glue down the pieces to make the finished texture collage.

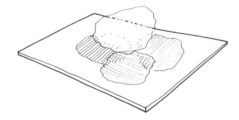 

VARIATIONS

- Have the children bring in materials of different textures to glue on the board.
- Once the collage is complete, the children can make "rubbings," using colored chalk on newsprint paper.

NOTES FOR NEXT TIME: _____

_____

_____

_____

Beginning Collages

MATERIALS

- ☐ paper of various kinds (e.g., construction, wallpaper, giftwrap, metallic paper, tissue paper, newspaper, colored magazine pages)
- ☐ paste
- ☐ scissors (optional)
- ☐ crayons
- ☐ markers

💡 HELPFUL HINTS

- A collage is a good activity for young preschoolers, as it can be completed quickly and is within the interest span of most young preschoolers. As the children paste together a collage, talk about the feel, shape, and color of the many things the children paste.

- Young children tend to taste the paste as they work. This is natural for this age group. This is also why you need to be sure to always use non-toxic materials!

DEVELOPMENTAL GOALS

Develop creativity, small motor development, and hand-eye coordination; explore a new use for a variety of papers; and learn about the design concepts of pattern, placement, size, and shape.

PREPARATION

Talk about what a collage is—a picture made of torn/cut pieces of paper. The word *collage* means "to paste" in French. A collage may be a design or a picture. Talk about how things may be placed in different places on the paper. Use the words *center*, *side*, *top*, and *bottom* when talking about placement.

PROCESS

1. Give the children pieces of various kinds of paper that tears easily.

2. Show the children, if necessary, how to tear large and small pieces.

3. Paste these torn pieces on colored construction paper in any way the children prefer.

4. Add details with crayons or markers.

VARIATIONS

- Have scissors available for children who want to try cutting the pieces to paste on the collage.

- Provide different materials for the backing of the collage, such as cardboard, shoebox lids, or pieces of burlap.

- Add different materials to the collage. Some good things to add are large buttons, bits of cloth and paper in different colors, textures and shapes, and bottle caps.

NOTES FOR NEXT TIME: _____

_____

PAPER ART

Box-Lid Collages

MATERIALS

- ☐ box lids
- ☐ paste
- ☐ construction paper
- ☐ fabric and trim scraps
- ☐ buttons
- ☐ seeds
- ☐ tissue paper

HELPFUL HINTS

- When working with beginners, limit the number of collage materials; this lessens confusion.

- Encourage the children to use materials in their own ways. Instead of giving exact directions, suggest ways of selecting materials for variety of shape, size, color, and texture.

DEVELOPMENTAL GOALS

Develop creativity, small motor development, and hand-eye coordination and explore a new use for recycled box lids.

PREPARATION

Talk about collages. Discuss how things can be arranged in many different ways. Talk about the shapes, sizes, and colors of materials collected for this activity.

PROCESS

1. Give each child a box lid.
2. Have the children arrange and rearrange materials in the box lid.
3. The children may form a picture or compose an abstract design.
4. When the child is satisfied with the arrangement, have the child glue the items in the box lid.

VARIATIONS

- Create three-dimensional effects by crumpling flat pieces of material and attaching them to the background in two or three places.
- Other techniques include overlapping, bending, folding, rolling, curling, and twisting paper.
- Create a nature collage using all natural materials.
- Make a paper or cloth collage, exploring a variety of one kind of material.
- Make a collage with leaves, buttons, or one kind of material children enjoy.

NOTES FOR NEXT TIME: _____

_____

_____

PAPER ART

Cardboard Puzzles

MATERIALS

- ☐ paper
- ☐ pieces of cardboard
- ☐ paste
- ☐ scissors
- ☐ crayons
- ☐ markers
- ☐ paint
- ☐ brushes

💡 HELPFUL HINTS

- This activity is most appropriate for children able to use scissors.

- For children unable to use scissors, an adult will need to cut the puzzle pieces.

DEVELOPMENTAL GOALS

Develop creativity, small motor development, and hand-eye coordination; explore a new use for cardboard; and practice putting patterns together.

PREPARATION

Discuss the puzzles children play with and how the children can learn to make their own puzzles.

PROCESS

1. Have the child make a drawing or painting on the desired size of paper.

2. Paste the picture to a piece of cardboard.

3. Press the picture under books or other flat heavy objects until dry.

4. When dry, cut into odd shapes.

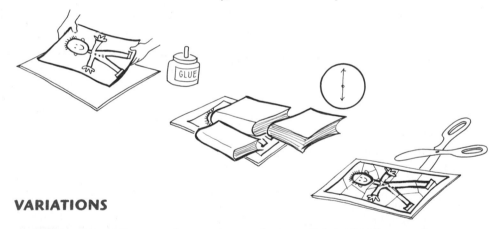

VARIATIONS

- Make a decorative envelope or paper-bag container for the puzzle.

- For scissoring practice, glue a magazine picture to a piece of cardboard. After the cardboard is dry, draw black marker lines for the child to cut into puzzle pieces.

NOTES FOR NEXT TIME: _____

_____

_____

_____

PAPER ART

Colored-Magazine-Page Art

A All Ages

MATERIALS

- ☐ old magazines with colored pictures
- ☐ scissors (optional)
- ☐ paste
- ☐ construction paper
- ☐ crayons
- ☐ markers

HELPFUL HINTS

- Encourage the children to think creatively by talking about the shapes as the children tear (or cut) them. "What do you think this could be?" "Isn't this an interesting shape?" "How can you arrange the shapes?"

- Toddlers enjoy the simple act of tearing pieces from magazines. They can be encouraged to paste these pieces onto a sheet of paper

DEVELOPMENTAL GOALS

Develop creativity, small motor development, and hand-eye coordination and explore a new use for magazine pages.

PREPARATION

The children cut or tear shapes from colored pictures from shiny-page magazines.

PROCESS

1. Have the child glue the shapes to a piece of colored construction paper.

2. Details may be added to the shapes.

3. The background may be colored in.

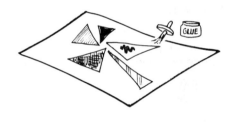

VARIATIONS

- Round shapes can become flowers with stems and leaves colored in.
- Triangles and rectangles can become buildings or houses using markers for details.
- Shapes can be animals, real or imagined, with details colored in.

NOTES FOR NEXT TIME: _____

_____

_____

_____

PAPER ART

Construction-Paper Buildings

MATERIALS

- ☐ construction paper
- ☐ crayons
- ☐ markers
- ☐ tape
- ☐ stapler and staples
- ☐ markers

HELPFUL HINT

- This activity is suitable for children with small motor skills developed enough to roll construction paper into shapes.

DEVELOPMENTAL GOALS

Develop creativity, small motor development, and hand-eye coordination and explore a new use for construction paper.

PREPARATION

Discuss types of buildings with the children, such as houses, barns, silos, and apartment buildings. Talk about the shapes, colors, and details on these buildings.

PROCESS

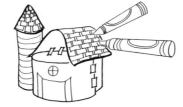

1. Give each child a supply of colored construction paper.
2. Roll paper and tape on the ends for round shaped buildings.
3. Fold paper for roofs.
4. Tape four pieces of paper to make square or rectangular buildings.
5. Add such details as windows and doors with crayons, markers, or paint.

VARIATIONS

- Add cut-paper windows and doors, chimneys, and balconies.
- Make several buildings to create a city, small town, or farm.
- Store windows can have merchandise painted on, cut out or made and set behind cellophane window panes.

NOTES FOR NEXT TIME: _____

_____

_____

PAPER ART

Construction-Paper Characters

MATERIALS

- ☐ construction paper
- ☐ tape
- ☐ glue
- ☐ scissors
- ☐ crayons
- ☐ markers
- ☐ tempera paint
- ☐ brushes
- ☐ yarn
- ☐ buttons
- ☐ pieces of trim, fabric scraps

💡 HELPFUL HINTS

- Younger children may find it easier to add details with markers.
- Some children may need help taping the construction-paper ends together.

DEVELOPMENTAL GOALS

Develop creativity, small motor development, and hand-eye coordination and explore a new use for construction paper.

PREPARATION

Talk about the people who are important in the child's life. Talk about those people's sizes, shapes, and other characteristics. Think about these things when making the construction-paper creations.

PROCESS

1. Form the body by rolling the paper into a tube and taping it on the ends.
2. The tube is both the body and the head of the person.
3. Cut-out feet from construction paper can be taped on the bottom of the tube.
4. Glue on features made of pieces of construction paper.
5. Glue on yarn or pieces of construction paper for hair.
6. Add fabric or trim scraps for clothing details.
7. Features can be drawn on with crayons, markers, or paint.

VARIATIONS

- Make a family of construction-paper characters.
- Older children may want to make favorite characters from storybooks.
- Famous characters from history make good topics for older children.

NOTES FOR NEXT TIME: _____

_____

_____

_____

Corrugated-Cardboard Designs

MATERIALS

- ☐ pieces of colored construction paper
- ☐ corrugated cardboard
- ☐ paste
- ☐ tempera paint
- ☐ brushes
- ☐ markers
- ☐ crayons

💡 HELPFUL HINTS

- Collect pieces of packaging cardboard. This material does not have the top layer of paper and can be used as is.

- Save cardboard boxes. Cut up into small, sheet-sized pieces to use in this activity. The sheets need not be cut perfectly—Irregular shapes are more interesting!

DEVELOPMENTAL GOALS

Develop creativity, small motor development, and hand-eye coordination and explore a new use for cardboard.

PREPARATION

Tear off the top lining of paper on the cardboard to uncover the lined side of the cardboard.

PROCESS

1. Give each child a piece of cardboard.

2. Have the child draw a picture or design on the cardboard using crayons, markers, or paint.

3. Add pieces of construction paper to the design.

VARIATIONS

- Older children may enjoy cutting out pieces of cardboard to make a collage of cardboard shapes.

- Interesting effects are created by painting directly on the corrugated cardboard. Try painting in the ridges, on the ridges, or across the ridges.

- Use one color inside the ridges and another on the ridges.

- Use the cardboard design in a printing activity. Brush a thin coat of tempera paint onto the design. Place another piece of paper over the cardboard and rub with the hand to get a print of the design.

NOTES FOR NEXT TIME: _____

_____

_____

_____

PAPER ART

Creative Bird Binoculars

MATERIALS

- ☐ two paper rolls (about 4" to 5" long) per child
- ☐ single-hole punch
- ☐ glue
- ☐ yarn or string
- ☐ crayons
- ☐ markers
- ☐ stickers

💡 HELPFUL HINTS

- Have books about birds available while children are decorating their paper rolls.
- Talk about the colors and specific markings of birds in the pictures.
- Older children can keep journals on the birds they see.
- Older children can make graphs showing how many times each type of bird is seen.

DEVELOPMENTAL GOALS

Develop creativity, small motor development, and hand-eye coordination and explore a new use for paper tubes.

PREPARATION

Give each child two paper rolls and have them decorate them with crayons, markers, and stickers.

PROCESS

1. Have the child glue the two paper rolls together.
2. Help the child put a hole in each side of the binoculars.
3. Tie the ribbon/yarn through the holes.
4. Send the children outside to look for birds through their creative binoculars.
5. Talk about the birds the children see with their binoculars.

VARIATIONS

- Use one paper roll as a telescope for viewing the birds.
- Encourage the children to draw or paint pictures of the birds they saw with their binoculars.

NOTES FOR NEXT TIME: _____

_____

_____

PAPER ART

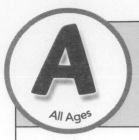

All Ages

Crumpled-Paper Designs

MATERIALS

- ☐ colored tissue
- ☐ colored comics from the newspaper
- ☐ paste
- ☐ construction paper

 **HELPFUL HINT**

- Have the children tear the tissue and/or colored comics into small pieces. It is a great exercise for the small muscles in the hands and fingers.

DEVELOPMENTAL GOALS

Develop creativity, small motor development, and hand-eye coordination and explore a new use for tissue paper.

PREPARATION

Tear the tissue or colored newspaper into small pieces.

PROCESS

1. Crumple the colored tissue or colored comics into small wads.
2. Dip the wads into paste.
3. Paste the wads to colored construction paper.

 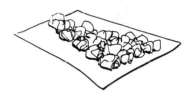

VARIATIONS

- A group of children might want to work together to make a cooperative collage for the room.
- Fill an outlined shape with crumpled paper wads.
- Draw a picture and fill sections of it with these colorful wads.

NOTES FOR NEXT TIME: _____

_____

_____

_____

Cupcake-Liner Art

MATERIALS

- ☐ cupcake liners (large and small)
- ☐ construction paper
- ☐ white paper plates
- ☐ scraps of fabric and trim
- ☐ buttons
- ☐ paste
- ☐ crayons
- ☐ markers

💡 HELPFUL HINT

- Very young children will enjoy the gluing more than the decorating process. You will need fewer additional materials for this age group in this activity.

DEVELOPMENTAL GOALS

Develop creativity, small motor development, and hand-eye coordination and explore a new use for cupcake liners.

PREPARATION

Discuss flowers with the children. Talk about such details as color, size, and shape. Talk about other things in nature, such as trees, bushes, and weeds.

PROCESS

1. Decorate the cupcake liners with markers and crayons.
2. Glue the cupcake liners to a piece of construction paper or a paper plate.
3. Glue on such details as buttons and fabric and trim scraps.
4. Draw stems with crayons and markers.
5. Add more background details with crayons and markers.

VARIATIONS

- Paper plates decorated with cup cake liner flowers can be made into hats. Punch holes in either side of the paper plate. Tie a ribbon or piece of yarn into each hole.
- Spread glue on some flowers and sprinkle glitter onto the glue for a fun and shiny effect.
- Glue on twigs or pipe cleaners for flower stems.

NOTES FOR NEXT TIME: _____

_____

_____

_____

PAPER ART

Cut or Torn Paper Snowflakes

MATERIALS

- ☐ foil paper
- ☐ tracing paper
- ☐ poster paper
- ☐ construction, or any decorative wrapping paper
- ☐ scissors

💡 HELPFUL HINTS

- This activity is most appropriate for children who can use scissors easily.

- Children just beginning to use scissors will be able to cut a few notches along the two folded edges. As they grow in scissoring skills, they will be able to cut more notches.

- Snowflakes can be made by tearing holes into the folded paper. This way, children who are not yet adept at using scissors can still partici-pate in this activity.

DEVELOPMENTAL GOALS

Develop creativity, small motor development, and hand-eye coordination and explore new ways to cut paper.

PREPARATION

Cut the paper into squares of many sizes.

PROCESS

1. Fold the squares in half, then in half again, making a smaller square.

2. Fold the square to make a triangle.

3. Keep in mind where the center of the paper is. Mark it with a crayon.

4. Cut a V into the open edges to get the points of the snowflakes.

5. Cut notches of different sizes along the two folded edges.

6. The more pieces that are cut out, the fancier the snowflake.

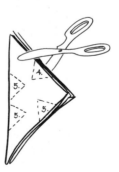

VARIATIONS

- Make mobiles with several snowflakes.
- Decorate windows with snowflakes.

NOTES FOR NEXT TIME: _____

_____

_____

_____

PAPER ART

Cutting-Paper Fun—Spirals

5 Years Old and UP

MATERIALS

- ☐ colored paper
- ☐ scissors
- ☐ pencil

💡 HELPFUL HINTS

- This is a good activity for children learning to use scissors. The farther apart the lines, the easier the paper is to cut.

- For children more adept at scissoring, draw the lines closer together to make this activity more of a challenge.

DEVELOPMENTAL GOALS

Develop creativity, small motor development, and hand-eye coordination and explore new ways to use paper and scissors.

PREPARATION

Be sure the children have blunt-tipped scissors for this activity. Practice cutting paper with scissors, if necessary.

PROCESS

1. Cut colored paper into a large circle. (Use a plate to trace a circle onto the paper and cut around the traced lines.)

2. Draw lines in a spiral formation on the round sheet of paper.

3. Cut along the lines from the outside edge of the circle toward the center.

4. When all the lines have been cut, you have a dangling spiral of paper.

VARIATIONS

- Let the children draw the lines on the paper.
- Use foil or metallic paper for a shiny, interesting, spiral decoration.
- Cut two spirals and glue them together at their widest ends. Hang a pinecone, a cut-paper decoration, or another object through the center.
- Make a picture or a design on the paper before cutting it for a colorful spiral.
- Add glitter to the picture or design before cutting it for a sparkly spiral.

NOTES FOR NEXT TIME: _____

_____

_____

PAPER ART

Cutting-Paper Fun—Squares and Triangles

MATERIALS

- ☐ colored paper
- ☐ scissors
- ☐ pencil

💡 HELPFUL HINTS

- Triangles and squares may be difficult for children just beginning to use scissors.

- Draw lines farther apart for easier cutting. To make cutting more of a challenge, draw the lines closer together.

DEVELOPMENTAL GOALS

Develop creativity, small motor development, and hand-eye coordination and explore a new use for scissors and paper.

PREPARATION

Be sure children use blunt-tipped scissors for this exercise. Give the children time to practice cutting with scissors before starting the activity if they feel the need.

PROCESS

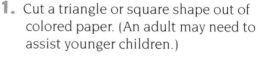

1. Cut a triangle or square shape out of colored paper. (An adult may need to assist younger children.)

2. Draw a series of lines from the outside toward the center of the square or triangle.

3. Cut along the lines from the outside edge toward the center.

4. When all the lines have been cut, you have a dangling triangle or square.

VARIATIONS

- Use foil or metallic paper for a different effect. You will need to use markers to draw on the lines.

- Draw a picture or design on the paper before drawing the lines to cut along.

- Apply glue to parts of the picture or design. Sprinkle on glitter for a sparkly effect.

- Let the children draw the lines on the paper.

NOTES FOR NEXT TIME: _____

_____

_____

_____

PAPER ART

344 PAPER ART

Dioramas

MATERIALS

- ☐ shallow boxes
- ☐ markers
- ☐ crayons
- ☐ paint
- ☐ paintbrushes
- ☐ construction paper
- ☐ glue
- ☐ tape
- ☐ stapler and staples
- ☐ pipe cleaners
- ☐ straws
- ☐ clay or play dough

☼ HELPFUL HINTS

- Child-sized shoe-boxes are great for making dioramas. The boxes should be relatively shallow, as deep boxes are difficult to manipulate.

- This activity is suitable for children with small motor skills developed enough that they can do the taping and gluing that are parts of this activity.

DEVELOPMENTAL GOALS

Develop creativity, small motor development, and hand-eye coordination; learn about dioramas; and explore a new use for recycled boxes.

PREPARATION

Talk about what a diorama is—a three-dimensional display in a box. Discuss which scenes the children would like to display in the box. Talk about the things, people, animals, plants, and so on that would be in the scene.

PROCESS

1. Give each child a box.
2. Draw or paint a background in the bottom of the box, or use cut-paper objects for the background.
3. Paper or cardboard figures can be made to stand by folding the lower part for a base.
4. Make other figures with pipe cleaners or straws.
5. Smaller objects can be made of clay or play dough.
6. The children should experiment with the arrangement of the objects before fastening them into the box with glue, tape, or staples.

VARIATION

- Add painted bits of sponges or twigs for trees, small gravel for rocks, cotton for snow, or a mirror for water.

NOTES FOR NEXT TIME: _____

_____

_____

Egg-Carton Baskets

MATERIALS

- ☐ egg cartons cut into four piece sections
- ☐ colored construction paper
- ☐ paste
- ☐ fabric scraps
- ☐ bits of trim
- ☐ tempera paint
- ☐ brushes
- ☐ markers
- ☐ crayons
- ☐ pipe cleaners (optional)
- ☐ stapler, staples

💡 HELPFUL HINT

- Younger children may need help stapling handles to their baskets. Let them try to do so first before doing it for them!

DEVELOPMENTAL GOALS

Develop creativity, small motor development, and hand-eye coordination and explore a new use for egg cartons.

PREPARATION

Cut the egg cartons into sections with four cups. This makes three baskets from one egg carton.

PROCESS

1. Have the child decorate the four-egg-cup section with crayons, markers, or paint.
2. Bits of colored construction paper can be glued on for added designs.
3. Glue on pieces of trim or fabric scraps for more design possibilities.
4. Staple on a strip of construction paper for a handle.
5. Alternatively, punch a pipe cleaner into the side for a handle.

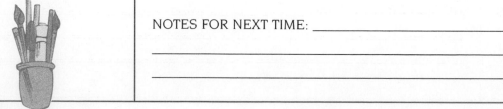

VARIATIONS

- Spread glue on the egg-cup sections. Sprinkle glitter on for a sparkly effect.
- These baskets are fun to take on outdoor walks. They are great for carrying such treasures as pretty rocks, twigs, and acorns.

NOTES FOR NEXT TIME: _____

_____

_____

Years Old and Up

Egg-Carton Buggy Things

MATERIALS

- ☐ egg cartons cut into single cups
- ☐ pipe cleaners cut into small pieces
- ☐ buttons
- ☐ scraps of fabric and trim
- ☐ crayons
- ☐ markers

HELPFUL HINT

- Markers work best for adding details when Styrofoam egg cartons are used.

DEVELOPMENTAL GOALS

Develop creativity, small motor development, and hand-eye coordination; explore a new use for egg cartons; and relate science to art activities.

PREPARATION

Discuss bugs, real and imaginary, with the children. Talk about colors, shapes, "feelers," legs, and textures. Talk about other creatures, real or imaginary.

PROCESS

1. Give each child one egg cup.
2. Attach pieces of pipe cleaners for legs.
3. Use buttons for eyes.
4. Use pieces of pipe cleaners for antennae ("feelers").
5. Add details with crayons or markers.
6. Add pieces of fabric or trim for more details.

VARIATIONS

- String a thread through the top of the egg cup to hang the creations.
- Make a family of creatures. Tell stories about the creatures' adventures in the bug world.
- Make houses for the bug creatures out of milk cartons or other recycled boxes. Decorate the houses with markers or crayons.

NOTES FOR NEXT TIME: _____

_____

_____

_____

PAPER ART

Egg-Carton Creatures

MATERIALS

- ☐ egg cartons
- ☐ scissors
- ☐ tempera paint
- ☐ crayons
- ☐ markers
- ☐ string
- ☐ pipe cleaners (optional)

HELPFUL HINTS

- When using Styrofoam egg cartons, use pens or markers to draw the face and decorate.

- Children aged 8 and older can cut the egg carton into sections with blunt-tipped scissors.

DEVELOPMENTAL GOALS

Develop creativity, small motor development, and hand-eye coordination and explore a new use for egg cartons.

PREPARATION

An adult cuts an egg carton into four parts, each part three sections long. Turn the parts upside down and carefully punch a hole near the bottom of the front and back of each part.

PROCESS

1. Give each child four parts of the egg carton.
2. The children paint a face on one end of the egg carton.
3. The children decorate the body with crayons, paint, or markers.
4. Add pipe cleaners for feelers.
5. When the children are finished decorating the egg-carton pieces, string the pieces together to form a moveable creature.

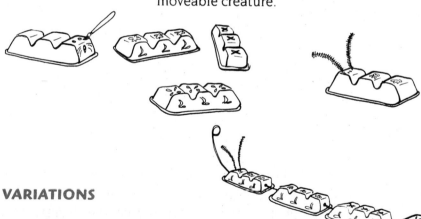

VARIATIONS

- String the egg carton pieces vertically instead of horizontally for a different kind of creature.

- Glue on sequins, buttons, feathers, or bits of trim for even more fanciful creatures.

NOTES FOR NEXT TIME: _____

_____

PAPER ART

Egg-Carton Gardens

MATERIALS

- ☐ tops from Styrofoam egg cartons
- ☐ scissors
- ☐ pipe cleaners
- ☐ toothpicks
- ☐ construction paper
- ☐ crayons
- ☐ markers
- ☐ glue
- ☐ glue brushes
- ☐ glitter (optional)
- ☐ twigs

💡 HELPFUL HINTS

- Flat pieces of Styrofoam from packing cases can be used in place of egg-carton tops.
- When using toothpicks with preschool children, be sure to supervise this activity very closely.

DEVELOPMENTAL GOALS

Develop creativity, small motor development, and hand-eye coordination and explore a new use for egg cartons.

PREPARATION

Give each child a top from a Styrofoam egg carton. Talk about flower gardens, real or imagined. ("Which kind of flowers can you see in your mind?" "Which kinds of flowers do you see in a garden?" "Think of colors and shapes.")

PROCESS

1. Have the children cut or tear the construction paper into flower shapes.
2. Have the children decorate the flower shapes with crayons and/or markers.
3. Glitter can be applied to flower shapes that have been brushed with glue.
4. Insert a toothpick or pipe cleaner into the flower.
5. Poke the flower into the Styrofoam egg carton top.
6. Add twigs to fill the egg carton top as desired.

VARIATIONS

- Make an egg-carton zoo. Fill the egg-carton top with paper animals.
- Create an egg-carton top filled with paper "people." Classmates, family members, and characters from a favorite story book all make fun additions!
- Older children might enjoy creating a scene from a favorite story in the egg- carton top.

NOTES FOR NEXT TIME: _____

_____

_____

PAPER ART

Folded-Paper Masks

MATERIALS

- ☐ newsprint paper—one sheet per child
- ☐ colored construction paper—one sheet per child
- ☐ scissors
- ☐ pencils
- ☐ crayons
- ☐ markers

💡 HELPFUL HINTS

- This activity is suitable for children able to use scissors.
- Children who cannot yet use scissors can tear the eye and mouth shapes from construction paper.
- Have a book with pictures of different kinds of masks available for the children to see before this activity. It may provide some real inspiration!

DEVELOPMENTAL GOALS

Develop creativity, small motor development, and hand-eye coordination; explore a new use for newsprint; and reinforce the design concepts of pattern, shape, size, and placement.

PREPARATION

Show the students how to fold their paper by matching the corners of paper and pressing a fold. Use the newsprint paper to practice folding and making holes along the fold (see the following "process" section). With some children you may need to fold the paper for them.

PROCESS

1. Find the middle of the folded edge and cut into the fold, making one shape for both eyes.
2. Cut different shapes on the fold for the nose and mouth.
3. Trim the outer edge of paper as desired.

VARIATIONS

- Make a folded mask from construction paper.
- Decorate the mask with crayons and markers.

NOTES FOR NEXT TIME: _____

_____

_____

_____

PAPER ART

Fun with Paper

DEVELOPMENTAL GOALS

Develop creativity, small motor development, and hand-eye coordination and explore new ways to cut paper.

MATERIALS

- ☐ construction paper
- ☐ lightweight colored paper (e.g., copy paper)
- ☐ scissors
- ☐ paste
- ☐ crayons
- ☐ markers

💡 HELPFUL HINTS

- Recycled colored copy paper is a good source of paper for this activity.
- This activity is appropriate for children able to use scissors.

PREPARATION

Cut some of the paper into strips about 1-1/2" to 2" wide and 6" to 8" long. Give each child a supply of paper, paper strips, and scissors.

PROCESS

1. Have the children fringe the paper by making short scissor snips close to each other in the paper.
2. Wind the strips around a pencil to make curly paper strips.
3. Fold the paper strips back and forth to make accordion strips.
4. Glue the paper cutouts to a piece of construction paper.
5. Fill the design with crayons and markers.

VARIATION

- Try the same cutting activities with cellophane, tissue paper, and even newspaper.

NOTES FOR NEXT TIME: _____

_____

_____

_____

Imaginary Animals

MATERIALS

- ☐ collection of boxes of various sizes and shapes
- ☐ paste
- ☐ masking tape
- ☐ stapler and staples
- ☐ scraps of colored paper, fabric, trim
- ☐ buttons
- ☐ yarn

💡 HELPFUL HINT

- Boxes with waxed surfaces can be covered with a layer of newspaper and wallpaper paste and allowed to dry before painting.

DEVELOPMENTAL GOALS

Develop creativity, small motor development, and hand-eye coordination and explore a new use for recycled boxes.

PREPARATION

Talk about animals and their shapes, sizes, and colors. Give the children a collection of boxes of various sizes and shapes.

PROCESS

1. Have the children stack the boxes and rearrange them until they are satisfied with the arrangement.

2. Shapes and sizes of boxes may suggest certain animals, such as an oatmeal box for an elephant or a long, narrow box for a giraffe's neck.

3. Smaller boxes or toweling rolls can be used for legs or a head.

4. Fasten boxes together with glue, masking tape, or a stapler.

5. Glue on details using scraps of colored paper, fabric, trim, buttons, or yarn.

VARIATIONS

- Textured surfaces can be created by using corrugated paper or egg cartons for bodies of animals.
- Wood shavings, bark, or wrinkled-paper scraps can be glued to boxes to create interesting textures.
- Exaggerated features help create dramatic effects, such as large buttons for eyes, frayed string or rope for a mane or tail, or pieces of cloth for ears.

NOTES FOR NEXT TIME: _____

_____

_____

PAPER ART

Junk-Mail Jewels

MATERIALS

- ☐ junk mail with coated, shiny surfaces
- ☐ ruler
- ☐ pencil
- ☐ scissors
- ☐ white glue
- ☐ round toothpicks
- ☐ strong, thin string (e.g., kite string)
- ☐ large, blunt needle for threading beads

💡 HELPFUL HINTS

- Use magazine covers and other slick papers to make beads. Even consider using materials with some printing work, because only the last inch or so of the bead is visible.

- This activity is appropriate for children whose small motor skills are developed enough to roll the paper onto a toothpick.

DEVELOPMENTAL GOALS

Develop creativity, small motor development, and hand-eye coordination and explore a new use for junk mail.

PREPARATION

Collect junk-mail letters, flyers, and brochures. Cut the paper into small strips, approximately 3/4" wide by 4-1/2" long.

PROCESS

1. Roll each bead by wrapping the paper strips tightly around a toothpick.

2. Complete the bead by gluing the last 1/2" of the strip.

3. Remove the toothpick and repeat until all desired beads are made.

4. String the beads on the kite string.

5. Tie a knot in the string to complete the necklace.

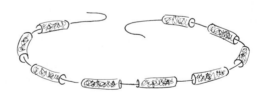

VARIATIONS

- Make beads of different sizes by varying the dimensions. To make bigger beads, use longer strips of paper. Change the width of the strips to make wider or narrower beads.

- Use beads from broken necklaces and bracelets to alternate with the paper beads for variety.

NOTES FOR NEXT TIME: _____

_____

_____

PAPER ART

PAPER ART 353

Me-Mobiles

MATERIALS

- ☐ selection of magazines (e.g., school and department store catalogs, nature, sports, and popular family magazines)
- ☐ scissors
- ☐ paste
- ☐ construction paper
- ☐ wire hangers
- ☐ yarn or string
- ☐ name tags large enough to fit in the central triangle of the hanger

💡 HELPFUL HINTS

- Encourage the children to talk about their selections.
- Hangers can be hung on a clothesline in the room or in any other appropriate place.

DEVELOPMENTAL GOALS

Develop creativity, small motor development, and hand-eye coordination and explore a new use for magazine pages.

PREPARATION

Tie the child's name tag to the central portion of the hanger and allow at least three strings or pieces of yarn to dangle from the bar of the hanger.

PROCESS

1. Have the children look through the magazines.
2. Direct the children to cut or tear out three or more pictures that reflect a favorite thing or activity.
3. Have the children paste the pictures to the construction paper.
4. Have the children tie or staple the pictures to the strings attached to the hanger. (Adult help may be required.)

VARIATIONS

- The children can draw pictures reflecting their favorite thing or activity.
- The children bring in photos from home for this activity.
- Choose a favorite story book or cartoon character and cut out pictures reflecting a favorite thing or activity.

NOTES FOR NEXT TIME: _____

_____

_____

_____

Milk-Carton Birdhouses

MATERIALS

- ☐ milk carton
- ☐ stapler and staples
- ☐ masking tape
- ☐ soft cloth or rag
- ☐ brown tempera paint (or shoe polish)
- ☐ scissors
- ☐ twine

HELPFUL HINT

- Be sure to avoid excessive decorations on the birdhouse. They will scare the birds away!

DEVELOPMENTAL GOALS

Develop creativity, small motor development, and hand-eye coordination and explore a new use for milk cartons.

PREPARATION

Have a milk carton for each child. Clean and dry the milk carton thoroughly. Staple the top of the carton shut.

PROCESS

1. Tear off small pieces of masking tape and cover the carton with the pieces of tape.

2. Using a soft cloth, rub brown shoe polish all over the tape. This will give the carton a rough, bark-like finish. Alternatively, paint the tape with brown tempera paint.

3. With an adult assisting, have the child cut a hole about 4" above the bottom of the carton. This hole should be approximately 1" to 1-1/2" in diameter so the birds can get in and out of the house.

4. Poke a few drainage holes in the bottom of the carton and two air holes in the top of the carton.

5. Poke a hole through the top of the feeder, string a piece of twine through the hole, and hang the feeder on a tree.

VARIATIONS

- Glue on twigs for decoration.
- Hang the feeder where the child can see when the birds are using it.
- Draw designs on the birdhouse with markers instead of painting it brown.

NOTES FOR NEXT TIME: _____

_____

_____

PAPER ART

Milk-Carton Construction Fun

MATERIALS

- [ ] milk
- [ ] juice, or cream cartons (different sizes—all cleaned and dry)
- [ ] white acrylic paint
- [ ] gesso or white latex house paint
- [ ] pencils
- [ ] paintbrushes
- [ ] tempera paint
- [ ] containers for water

💡 HELPFUL HINT

- This is a good activity to tie into a social studies lesson on the community. Older children (over age 8) can research communities and replicate them with milk-carton constructions.

DEVELOPMENTAL GOALS

Develop creativity, small motor development, and hand-eye coordination and explore a new use for milk cartons.

PREPARATION

Discuss homes and neighborhoods with the children. Talk about the different styles of places to live: houses, apartments, condos, and so on. Talk about shapes and sizes and such details as windows, doors, roofs, and stairways.

PROCESS

1. Have the child cover the carton with white acrylic, gesso, or latex house paint.

2. Let the paint dry thoroughly.

3. Draw windows, doors, and so on onto the carton.

4. Paint the carton (using tempera paint) to look like a house.

VARIATIONS

- Make several houses for a neighborhood.
- Create a town/village from a favorite story.
- Paste cutout pictures of people to the houses.

NOTES FOR NEXT TIME: _____

_____

_____

_____

PAPER ART

Nesting Cup Toys

MATERIALS

- ☐ paper or Styrofoam cups (in three different sizes that fit one inside the other)
- ☐ markers
- ☐ crayons

💡 HELPFUL HINTS

- Markers work best on Styrofoam cups.
- Bring in a set of nesting dolls/toys for the children to see and play with.

DEVELOPMENTAL GOALS

Develop creativity, small motor development, and hand-eye coordination and explore a new use for paper or Styrofoam cups.

PREPARATION

Talk about "nesting" toys. An example is the nesting Russian mother dolls, called "Marushka" dolls. These nesting toys fit one inside the other. A real-life example is great to have to show to the children for this activity.

PROCESS

1. Draw designs or faces on the cups.
2. Hands and arms may be drawn on the sides of the cups.
3. Clothing details may be drawn on, as well.

VARIATIONS

- Make nesting animals, imaginary or real.
- Make a family of nesting dolls or animals.

NOTES FOR NEXT TIME: _____

_____

_____

_____

PAPER ART

Paper-Bag Creations

MATERIALS

- ☐ small brown-paper bags
- ☐ small pieces of colored tissue paper
- ☐ glue

💡 HELPFUL HINTS

- Let the older children tear the tissue into small pieces. It is good exercise for the small muscles in the hands and fingers.

- Younger children may have a hard time tearing tissue paper because it is flimsy. Give these children cut squares of tissue paper for this activity.

DEVELOPMENTAL GOALS

Develop creativity, small motor development, and hand-eye coordination and explore a new use for paper bags.

PREPARATION

Discuss trees and other things found in nature, like bushes and flowers. Talk about color, shapes, and sizes.

PROCESS

1. Give each child a small brown-paper bag.
2. Twist the bag to form a trunk or stem.
3. Once the bag is twisted, start ripping the top part of the bag into small sections.
4. Twist each torn section to form branches for a tree, petals for a flower, leaves for a bush, and so on.
5. Once the branches are formed, glue pieces of colored tissue paper to them to form leaves.

VARIATIONS

- Make paper-bag vegetables.
- Make trees in different seasons of the year.
- Use bags of different sizes to make a forest.

NOTES FOR NEXT TIME: _____

_____

_____

_____

PAPER ART

Years Old and UP

Paper-Bag Fish

MATERIALS

- ☐ old newspapers
- ☐ paper lunch bag
- ☐ large rubber bands
- ☐ scissors
- ☐ construction paper
- ☐ glue
- ☐ poster paint
- ☐ markers
- ☐ sequins
- ☐ trim pieces
- ☐ paint brushes

💡 HELPFUL HINTS

- Because this activity involves waiting for the paint to dry, be sure to tell the children ahead of time that their projects will take two steps with waiting involved.

- This is a good activity to do before going outside so the children can let their bags dry while playing.

DEVELOPMENTAL GOALS

Develop creativity, small motor development, and hand-eye coordination and explore a new use for paper bags.

PREPARATION

Give each child a paper lunch bag, a paintbrush, and access to the materials listed.

PROCESS

1. Have the child paint the paper bag.
2. While it is still wet, add glitter to the creature.
3. Allow the bag to dry thoroughly (at least 30 minutes) by opening the bag all the way and standing it on its open end.
4. Once the paint is dry, wad some sheets of newspaper and stuff them inside the lunch bag until it is about half full.
5. Squeeze the open end of the bag together and tie it off tightly with a rubber band.
6. Fan out the top of the bag for a fish tail.
7. Using the construction paper and scissors, cut out features like fins, eyes, and a mouth.

VARIATIONS

- Make other animals out of paper bags, such as dogs, cats, rabbits, or even birds.
- Older children can use their science books to choose specific kinds of fish to make out of paper bags.
- The book by Dr. Seuss "One Fish, Two Fish, Red Fish, Blue Fish" is a natural follow-up to this activity.

NOTES FOR NEXT TIME: _____

_____

PAPER ART

PAPER ART 359

4 Years Old and Up

Paper-Bag Kites

MATERIALS

- ☐ paper bags (lunch-bag size)
- ☐ construction paper
- ☐ glue
- ☐ crayons
- ☐ markers
- ☐ scissors
- ☐ paste
- ☐ string
- ☐ tissue-paper or crepe-paper strips

💡 HELPFUL HINT

- Younger children may need help cutting the hole in the bottom of the bag. For other children, you may help by starting the cutting and letting them finish cutting the hole.

DEVELOPMENTAL GOALS

Develop creativity, small motor development, and hand-eye coordination and explore a new use for paper bags.

PREPARATION

Cut a large circle out of the bottom of the paper bag. This will allow the bag to fly in the air.

PROCESS

1. Draw pictures or designs on both sides of the paper bag.
2. Glue on pieces of construction paper for added details.
3. Glue colorful strips of tissue paper or crepe paper onto the end of the bag, opposite the hole.
4. Punch two holes in the bottom of each sack (in the corners above the hole).
5. Tie a piece of string through the holes to make a handle.
6. Go outside and move the kites in the wind.

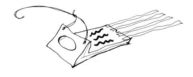

VARIATIONS

- Hang the kites on a pole or from the ceiling near a window. Enjoy the way the air moves the kite.
- Make animal or fish kites.
- Older children enjoy researching specific types of fish and making accurate designs and markings on the kite.

NOTES FOR NEXT TIME: _____

_____

PAPER ART

Paper Batik

MATERIALS

- ☐ crayons
- ☐ construction paper or plain white drawing paper
- ☐ shallow container of water
- ☐ paper towels
- ☐ tempera paint
- ☐ paint brushes

💡 HELPFUL HINTS

- Young children love working with water! That is why this activity is such fun. Be prepared for a messy but fun experience.

- Bring in samples of batik fabric from a fabric store for the children to see. Batik fabric is usually found in the cotton fabrics section.

DEVELOPMENTAL GOALS

Develop creativity, small motor development, and hand-eye coordination; explore a new use for paper; and learn about batik.

PREPARATION

Instruct the children to make drawings with crayons on construction paper.

PROCESS

1. After completing a drawing with crayons, soak the paper in water.
2. Crumple the paper into a ball.
3. Uncrumple the paper.
4. Flatten the paper and blot off the excess water with a paper towel.
5. Using a wet paintbrush, flow a watercolor or a diluted tempera paint over the surface.
6. Because the color will be more intense in the creased area, the finished drawing will have dramatic contrasts.

VARIATIONS

- Cut open a paper bag and make the drawing on the bag. Follow the preceding procedure for another interesting effect.
- Batik paper designs make lovely wrapping papers.

NOTES FOR NEXT TIME: _____

_____

_____

_____

PAPER ART

Paper Floats

MATERIALS

- ☐ construction paper
- ☐ scissors
- ☐ plastic dishpan with water
- ☐ colored chalk
- ☐ grater

💡 HELPFUL HINT

- Be sure to cover the area and the children well for this activity. It is messy fun!

DEVELOPMENTAL GOALS

Develop creativity, small motor development, and hand-eye coordination and explore a new use for construction paper.

PREPARATION

Fill the plastic dishpan with water. Help the children grate various colors of chalk.

PROCESS

1. Have the children cut or tear construction paper into desired shapes.
2. Have the children choose two or three colors of chalk to sprinkle on the water.
3. Have the children float the paper shapes on the water to absorb the chalk design.
4. Hang the shapes on a line or lay them flat to dry.

VARIATION

- Use India ink on the water instead of chalk. Swirl the ink to make a design, then lay the paper on the water's surface to absorb the design.

NOTES FOR NEXT TIME: _____

_____

_____

_____

PAPER ART

Paper-Plate Color Mixing

MATERIALS

- ☐ two primary color paints
- ☐ Styrofoam or paper plate
- ☐ 9" × 12" white paper

💡 HELPFUL HINTS

- Cover the work area with newspaper. Be sure the children wear their art clothes or other types of coverups.

- Some children may want to avoid getting paint on their hands. Do not force these children to participate in this activity. Have an alternative activity for them after encouraging, but not forcing, the children to participate.

- Plan to have an activity for children who finish this activity quickly. Finger painting with tempera paint is a handy extra activity for these children. Or they may enjoy making finger print designs.

DEVELOPMENTAL GOALS

Develop creativity, small motor development, and hand-eye coordination and explore a new use for paint and paper plates.

PREPARATION

Give each child a Styrofoam or paper plate and a piece of white paper.

PROCESS

1. Put two primary colors on the plate (e.g., red and yellow).

2. Have the child put the hand in the red paint, then make a handprint on the paper.

3. Have the child put the other hand in the yellow paint and make a hand print on the paper.

4. With the paint still on the hands, have the child rub the hands together to see which color results.

5. Have the child make a hand print with the paint just made.

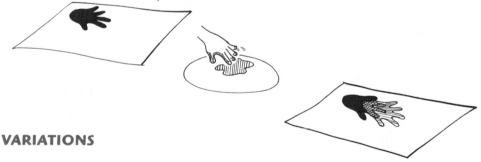

VARIATIONS

- Use different primary colors, such as red and blue.
- Let the children choose the two colors they use. Talk about the results.
- Try using crayons to mix primary colors. Discuss the difference between crayons and paint color mixing.

NOTES FOR NEXT TIME: _____

_____

_____

_____

PAPER ART

A

All Ages

Paper-Plate Color

MATERIALS

- ☐ white paper plates
- ☐ primary colors of tempera paint in plastic bottles
- ☐ plastic wrap

💡 HELPFUL HINTS

- Students will be amazed when they create greens and purples and oranges that were not there when they started. This is why this is a great way to teach children about color; they get to see the colors first-hand by mixing the colors themselves!

- These paintings make wonderful abstract pieces with great colors!

DEVELOPMENTAL GOALS

Develop creativity, small motor development, and hand-eye coordination; explore a new use for paper plates; and learn how primary colors mix.

PREPARATION

Put a dab of primary colors on each child's paper plate, about the size of a half-dollar.

PROCESS

1. Put the plastic wrap on top of the paint.
2. Have the child mix the colors with the fingers on the plastic wrap.
3. Colors mix similar to finger paint without the mess.
4. When the child is finished mixing colors, pull the plastic off and let the painting dry.

VARIATIONS

- Sprinkle glitter into the tempera paint for a sparkly effect.
- Have the children choose the colors they want to mix.

NOTES FOR NEXT TIME: _____

_____

_____

_____

PAPER ART

Paper-Plate Hats

3 Years Old and Up

MATERIALS

- ☐ paper plates
- ☐ tape
- ☐ glue
- ☐ markers
- ☐ crayons
- ☐ crepe-paper strips
- ☐ stickers
- ☐ glitter
- ☐ scraps of fabric and trim
- ☐ construction paper
- ☐ scissors (optional)

💡 HELPFUL HINTS

- Older children can

DEVELOPMENTAL GOALS

Develop creativity, small motor development, and hand-eye coordination; explore a new use for paper plates; and reinforce the design concepts of pattern, color, and size.

PREPARATION

Cut the paper plate halfway through, roll it into a cone shape to fit the child's head, and tape the edges in place. Talk about how the children would like to decorate the paper-plate hats. Discuss the patterns, shapes, colors, and sizes of available materials.

PROCESS

1. Decorate the paper plate with markers and crayons.
2. Use the materials to decorate their hats in any ways the child wishes.
3. When finished, attach yarn to sides of the hat for ties.

4 Years Old and UP

Paper-Plate Insects and Such

MATERIALS

- ☐ paper plates
- ☐ crayons
- ☐ markers
- ☐ paint
- ☐ paintbrushes
- ☐ stapler and staples
- ☐ construction paper
- ☐ scissors
- ☐ paste
- ☐ pipe cleaners
- ☐ hole punch
- ☐ buttons

💡 HELPFUL HINTS

- Children enjoy practicing with a stapler on this kind of activity. To avoid too much frustration and a jammed stapler, take turns stapling the plates together—an adult one time and a child the next.
- This is a good follow-up activity to a science lesson on insects.
- Have a book with pictures of insects available to inspire the children in this activity.

DEVELOPMENTAL GOALS

Develop creativity, small motor development, and hand-eye coordination; explore a new use for paper plates; and relate science to art activities.

PREPARATION

Talk about the kinds of insects familiar to the child, such as ladybugs, flies, ants, bees, and spiders. Talk about the colors, shapes, and details on these insects. Talk about things in the insect world the children may be interested in making.

PROCESS

1. Give each child two paper plates.
2. Decorate the plates with designs and/or insect details using buttons for eyes or any other bits and pieces glued on for detail.
3. Cut insect legs from construction paper.
4. Staple the legs to the sides of one paper plate.
5. Staple the paper plates together.
6. Punch two holes at the top of the plates for the antennae. Thread a pipe cleaner through the holes.

VARIATION

- Make paper-plate insect puppets. When stapling the paper plates together, leave one end of the paper plate open. Cut off the rim of the plates where they were not stapled. This way the insect can be used as a puppet by placing your hand inside the two plates.

NOTES FOR NEXT TIME: _____

_____

_____

_____

PAPER ART

366 **PAPER ART**

Paper-Plate Lacing Designs

4 Years Old and Up

DEVELOPMENTAL GOALS

Develop creativity, small motor development, and hand-eye coordination; explore a new use for paper plates; and introduce lacing.

MATERIALS

☐ white paper plates
☐ crayons
☐ markers
☐ tempera paint
☐ brushes
☐ hole punch
☐ yarn or long shoe strings
☐ tape

💡 **HELPFUL HINT**

• To save time and involve the children even more in this activity, let the children punch the holes in the paper plates. It is good exercise for the small muscles in their fingers and hands, and the children love doing it!

PREPARATION

Cover the ends of the yarn with tape to make them easier to lace through the paper plates. Give each child a paper plate with a few holes in it and a piece of yarn. Work together practicing how to lace the yarn through the paper plate.

PROCESS

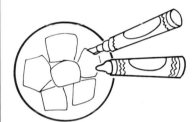

1. Decorate a paper plate with a picture or a design using crayons, markers, or tempera paint.
2. Punch holes around the picture or design.
3. Using a long shoelace (or a piece of yarn with the ends taped), have the child weave the shoelace through the picture or design.
4. Remove the shoelace to start relacing.

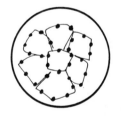

VARIATIONS

• Punch holes in the plates before giving them to the children. Their designs/pictures can be made around the holes or made to include the holes.
• Punch the holes in shapes, letters, or numbers in the paper plates.

NOTES FOR NEXT TIME: _____

_____

_____

_____

PAPER ART

Paper-Plate Masks

MATERIALS

- ☐ paper plates
- ☐ paint
- ☐ crayons
- ☐ markers
- ☐ yarn
- ☐ buttons
- ☐ construction paper
- ☐ paste

💡 HELPFUL HINTS

- These masks can be used by holding them up close to but not over the face. This makes them especially appropriate for children who do not like having their faces covered.

- Have a book with a variety of of masks to inspire the children in their mask making.

DEVELOPMENTAL GOALS

Develop creativity, small motor development, and hand-eye coordination and explore a new use for paper plates.

PREPARATION

Give each child a paper plate and easy access to the materials.

PROCESS

1. Have the child decide which animal, person, or book character on which to model a mask.

2. Have the children paint paper plates the color(s) of their choice.

3. If they choose, have the children color their plates instead of painting them.

4. Glue on yarn pieces for hair.

5. Make features and details with buttons, cut out pieces of construction paper, and so on. Glue these onto the paper plate.

VARIATIONS

- Older children can work together to make masks for several characters in a story they might like to act out for the class.

- Older children (over age 8) can research a historical character and make a mask of that person.

NOTES FOR NEXT TIME: _____

_____

_____

PAPER ART

Paper-Posies Potpourri

A All Ages

MATERIALS

- ☐ cupcake liners (small and large)
- ☐ white paper plates
- ☐ tissue paper
- ☐ egg cartons (cut into single-egg cups)
- ☐ construction paper
- ☐ fabric scraps
- ☐ bits of trim
- ☐ buttons
- ☐ markers
- ☐ crayons
- ☐ paste

💡 HELPFUL HINTS

- This activity ties in many of the previous activities on types of paper flowers. This is a good follow-up activity to these activities.

- Flowers are just one thing to make out of paper liners and egg cups. Let the children create anything they can imagine with these materials!

- Have a print of a Georgia O'Keefe flower painting available to inspire young artists in this activity.

DEVELOPMENTAL GOALS

Develop creativity, small motor development, and hand-eye coordination; explore a new use for colored paper; and relate science to art.

PREPARATION

Discuss flowers with the children. Talk about colors, shapes, and details. Have the the children think about which flowers they would like to create.

PROCESS

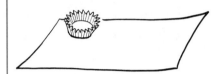

1. Use a piece of construction paper or a white paper plate for a base.

2. Glue cupcake liners to the base as one type of flower.

3. Crumpled bits of tissue paper can be glued on as another type of flower.

4. Egg carton cups can be glued on as another type of flower.

5. Buttons, bits of fabric and trim, and crayons/markers can be used to add details to the flowers.

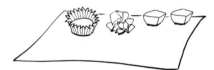

VARIATIONS

- Use a piece of cardboard or a shoe box lid for the base.
- Rub paste on some parts of the flowers and sprinkle glitter on for a sparkly effect.
- Add cotton balls, buttons, or beads for details on the flowers.

NOTES FOR NEXT TIME: _____

_____

_____

_____

PAPER ART

Paper Texture Collage

MATERIALS

- ☐ collection of papers with textures (e.g., metallic paper, newspaper, cardboard, sandpaper pieces, plastic wrap, wax paper, tissue paper, construction paper)
- ☐ paste

 **HELPFUL HINT**

- Encourage the children's awareness of texture by passing various materials for the children to touch and examine.

DEVELOPMENTAL GOALS

Develop creativity, small motor development, and hand-eye coordination and explore different textures of paper through making a collage.

PREPARATION

Discuss textures with the children. Talk about how each of the materials feels, how the materials look, and how they might be used in a collage.

PROCESS

1. Have the child select pieces of paper with different textures.
2. Have the child arrange and rearrange the shapes on a piece of background paper.
3. The shapes may form a picture or an abstract design.
4. Glue down the pieces when child is satisfied with the placement of the pieces.

VARIATIONS

- Glue the paper pieces to a piece of cardboard.
- Include buttons, braids, fabric scraps, or yarn for added interest and accent.
- Make a cloth collage, exploring a variety of different kinds of cloth.

NOTES FOR NEXT TIME: _____

_____

_____

_____

PAPER ART

Paper-Tube Creations

MATERIALS

- ☐ paper tubes from paper towels or toilet tissue
- ☐ paste
- ☐ pieces of trim
- ☐ small Styrofoam balls
- ☐ buttons
- ☐ pom-poms
- ☐ pieces of fabric
- ☐ feathers

💡 HELPFUL HINT

- Make a habit of saving paper tubes so that you will have a good supply whenever children want to use them in projects. Ask friends to do the same!

DEVELOPMENTAL GOALS

Develop creativity, small motor development, and hand-eye coordination and explore a new use for crayons.

PREPARATION

Give each child a paper tube and easy access to other art materials listed above. Discuss such art concepts as patterns, length, short and tall, beginning, middle, and end. Talk about how these concepts relate to animals and other things in nature.

PROCESS

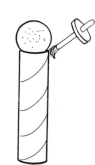

1. The paper tube is the creature's body.
2. Glue the Styrofoam ball to the tube to become the creature's head.
3. Glue on buttons for eyes.
4. Glue on pom-poms for a nose, ears, or eyes.
5. Glue on pieces of trim for hair, hats, or other features.

VARIATIONS

- Make paper-tube animals for an imaginary zoo. Animals can be true to life or made up.
- Make a family of paper-tube creatures to represent a child's real-life family.
- Choose a favorite character from a fairy tale or storybook and make a paper-tube representation of it.

NOTES FOR NEXT TIME: _____

_____

Paper-Tube Sliding Things

MATERIALS

- ☐ toilet-tissue or paper-towel tubes
- ☐ crayons
- ☐ yarn
- ☐ construction paper
- ☐ markers
- ☐ tempera paint and paintbrushes
- ☐ scissors
- ☐ glue
- ☐ tape

💡 HELPFUL HINT

- Young children may need assistance fastening the yarn to the tubes.

DEVELOPMENTAL GOALS

Develop creativity, small motor development, and hand-eye coordination and explore a new use for paper tubes.

PREPARATION

Cut the tubes into various sizes. Give each child at least five pieces.

PROCESS

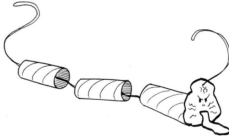

1. Have the children paint the tubes.
2. The children may want to color the tubes with markers or crayons instead of paint.
3. Cut out a head and tongue. Decorate the pieces by drawing features with crayons or markers.
4. Glue or tape the head and tongue to one tube piece.
5. When decorating with paint, wait until the tube pieces are dry.
6. Measure a piece of yarn long enough to extend through all pieces of tubes.
7. String the yarn through the tubes, fastening it to the first and last tube pieces.

VARIATIONS

- String beads between the tubes for a colorful effect.
- Glue on such natural objects as acorns, leaves, and grasses for an interesting effect.

NOTES FOR NEXT TIME: _____

_____

_____

_____

PAPER ART

Paper Weaving

MATERIALS

- ☐ paper
- ☐ scissors
- ☐ paste

HELPFUL HINTS

- Fold the paper in half and then cut the slits. This makes cutting easier.
- This activity is suitable for children who have developed enough small motor skill to do the weaving and cutting in this activity.

DEVELOPMENTAL GOALS

Develop creativity, small motor development, and hand-eye coordination; explore a new use for paper; and learn about weaving.

PREPARATION

Cut strips of colored construction paper, colored magazine pages, and wall-paper strips.

PROCESS

1. Cut a series of slits in a piece of construction paper.
2. Be sure to keep a border on all sides of the paper.
3. Weave the strips of colored paper through the slits in the paper.
4. Hold strips in place with a bit of paste, if necessary.

VARIATIONS

- Add strips of metallic paper for a shiny effect.
- Include some strips of fabric for an interesting effect.

NOTES FOR NEXT TIME: _____

_____

_____

_____

Small-Grained Paste Creations

MATERIALS

- ☐ white glue or liquid starch
- ☐ sand
- ☐ salt
- ☐ flour, or cornmeal
- ☐ salt shakers
- ☐ dry tempera paint
- ☐ paper
- ☐ brushes
- ☐ crayons
- ☐ markers

💡 **HELPFUL HINT**

- Very young children may want to taste the grains. Be sure the children are not allergic to any of the grains used in this activity before starting!

DEVELOPMENTAL GOALS

Develop creativity, small motor development, and hand-eye coordination and explore a new use for paste and grains.

PREPARATION

If using white glue, mix in a little water to make it thin enough to apply with a brush. Put the grains into shakers with large or small holes. Dry tempera can also be added to the grains for color.

PROCESS

1. Paint an area of paper with the white-glue mixture or liquid starch.
2. Shake on any small-grained media.
3. Add details with crayons or markers.

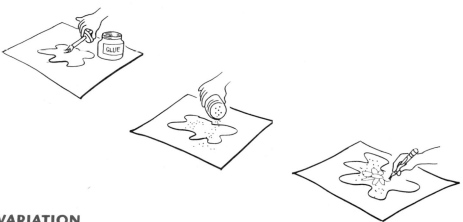

VARIATION

- Add spices to each shaker—cinnamon to one, cloves to another, nutmeg to another. Talk about the smells and the colors.

NOTES FOR NEXT TIME: _____

_____

_____

_____

PAPER ART

Tearing, Punching, Stapling

MATERIALS

- ☐ stack of old magazines and newspapers
- ☐ paper punch
- ☐ stapler, staples
- ☐ paper of various textures (e.g., smooth, bumpy, heavy, tissue thin) all in different colors
- ☐ crayons
- ☐ markers

💡 HELPFUL HINT

- If you lack a paper punch or if the child is too young to use it, the child can use the handle of a wooden spoon to punch large holes in the paper.

DEVELOPMENTAL GOALS

Develop creativity, small motor development, and hand-eye coordination; explore new ways to work with paper; and explore different textures of paper.

PREPARATION

Talk about the kinds of shapes the child would like to make. Discuss the different kinds of paper available to make shapes. Practice with the hole punch and stapler.

PROCESS

1. Challenge the child to tear a shape—a tiny shape, an enormous shape, a wide shape, and so on.

2. Have the child tear shapes from as many different kinds of papers as desired.

3. Have the child paste or staple the shapes to a piece of paper.

4. Details may be added with crayons or markers.

VARIATIONS

- The children might enjoy pasting or stapling all the interesting, ragged shapes on a long piece of paper for a big, colorful mural.

- Save the circles the child punches from wax paper. Put them in a plastic jar full of water. After you fasten the lid tightly, the child can shake the jar and make a "snowstorm" inside.

- Save the circles cut out of colorful paper and use them later in pasting activities for added details.

NOTES FOR NEXT TIME: _____

_____

Tissue-Paper Art

MATERIALS

- ☐ torn pieces of tissue in various colors
- ☐ paste
- ☐ construction paper or any other type of paper

HELPFUL HINTS

- Tissue paper is very flimsy and can be hard to tear. The color can also rub off on the hands. For younger artists, provide small, cut squares of tissue.

- Older children who have better-developed small motor control can help cut the tissue into pieces. Cutting is good exercise for the small muscles in the fingers and hands, and the children love doing it, too!

DEVELOPMENTAL GOALS

Develop creativity, small motor development, and hand-eye coordination and explore a new use for tissue paper.

PREPARATION

Give each child a supply of torn pieces of variously colored tissue, paste, and a piece of construction paper.

PROCESS

1. Have the child paste pieces of tissue onto construction paper.

2. Make the torn pieces overlap, superimpose each other, or rest next to each other.

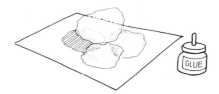

VARIATIONS

- Liquid starch can be used instead of paste. The child dips a brush into the liquid starch, then paints the piece of tissue paper onto the construction paper.

- Torn pieces can be crumbled, then pasted onto the construction paper. This gives a three-dimensional effect.

- Tissue pieces can be glued onto plastic jars, bottles, and boxes for colorful, original gifts.

- Line drawings can be filled by pasting on crumbled pieces of tissue paper.

NOTES FOR NEXT TIME: _____

_____

_____

_____

PAPER ART

Tissue-Paper Jewelry

MATERIALS

- ☐ 3-inch circles, squares, and triangles of different colors of tissue paper
- ☐ yarn
- ☐ pieces of drinking straws cut into small pieces 1-1/2" to 2" long

💡 HELPFUL HINTS

- To speed cutting, cut several layers of tissue at a time when cutting out the circles, squares, and triangles.

- Children who have learned to use scissors can help cut out the tissue circles, squares, and triangles for this activity.

DEVELOPMENTAL GOALS

Develop creativity, small motor development, and hand-eye coordination and explore a new use for tissue paper.

PREPARATION

Poke holes in the centers of the tissue-paper pieces. Cut pieces of yarn about 2 feet long. Knot one end of the yarn. Tape the other end to make a "needle."

PROCESS

1. Give each child a supply of tissue-paper and straw pieces.
2. String the tissue paper onto the piece of yarn.
3. String a straw piece following the tissue-paper piece.
4. Continue until the desired length is reached.
5. Tie the ends of the yarn to complete the jewelry.

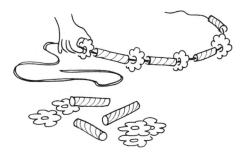

VARIATIONS

- String beads from old pieces of jewelry between the tissue-paper pieces.
- Older children can use blunt-tipped carpet needles threaded with yarn. This way they can string "popcorn" pieces of Styrofoam between the tissue-paper pieces.
- Cut out some squares, circles, and triangles from foil or metallic wrapping paper for an interesting effect.

NOTES FOR NEXT TIME: _____

_____

_____

Tissue-Paper Plaids

MATERIALS

- ☐ sheets of white construction paper
- ☐ strips of tissue paper of various widths
- ☐ liquid starch in a small container
- ☐ paint brushes
- ☐ scissors

💡 HELPFUL HINT

- This activity is appropriate for children with enough small motor skill to work with layering tissue paper and glue it as required in the activity.

DEVELOPMENTAL GOALS

Develop creativity, small motor development, and hand-eye coordination and explore a new use for tissue paper.

PREPARATION

Place three or four different color sheets of tissue paper in a stack. Using a paper cutter, cut into 1/2", 1/4", 3/4", 1" and 1-1/2" strips.

PROCESS

1. Give each child a sheet of white construction paper.
2. Paint the entire surface of the construction paper with a coat of liquid starch.
3. Lay on horizontal strips, three or more of each color.
4. Vary the widths and spaces between the strips.
5. Let the ends stick over the edge.
6. Fill the brush with starch and paint the entire surface horizontally.
7. Lay on vertical strips, three or more of each color.
8. Vary the widths of the strips and the spaces between. Let the ends stick over the edge.
9. Fill the brush with starch and paint the entire surface vertically.
10. When dry, trim off the ends of the tissue paper.

VARIATIONS

- Tissue plaids make beautiful cards or book or folder covers.
- Tissue plaids also are very striking when mounted on a paper of a complementary color.

NOTES FOR NEXT TIME: _____

_____

PAPER ART

A

All Ages

Torn-Paper Pictures

MATERIALS

☐ colored paper

☐ paste

 **HELPFUL HINTS**

- Random designs from torn paper are most appropriate for very young children.

- Very young children may try to taste the paste, which is natural. Remind the children to use their fingers and not their tongues! In addition, be sure to always use nontoxic glue.

DEVELOPMENTAL GOALS

Develop creativity, small motor development, and hand-eye coordination; explore a new use for colored paper; and reinforce the art elements of design, pattern, and shape.

PREPARATION

Discuss with the children the designs or pictures they would make from pieces of torn paper. Talk about the shapes, sizes, and colors the children might use in their pictures.

PROCESS

1. Have the child tear the paper into shapes.

2. Have the child arrange the torn shapes on a piece of paper as the background.

3. Paste each piece in place to complete the picture.

 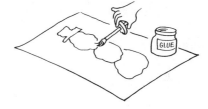

VARIATIONS

- Drawings can be added to provide details.

- Different textures of papers can be used for interesting effects.

- Glue on pieces of trim or fabric scraps to add interest to the design.

NOTES FOR NEXT TIME: _____

_____

_____

_____

Translucent Paper

MATERIALS

☐ cotton balls
☐ salad oil
☐ wax paper
☐ torn pieces of colored tissue paper
☐ aluminum pie tin

💡 HELPFUL HINTS

• Let the older children tear the tissue into small pieces. It is great exercise for the small muscles in the fingers and hands!

• Give the younger children cut squares of tissue paper, as they have a harder time trying to tear tissue paper.

DEVELOPMENTAL GOALS

Develop creativity, small motor development, and hand-eye coordination and explore a new use for tissue paper.

PREPARATION

Pour the oil into the pie tin. Give each child a cotton ball, a piece of wax paper, a supply of torn pieces of colored tissue, and easy access to the pie tin with salad oil.

PROCESS

1. Have the child dip the cotton ball into the salad oil.

2. Have the child brush the oil over the waxed paper.

3. Have the child press the tissue-paper pieces all over the waxed paper until the paper is completely covered.

4. The oil helps the tissue paper stick to the wax paper and makes the tissue paper translucent.

VARIATIONS

• When the paper dries, add a black frame to create a stained-glass window.

• Cut holiday shapes and use related colors of tissue paper.

• Use a rectangle sheet of waxed paper with assorted colors of tissue paper.

NOTES FOR NEXT TIME: _____

_____

_____

_____

PAPER ART

Index by Ages

PAPER ART

General Index

3 YEARS AND UP

4 YEARS AND UP